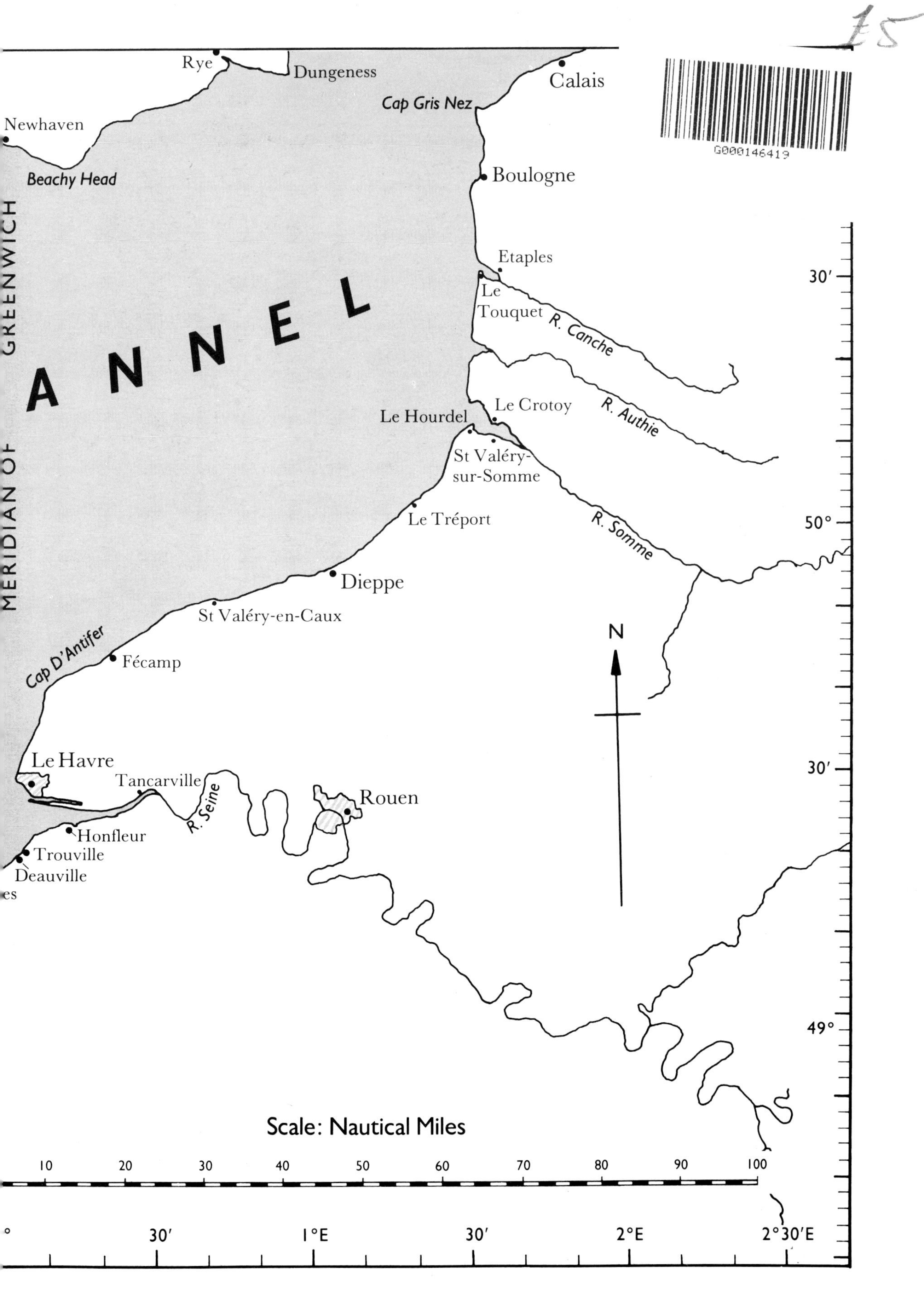

Rye
Dungeness
Calais
Cap Gris Nez
Newhaven
Beachy Head
Boulogne
MERIDIAN OF GREENWICH
Etaples
30′
Le Touquet
R. Canche
ANNEL
Le Crotoy
R. Authie
Le Hourdel
St Valéry-sur-Somme
Le Tréport
R. Somme
50°
Dieppe
St Valéry-en-Caux
N
Cap D'Antifer
Fécamp
Le Havre
30′
Tancarville
R. Seine
Rouen
Honfleur
Trouville
Deauville
49°
Scale: Nautical Miles
10
20
30
40
50
60
70
80
90
100
30′
1°E
30′
2°E
2°30′E

Mark Brackenbury

NORMANDY AND CHANNEL ISLANDS PILOT

Calais to St. Malo

Eighth Edition

ADLARD COLES NAUTICAL
London

To the Royal Cruising Club

Eighth edition published by Adlard Coles Nautical
an imprint of A & C Black (Publishers) Ltd
35 Bedford Row, London WC1R 4JH

First published as
Normandy Harbours and Pilotage by Edward Delmar-Morgan, 1969
Second edition 1973
Third edition revised by Mark Brackenbury 1978
Fourth edition revised by Mark Brackenbury 1980
Fifth edition as
Normandy and Channel Islands Pilot by Mark Brackenbury 1983
Sixth edition 1986
Seventh edition 1988
Revised reprint 1990
Eighth edition 1992

ISBN 0-7136-3507-x

A CIP catalogue record for this book is available from the British Library.

Printed in England by Butler & Tanner Ltd, Frome and London

Whilst every effort has been made to ensure that the contents of this book are as accurate as possible, readers are nevertheless warned that any of the information contained herein may have changed between the date on which the book was completed and the date of publication. Readers are advised to refer to all relevant official charts, publications and notices and neither the author nor the publishers can accept responsibility for the consequences of any error or omission contained in this book.

Contents

List of harbour plans and sketch charts

List of photographs and drawings

Introduction

The history of this book began with the publication of *Normandy Harbours and Pilotage* by Edward Delmar-Morgan in 1969. Sadly, he died shortly after completing the revisions for the second edition in 1973, and when the process of change and development along this coast made another completely revised edition necessary, the publishers, Adlard Coles Ltd, asked me to cruise the area and make the necessary corrections. This 1978 edition was followed by another fully revised edition in 1980.

At this time, there was a gap in the coverage provided by the Adlard Coles Pilotage Series, between Cherbourg (where *Normandy Habours* ended) and St Malo (where *North Brittany Pilot* began), spoiling the otherwise continuous coverage from Den Helder to La Coruña. In the discussions before the revision programme for the fifth (1983) edition, it was therefore agreed that as well as revising all the material on the area previously covered, Calais to Cherbourg, I should write completely new sections on the French coast between Cherbourg and St Malo, and also on the Channel Islands. This added more than a third to the size of the book, and in the original part very little remained of Edward Delmar-Morgan's early work owing to the tremendous changes that had taken place in almost every port covered. It was therefore decided that the time had come to allow Edward's name to retire from the front cover: however, I shall always be grateful to him for getting the book off to such a successful start.

I am grateful also to Mr Jack Coote for his help in the preparation of the sixth (1986) edition. I had been away on a long-planned circumnavigation in my ketch *Kiwa*, and he very kindly kept an eye on developments during my absence, and also provided some excellent photographs, which are credited where they appear.

Eighth Edition

I was able to visit virtually every harbour mentioned in the book during the summer of 1991, and found even more than the usual number of changes in detail, although the friendly and peaceful nature of the region remains happily unspoiled. The most important single change has been the opening of Port Guillaume, the splendid new marina just inside the entrance of the river Dives. Many old firms have disappeared, although in most cases they have, happily, been replaced by others. The new format for tidal information introduced in the seventh edition has proved popular, as has the cruise planning chart which makes up the endpapers, and I am continuing to add to the historical and general notes on the ports as opportunity offers.

Description of the cruising areas

(See endpapers chart.) From Calais to Boulogne the coast consists of chalk cliffs similar to those on the opposite side of the Dover Strait. Strong tidal streams make it important to get the tides right between these ports, especially near springs. South of Boulogne the cliffs fade away and give place to the estuaries of the Canche, Authie and Somme, with sandbanks extending well offshore. The Canche and Somme both have pleasant harbours for the shoal-draft yacht, but neither should be entered in strong onshore winds.

Beyond the Somme cliffs appear again, but these have a character of their own, being lower and flat-topped, with small harbours often well concealed in gaps in the cliff line. The first of these, Le Tréport, cannot safely be entered in onshore gales except during the hour before high water, so the yachtsman should always bear in mind that the 53 miles between

Boulogne and Dieppe can be a long and inhospitable stretch in heavy onshore weather. However, in normal summer conditions it offers an interesting and uncrowded cruising ground, especially for a boat that can dry out upright.

The general character of the coast remains much the same as far as Le Havre and the estuary of the Seine, which includes the charming and unique harbour of Honfleur. Westwards from here lies Calvados, an area of low shoreline with the hills standing well back. Several interesting harbours lie along this stretch, including Carentan, a favourite of mine – a typical French market town whose excellent marina, reached by estuary, river and canal, has an almost inland Dutch feel about it.

Northwards from here projects a much craggier and grander feature, the great rocky peninsula of the Cotentin. Here are tide-races and offlying reefs, small fishing harbours and the great port of Cherbourg, and here at last (for those who like them) we are in real lobster and crab country. Round the peninsula and going southward again, the rocks and cliffs give way to low sandy beaches with a few high headlands, and when we continue south to Granville, we have reached the port with the greatest tidal range in Europe.

Offshore lie the Channel Islands, a region of big tides and strong streams, strewn with detached rocks and intricate channels, but one which can provide some of the most interesting and satisfying cruising to be found in the whole area. They offer their own variety, from the medieval tranquillity of Sark to the bustle of St Peter Port or St Helier, not forgetting the remoteness of the Ecrehous (weekends excluded!) and the typically French atmosphere of France's own Channel Islands, the Iles Chausey.

The area covered in this book is a splendid and varied cruising ground, and it would take the average family cruising yatch several seasons to explore all that it has to offer. The French holiday season remains restricted to July and the first ten days of August, so anyone who can take an early or late season cruise will find the ports and facilities uncrowded, but even in high season there are only one or two ports (mentioned in the text) which suffer from serious overcrowding.

Detailed passage notes, considerably extended in comparison with previous editions, will be found listed in the Contents. Recommendations on charts and other reference books including notes on tide tables, tidal stream atlases and tidal calculations appear in the Appendix. In response to demand, waypoints have been included in the approach notes for appropriate harbours. Readers are reminded that it is their responsibility to ensure that the course from their position to the waypoint is a safe one, with no intervening hazards.

I wish my readers happy cruising in this fascinating area, and I hope they will find the information in this book useful in helping them to get the maximum enjoyment from their cruises. If any errors are detected, please do not hesitate to write to me care of the publishers. Finally, a word about the title. Nobody has ever been able to find one that is strictly accurate as well as being descriptive, without it becoming unduly cumbersome. However, it should be stated for the record that the northern boundary of Normandy runs through the middle of the port of Le Tréport: places north of that which appear in the book are, in fact, in Picardy. Similarly, Rothéneuf and St Malo are in Brittany.

Mark Brackenbury 1992

Calais

Charts Nos. 1892 and 1352

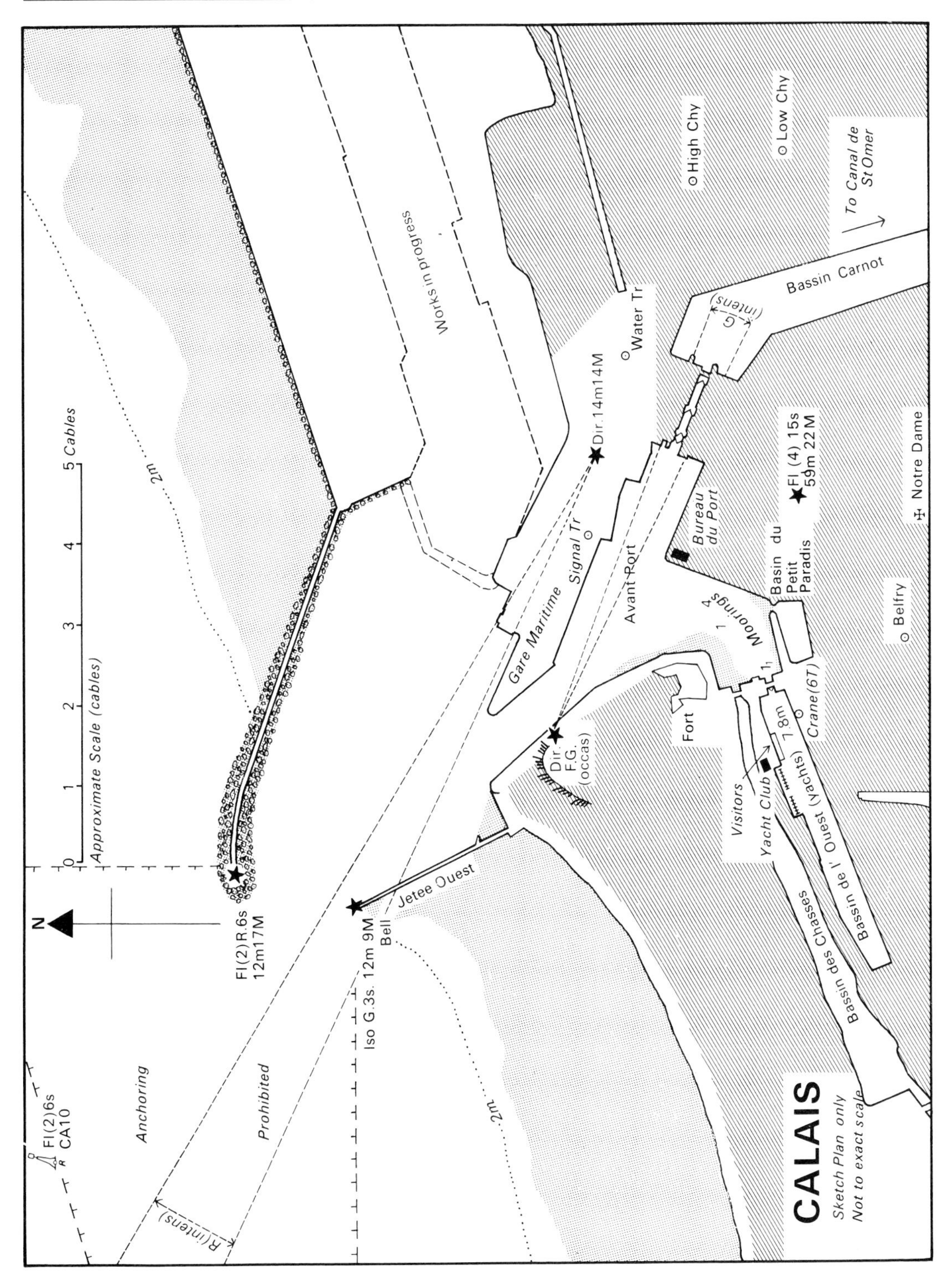

Plan 1 Calais.

Calais

Calais is surprisingly little affected by its status as a major ferry port, and it has a character of its own. It offers good accommodation for yachts in a tidal basin, but it is well to try to arrive near high water, as berths in the outer harbour are inadequate and uncomfortable.

Tidal notes

Heights: 7.1 m MHWS, 0.9 m MLWS, 5.9 m MHWN, 2.1 m MLWN.
HW is HW Dover +0.33 (but remember the difference in time zone), HW Dunkerque −0.21.
The ENE-going stream starts at HW Cherbourg + $1\frac{1}{2}$ and reaches a peak of 2.9 knots (mean springs) at HW Cherbourg + $3\frac{1}{4}$. The WSW-going stream starts at HW Cherbourg − $4\frac{1}{2}$, and reaches a peak of 2.5 knots (mean springs) at HW Cherbourg − 1.

Approach

A sandbank, the Ridens de la Rade, lies to the north of Calais, with its shallowest part about $1\frac{1}{2}$ miles NE from the entrance. The least sounding here is 0.1 m, so it has only a metre over it at MLWS. Coming from the east, the shore should be given a berth of at least 2 miles until the main lighthouse (white with black top, 59 m) is bearing east of 170° (mag) before turning to steer for the entrance. In calm weather this precaution is only necessary below half-tide; conversely, in northerly gales it is wise to pass W of buoy CA8 (QR) before turning E for the harbour. From the west, the approach is quite straightforward from a navigational point of view, as a craft will naturally join and use the main entrance channel. Keep well S of the line of red approach buoys and keep a constant lookout for ferries: the traffic is almost continuous and plenty of room should be left for two ferries to pass each other S of the red buoys. Waypoints: from the north or east, 50°59′.2N, 1°50′.0E, then steer 183° (mag) for buoy CA10 (Fl(2) R 6s) and thence for the pierheads. From NW or west, or in northerly gales, use 50°58′.8N, 1°48′.0E, whence 130° mag for CA8 (QR) and then as in text.

Entrance

Boats equipped with VHF should contact port control on Channel 12 for permission to enter or leave. Except in emergency boats should not attempt to enter under sail, but should motor and keep well over to their starboard side. Without radio, a boat can wait just outside and keep an eye on the signals displayed from the Gare Maritime (see plan): if these are extinguished

1 Calais: the harbour entrance.

entry is permitted. It is also possible to follow *close* behind a ferry entering. Do not pass too close to either pierhead, as tidal streams are strong and there can be swirls and eddies in their vicinity. Once inside, proceed southwards keeping to starboard until the Avant-Port de l'Ouest opens up.

Berthing

There are a few mooring buoys for small craft in the area in front of the bridge and lock, and boats can lie two abreast to these. Do not try to anchor: the holding is bad and the bottom foul. It is also possible to moor alongside on the E wall of the Avant-Port de l'Ouest, but note that the southernmost third of this dries, and the bottom is dangerous with jagged rocks and other obstructions. Do not leave the boat untended here, as local fishermen consider this wall to be their private property, but it is a useful place to put a man ashore to find out the times of bridge opening, which are displayed at the control building at the S end of the bridge. Altogether this is a bad place for small craft, and it is far better to try to arrive near HW, and go straight into the inner basin. Ferry and other traffic causes scend in the Avant-Port, and in NE to NW winds it can be bad, so if mooring alongside another yacht, guard against damage caused by unsynchronised rolling.

The charming and comfortable Port de Plaisance (yacht harbour) is in the Bassin de l'Ouest, closed off by dock gates. These open 2 hours before HW Calais, and close at HW + 1. There is also a bridge, whose approximate opening times are HW – 2, and HW + 1, but check the notice (see above). Light signals are shown from the bridge: Amber – bridge will open in 10 minutes; Green – pass through; Red – do not pass through. Once in the basin, visitors berth

2 Calais: Avant-Port, southern limb.

3 Calais: entrance to the yacht harbour.

(often several deep) alongside the long pontoon on the starboard side, except boats over 12 m LOA, which lie alongside the S wall of the basin. Do not make up warps too tightly here, as the water level falls considerably during the period between openings.

Facilities

The yacht club (Société des Régates de Calais) is large and friendly. There are excellent shower and toilet facilities in an annexe W of the main building, and it has a pleasant bar overlooking the basin, tel: 21 34 55 23. It will also arrange duty-free stores. Harbour dues are collected by the harbourmaster of the yacht harbour, whose office is on the ground floor of the club building, tel: 21 97 02 34. Fuel from pontoon in the basin (see plan) which also has a tank for used oil. Water and electricity on pontoons. 3 ton crane. Duty-free stores through club (not Sundays). Customs in rue Lamy, tel: 21 34 75 40. An excellent new chandler, Ebaine, is to be found a few metres S of the bridge in the rue de la Mer, tel: 21 34 69 01. They stock charts, have good chandlery supplies, and can arrange sail and hull repairs. M. Michel Louf, the harbourmaster of the yacht harbour, is not only most helpful but also speaks almost perfect English.

General

Excellent shopping and a variety of restaurants will be found 200–300 metres S of the bridge (avoid the restaurants directly overlooking the yacht basin, which tend to be overpriced compared with those in town). The town centre is a good deal further – nearly a mile along the same road, past the railway station and town hall. Calais is a major city with every possible kind of shop, hotel or restaurant, and is well worth a visit.

4 Calais: Port de Plaisance. Visitors' moorings and clubhouse (with *tricolores* over it). *Reproduced with the permission of the Chambre de Commerce et d'Industrie de Calais.*

Founded around 1180, and already a ferry port when Richard the Lionheart landed there in 1189 on his way to the crusades, Calais was taken by Edward III in 1347. Angered by the town's 11-month resistance, the king demanded that six leading citizens should appear before him barefoot in only their shirts, offering themselves for execution: on this condition he would spare the town. The six volunteers appeared, but Queen Phillippa pleaded for their lives, and the king eventually relented. This story is commemorated in the powerful sculpture by Rodin outside the Hotel de Ville. The town remained in English hands until it was retaken by the Duc de Guise in 1558 – the last English possession on the French mainland. This was during the reign of Mary Tudor, who said of the event that when she died the word 'Calais' would be found engraved upon her heart.

Apart from the Rodin, visitors should not miss the cathedral of Notre-Dame, the nave dating back to the late 13th century, but with the upper parts, side-aisles and facade dating from around 1400 and therefore being English work. There is also a museum specialising in lace (25 rue Richelieu), and a museum of the 1939–45 war, in the Parc St Pierre just beyond the Hotel de Ville on the right. The Hotel de Ville (town hall) itself is a fake, having been built in 15th-century Flemish style between 1911 and 1925! It is a splendid construction, nonetheless, and it has some magnificent stained glass windows.

Passage Notes: Calais to Boulogne

Chart No. 1892

In reaching Calais or Boulogne from England, the main offshore problem is a man-made one – the traffic separation scheme in the Dover Strait. The lanes must be crossed on a course as nearly as possible at right angles to the lanes, and on a spring tide the flood stream will be setting the boat to the SW at an average rate of nearly 3 knots between HW Dover $-5\frac{1}{2}$ to $-2\frac{1}{2}$, and similarly the ebb will be setting NE at nearly the same rate between HW Dover and HW $+3$. These streams can be most useful, but only if they are properly allowed for in advance.

In sailing from Calais to Boulogne, it is most important to avoid wandering out into the NE-going traffic lane, which is only 2.6 miles offshore at its nearest approach to the coast. The lanes are clearly shown on Admiralty Chart No. 1892. Shoals extend nearly 2 miles offshore between Caps Blanc-Nez and Griz-Nez, so it is advisable to pass N of the green buoys CA3 (Fl G 4s) and the Abbeville W cardinal buoy (VQ(9) 10s) $2\frac{1}{2}$ miles to the WSW. From here a course can safely be steered to pass a mile W of Cap Griz-Nez, after which maintain that offing until Boulogne outer entrance can be seen, when it may be steered for.

The timing of this passage in either direction depends upon the tides, and in particular the opening times of the yacht basin at Calais. These are approximately between HW Calais $-2\frac{1}{2}$ and $+1$. It is 22 miles from Calais to Boulogne, and going southwards the passage cannot be ideally timed without accepting the discomforts of mooring in Calais outer harbour. When the gates first open the flood is already dying, and before the boat is halfway to Griz-Nez it will have the full strength of the ebb against it. It is best to leave it until the final opening, when the ebb is already slackening. Within 2 hours the stream is slack, and after Griz-Nez the beginnings of the fair stream will be felt. The advantage of this timing is that Gris-Nez is rounded in slack water, avoiding the unpleasant seas that are found when the tide is running hard, especially with the wind against the stream. The disadvantage is that it may be difficult to berth at Boulogne when arriving at LW, as you will be. The alternative, especially in easterly winds, is to wait in Calais outer harbour for a couple of hours, and then have a roaring fair tide all the way: but in a southwesterly this can result in a very unpleasant hour rounding Griz-Nez.

From Boulogne to Calais there is no problem: a boat leaving Boulogne at HW Calais -3 and maintaining 5 knots will be in Calais in plenty of time for the final opening, except perhaps at extreme neaps when a departure at HW $-3\frac{1}{2}$ is safer. In strong north-easterlies, however, it is safer to avoid the heavy wind-over-tide seas by leaving at HW Calais $-4\frac{1}{2}$ and keeping as close inshore as safety allows. This way Griz-Nez can be approached in some shelter, and the danger area off the cape will be traversed at around slack water.

Chart Nos. 438, 1892 and 2451

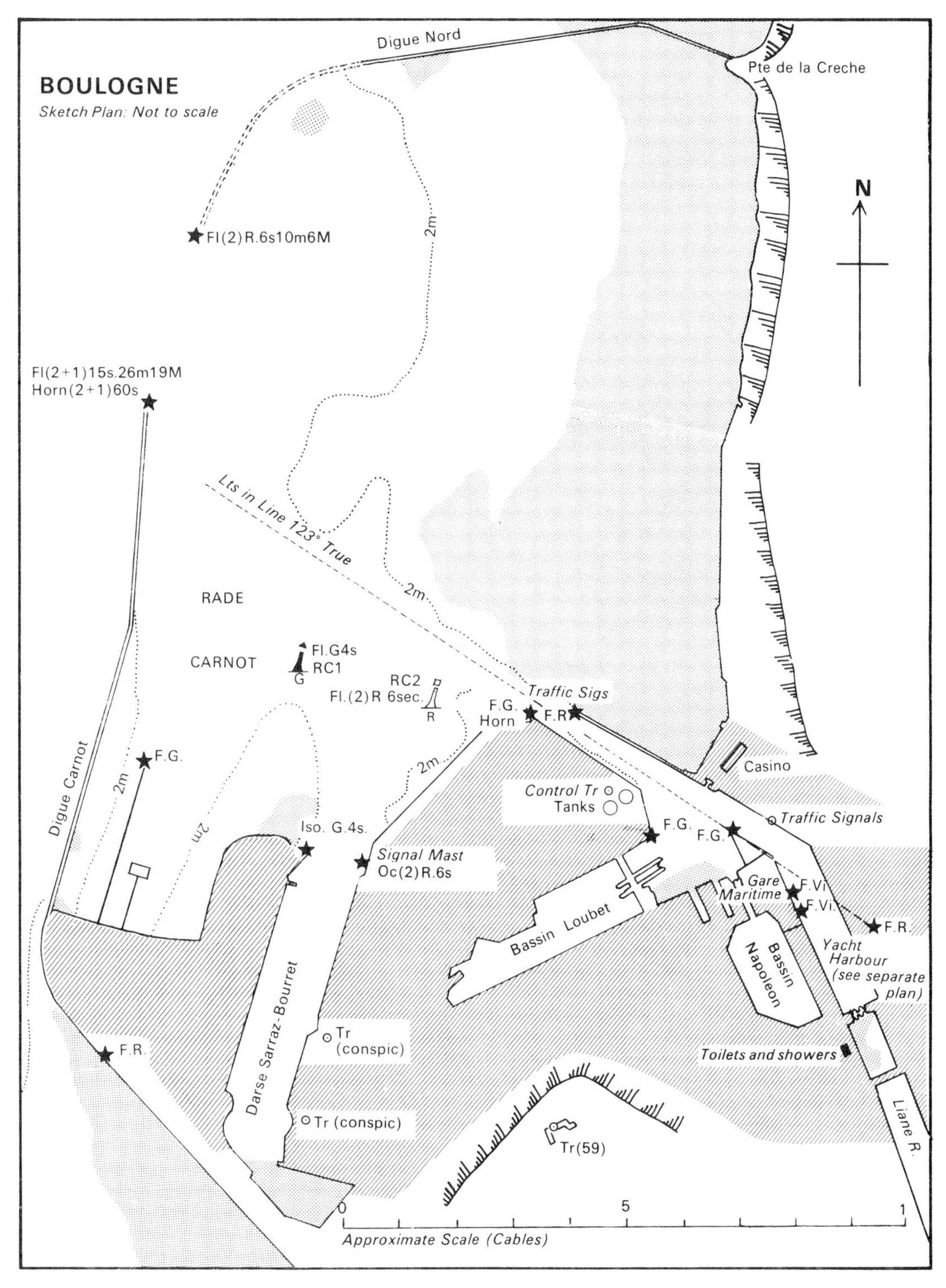

Plan 2 Boulogne.

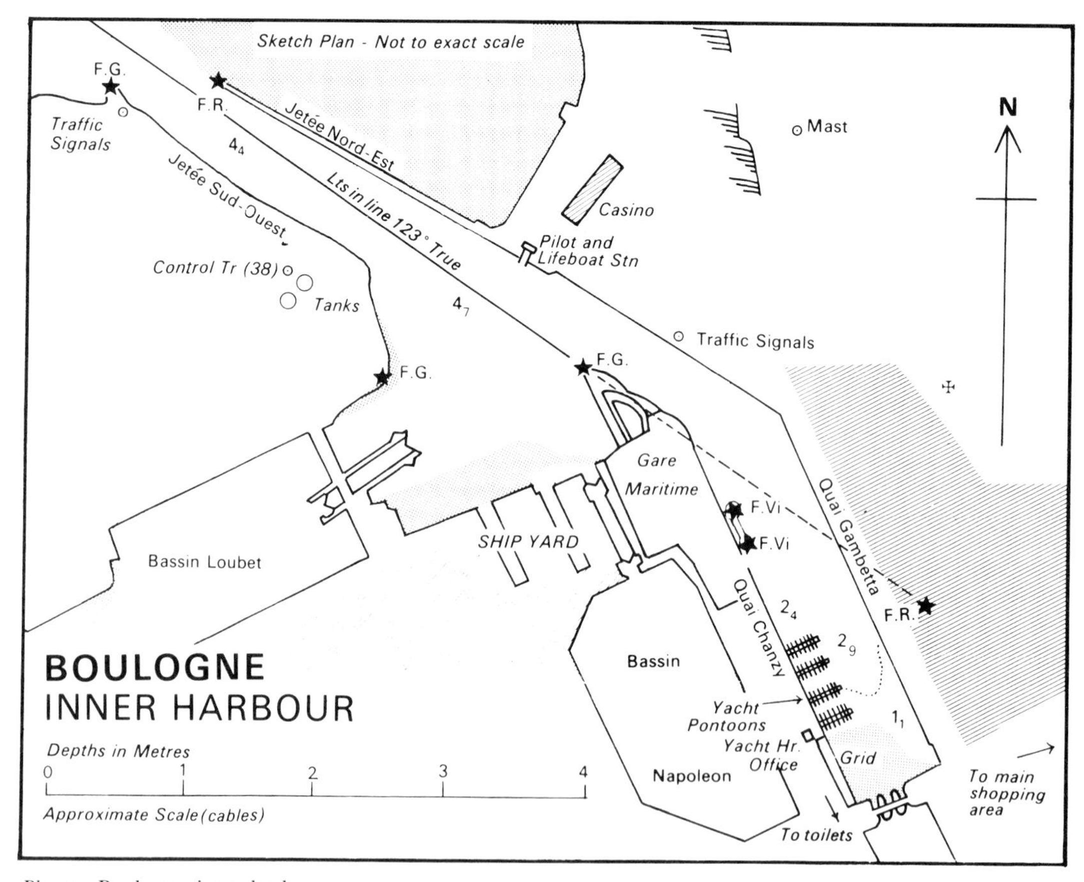

Plan 3 Boulogne, inner harbour.

Boulogne

Much improved in recent years, Boulogne is now once more one of the most valuable ports for eastern S coast and E coast British yachts to use as a first port of entry, although the yacht harbour still suffers from overcrowding during high season. It is a vital link in cruising this coast, and an attractive town. *Note: craft over 10 m should arrange for a berth before visiting. Tel (yacht harbour): 21 31 70 01.*

Tidal notes

Heights: 8.9 m MHWS, 0.8 m MLWS, 7.1 m MHWN, 2.6 m MLWN.

HW is HW Dover +0.04 (but remember the difference in time zone), HW Dunkerque −0.50. The N-going stream begins at HW Cherbourg $+\frac{1}{4}$ and reaches a peak of 2.5 knots (mean springs) at HW Cherbourg $+2\frac{1}{4}$. The S-going stream begins at HW Cherbourg $-4\frac{1}{2}$ and reaches a peak of 2.3 knots (mean springs) at HW Cherbourg −2.

Approach

There are no offshore dangers for small craft to worry about. Approaching from the north the breakwaters are conspicuous. Coming along the coast from the south, the harbour is concealed until Cap d'Alprech is abeam. There are usually plenty of ferries to aid identification. Waypoint: 50°45'.0N, 1°33'.0E, then steer 125° (mag) for the entrance.

Entrance

The outer part of the northern breakwater is submerged, and I have seen local yachts cutting across here near HW, but I do not recommend the practice: the outer harbour should be entered between the two light structures. The entrance can be very rough in gales between W and N.

Immediately upon entering the outer harbour, course should be changed to 170° (mag) for about half a mile to avoid shallow ground to the east. Once the S side of the N inner mole can be seen, or at night when the light structure at the Gare Maritime (FG) is in line with the light tower (FR located on top of the last but one of the five blocks of flats) bearing 123° (True), the entrance is simple. Proceed straight down between the two moles, keeping a course parallel to the NE mole, and at the end of the Quai Gambetta the pontoons will be seen on the starboard hand. When entering the inner harbour, traffic signals may be ignored as long as one proceeds with caution, *except* if Green above White above Red is shown from the signal tower. This is 'La Grande Interdiction', prohibiting all movement in the inner harbour, and must be obeyed by vessels of any kind whatever.

Berthing

The outermost five berths on pontoon 1 (the one nearest to the entrance) are reserved for visitors, as are the outermost seven on each side of pontoon 2, the end pair on 3 and the northern end berth on 4. When these are all full, yachts moor alongside between the pontoons, if necessary several abreast. In working hours there are always harbour officials on the pontoons to advise and assist. For several years silting was a serious problem, but the basin has now been dredged (least depth 3 metres at LAT in 1991) and the pontoons have been

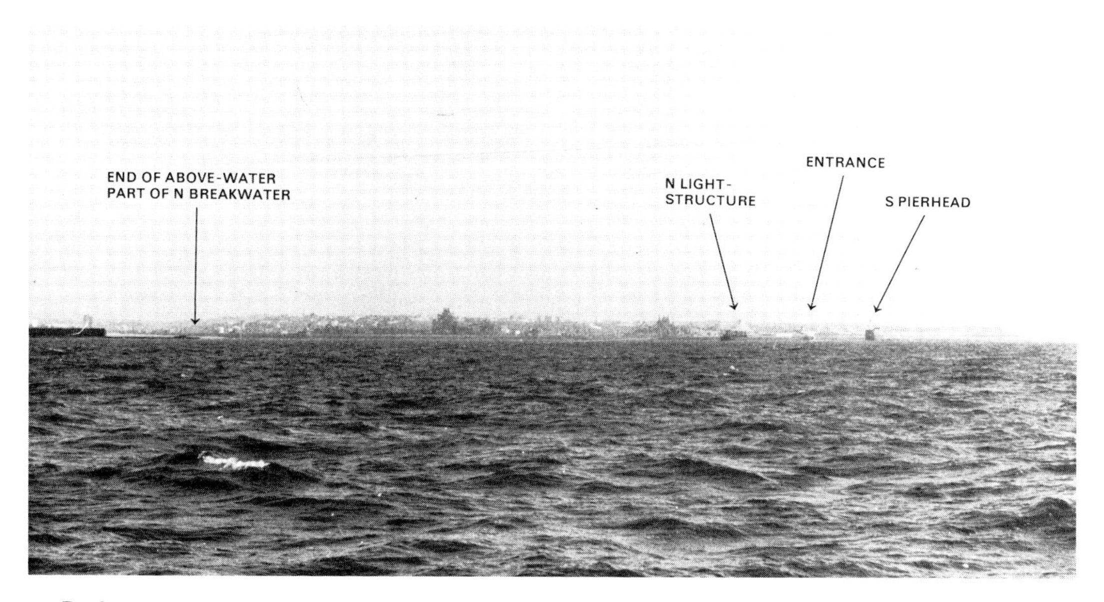

5 Boulogne entrance.

6 Boulogne: entrance to the inner harbour showing signalling station on southern pierhead and, to the right, the observation and control tower. Keep close along the mole on the left of the picture, to reach the yacht harbour.

replaced and extended. Do not, however, go beyond the line of the most southerly pontoon, as the bottom shelves sharply with rocks.

Facilities

Water by hose from pontoons. In 1991 it was hoped that diesel would be available alongside by the 1992 season. Toilets and showers in harbourmaster's building at top of ramp: the Y.C. Boulonnais is adjacent. There is a grid on which it is possible to dry for a tide: it is run by the Chambre de Commerce on the quai Gambetta, where enquiries for use should be made. The grid extends 2 m from the wall, with the position of the bearers marked in paint on the wall above. Have a good look at low water before trying to use it! For engine repairs ring Opale Marine on 21 30 36 19, or consult the harbour master. Some chandlery, charts etc at Angelo, 83 rue du Pot d'Etain, tel: 21 31 37 61.

General

There is a row of cafés and restaurants on the Boulevard Gambetta: others at all prices and standards and all kinds of shops can be found in the main town, and also in the walled city on the hill above, which is well worth a visit. Its walls, founded on Roman fortifications, date from the 13th century, and the base of the bell-tower within is Roman, although the upper parts are 13th-century gothic. The cathedral is 19th century, but just outside the walls to the east is the chateau, built by Philippe, Comte de Boulogne between 1227 and 1231. Although much restored the exterior is well worth seeing, but the inside is not yet open to the public.

Boulogne was the base from which Julius Caesar sailed in 55 B.C. on his invasion of Britain, and the Tour d'Ordre was built as a lighthouse following a visit by Caligula. The Emperor Claudius later visited the town on his way to Britain.

During more modern times, the town was taken by English troops after a siege in 1544 and remained an English possession until it was ransomed by Henri II in 1550.

7 Boulogne: yacht moorings and grid on the Quai Chanzy.

It was at Boulogne that Napoleon began to muster his armies for the invasion of England, and the Colonne de la Grande Armée was raised to commemorate the event. This is easily visible from seaward, and will be found on chart 1892. There is an interesting small Napoleonic museum in the town.

Passage Notes: Boulogne to Le Havre

The route southwards from Boulogne to Cayeux is notable for the three great estuaries – of the Canche, the Authie and the Somme – which break the otherwise rather monotonous coastline. Each of the rivers has built up a sandbar at its mouth which extends somewhat beyond the line of the coast to the N and S, but an offing of a generous mile from the visible shoreline clears all hazards. There are useful harbours in the Canche and Somme; the Authie should be avoided. Beyond the Somme, the only offshore hazards are the 1 m wreck about $1\frac{1}{4}$ miles NNW of Pte d'Ailly (pass N of the N cardinal buoy marking it or *at least* $\frac{1}{2}$ mile S of it) and the N cardinal buoy off Port Sussette (3 miles W of St Valéry-en-Caux) which marks the N end of a prohibited area extending to the shore.

Past Cap d'Antifer, the giant Antifer oil terminal comes into view. Ships using the main channel have absolute priority here, but small craft may cross the channel as long as they do not obstruct large vessels. They must cross at right angles, and motor if necessary to maintain a reasonable speed. Such crossing should be made offshore of buoys A22 and A21: these can be identified by knowing that buoys A26 and 25 are off the end of the huge breakwater, A24 and 23 are about $\frac{3}{4}$ mile to the NW, and A22 and 21 are about another $\frac{3}{4}$ mile NW. One is therefore required to give the end of the breakwater a berth of about $1\frac{1}{2}$ miles, which is roughly the length of the breakwater. Note that in wind over tide conditions near springs, severe tide-race conditions occur off the end of the breakwater, extending as much as two miles out to sea.

S from here to Le Havre the only offshore hazard likely to worry a yacht (apart from the innumerable fishermen's floats) is the Banc de l'Eclat, which carries a least depth of 0.5 m at LAT – about 1.5 m at MLWS. This is avoided by keeping close in ($\frac{1}{4}$ to $\frac{1}{2}$ mile) to Cap de la Hève, and then steering SSE for the final pair of buoys (LH15 and 16) before the harbour entrance. This is covered in more detail under Le Havre.

If proceeding S to the Seine or Trouville without visiting Le Havre, craft under 19.8 m LOA may cross the buoyed channel anywhere, but they must do so at right angles, maintaining a reasonable speed, and above all according absolute priority to commercial vessels using the channel.

It is worth making the point that along the part of the coast that consists of cliffs (i.e. from le Tréport to Fécamp) the harbours and coastal towns all lie in natural breaks in the cliff line. This has two effects: one is that they all look very similar and are difficult to tell apart, the other that they are often invisible from a boat sailing fairly close in along the coast until they are nearly abeam. It can be quite disconcerting to see a line of apparently unbroken cliffs stretching ahead for miles when your destination is a harbour that the chart says is only a couple of miles ahead, but if your navigation is right it will turn up on cue, appearing like magic out of an apparently smooth cliff.

The River Canche, Le Touquet and Etaples

Chart No. 2451

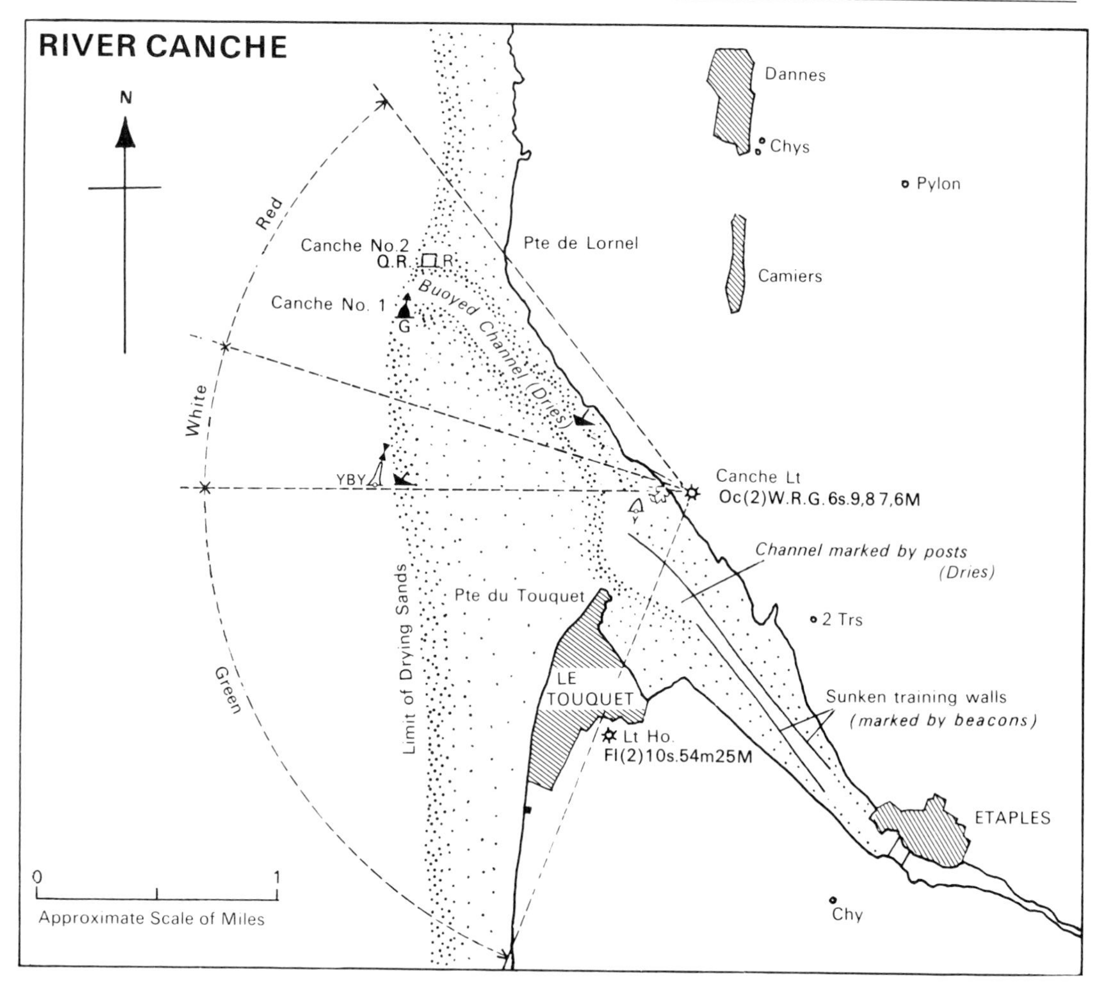

Plan 4 The River Canche, Le Touquet and Etaples.

This is a difficult and potentially dangerous estuary, and the entrance should not be attempted by the inexperienced or in strong onshore winds. But in fine weather it offers a delightful small marina at Etaples and, for the boat which can dry upright, a unique anchorage off Le Touquet.

Tidal notes

Heights: 9.0 m MHWS, 1.0 m MLWS, 7.2 m MHWN, 2.7 m MLWN.
HW is about 12 minutes after HW Dieppe. In the approaches, the N-going stream begins at HW Cherbourg, and the S-going at HW Cherbourg −6. Except at extreme springs, maximum rates, attained 2–3 hours after the above times, are less than 2 knots.

Approach

As shown on the plan, the entrance buoys lie at the N side of the estuary, so coming from the north, keep an offing of a mile until they are identified, and then steer for them. From the south, keep a mile offshore until Le Touquet is abeam, then maintain a course of N (True) until the buoys are seen, then proceed as before. Sound constantly when crossing the estuary, and turn more W if soundings begin to shoal. Arrival should be timed so that the entrance buoys are passed between 2 and 1 hours before the local HW. At HW on a low neap there will be 1.5 m in the channel as far as Le Touquet and 1 m from there to Etaples; on a mean tide these figures increase to $2\frac{1}{2}$ m and 2 m, and on a spring to $3\frac{1}{2}$ m and 3 m. The ideal time to visit is near springs but when the tides are still making, which avoids the danger of being neaped if one has the misfortune to go aground near HW. Waypoint: 50°24′.0N, 1°31′.0E, then steer east, sounding carefully, until the entrance buoys are sighted.

Entrance

From the entrance buoys, the channel is well marked, by buoys as far as Le Touquet and by beacons thereafter, although even in the upper channel buoys may be used to mark temporary sandbanks or obstructions. Allow for a strong N-going set in the outer part of the channel. The yellow buoy off Le Touquet must be left to port when entering, as it marks the seaward end of a wall running to the N shore. Always be alert for the possibility of a pair of buoys out of line with the others: to miss an 'elbow' of this kind can result in grounding. On a big spring (9 m at Dieppe), arriving $\frac{1}{2}$ h before HW I found a least depth of 3 m in the channel to Etaples in 1987. Keep at least 10 m off both port and starboard markers, as the obstructions they mark often project some distance beyond them.

Berthing and facilities: Le Touquet

Only boats that can dry upright can stay at Le Touquet, as the anchorage dries completely. There may be a free mooring: otherwise anchor just to the W of the moorings, taking local advice or investigating the bottom before drying, as there are one or two stony patches on what is otherwise flat sand. It is also wise to take advice before walking ashore, as there are patches of quicksand and deep mud.

8 A view from the NW of the YC du Touquet on the Pointe du Touquet. The channel buoys are seen on the left, and Etaples is visible in the centre background. The pier in the foreground is now partially destroyed. *Reproduced by kind permission of the artist, Petit-Paul of St Valéry-sur-Somme.*

9 Le Touquet from the anchorage: the yacht club is near the right. There is plenty of room to anchor and good holding, but look out for the few stones.

The yacht club (Cercle Nautique du Touquet) is friendly and hospitable. It is open at weekends from Easter to November 1st, and every day in July and August: snack meals (except Saturday evenings), toilets and showers, tel: 21 05 12 77. There is usually someone there who can advise on a proposed visit. The town ($\frac{3}{4}$ mile) has moderate shops but good restaurants: for best value keep away from the sea front.

Berthing: Etaples

Arriving at Etaples, the marina will be seen beyond the fishing quay. Visitors berth at the ends of the pontoons, and on arrival it is most important to turn and secure with bows downstream. This is because the flood arrives as a very strong current, almost a tidal bore, and when leaving one wants to do so well before HW to have the benefit of a rising tide for the shallow part of the channel. One can only do this if facing downstream, as with the tide sweeping one up under the low bridge it is dangerous to cast off facing upstream until slack water, as there is not room for the average yacht to turn.

Facilities

Toilets and showers by the Syndicat d'Initiative (tourist office) to the right at the top of the access bridges. Diesel has to be carried from a rather distant garage. Water and electricity on pontoons. 3 ton crane. Yacht club (YC Etaplois) near the marina, open July to mid-September, tel: 21 94 74 26.

General

Etaples is a charming little town, with good shops and restaurants, and in particular really excellent fish and vegetable markets just opposite the marina. For chandlery, repairs etc, there are Au Grand Large and Jean Lefèvre, both on boulevard Bigot-Descelers, the road running downstream along the river bank on the same side as the marina.

10 Etaples. The marina lies upstream from the fish quay. Remember to moor bow downstream to avoid being swept under the bridge when casting off with the flood making.

It is an ancient town. The pre-Roman Celtic port of Quentovic suffered numerous Norman invasions between 641 and 880, and was finally abandoned by its original inhabitants (who fled to and founded Montreuil) and then by the Normans. Etaples (from Stapula, Latin for market) was founded on the same site around AD 1000 and was an important commercial port before the encroaching sands choked the estuary and reduced it to the tidal fishing port which survives today.

Chart No. 2451

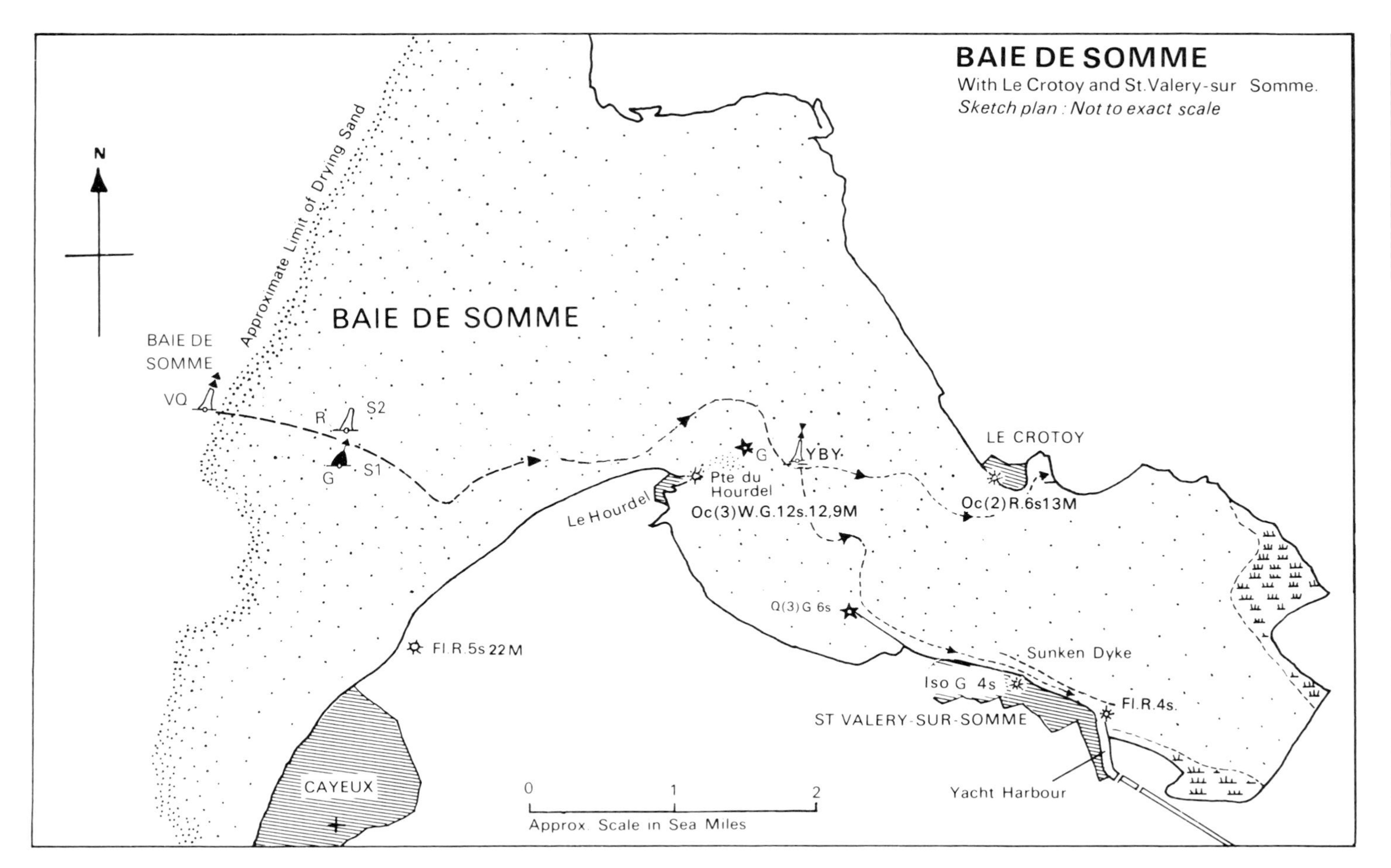

Plan 5 Sketch plan of Baie de Somme, showing position of offing and entrance buoys in 1991. Warning: substantial position changes may occur owing to shifting of the sands. (The dotted line ——→—— shows the general lie of the entrance channels – positions approximate and liable to change.) Principal lights only are shown.

The River Somme

The Somme reaches the sea by way of the largest of the three drying estuaries that lie between Boulogne and Le Tréport, but although the whole estuary dries at LW, the channels to the two principal ports are well marked, and deeper than those in the Canche. (It should be mentioned that the Authie should be avoided, as it is not only extremely shallow, but patches of soft mud mixed with hard sand mean that bilge-keelers attempting to dry have been known to roll over.) There are marinas at both St Valéry-sur-Somme and Le Crotoy, with good facilities for visitors.

Tidal notes
Heights (St Valéry): 10.0 m MHWS, 7.9 m MHWN.
HW St Valéry is HW Dieppe +0.27 (springs), +0.40 (neaps). In the approaches, the N-going stream begins at HW Cherbourg, the S-going at HW Cherbourg $+5\frac{1}{2}$. Maximum spring rates under 2 knots.

Approach
The approach buoy Baie de Somme (N cardinal, VQ) is moved to take account of changes in the channel, and I have known it to be at least a mile N or S of its 1991 position, shown on the plan. It cannot be too strongly emphasised that these radical shifts in position of the sandbanks in the estuary of the Somme take place from time to time, and both the plan and these notes must be used with this possibility constantly in mind. However, in calm weather or in offshore winds the entrance should present no problems. Coming from either direction, keep about a mile offshore until the beginning of the bay; then steer 015° or 210° (mag) as appropriate until the Baie de Somme buoy is identified. If from there the first pair of channel buoys can be seen, make for them. If not, in reasonable weather it is perfectly safe to steer E until the water shoals to less than 6 m (for those with echo sounders in feet, say 20 ft) by which time the buoys should be clearly visible. Once in the channel, it is very closely buoyed, and there are no problems, but helmsmen should constantly keep an eye on the last pair of buoys passed as well as the next ones, to guard against being set out of the channel by cross-currents. Buoys 1, 9, 15, 23 and 30 are lit, but no one in their senses would attempt an entry in the dark without first exploring in daylight.

In calm weather a shallow-draft vessel can safely begin the passage from the approach buoy 3 hours before HW, but if there is any sea to speak of it is wiser to delay until 2 hours before. In onshore winds over force 4, it is unwise to leave the buoy later than 1 hour before, as the seas become dangerous once the tide turns. Maintaining an average of $4\frac{1}{2}$ knots through the water, I find that it takes almost exactly 2 hours from the Baie de Somme buoy to St Valéry on an average tide, and a little less to Le Crotoy, so HW −2 or a few minutes earlier at the buoy is the ideal. The entrance should not be attempted in onshore winds over force 6; allowance must be made for the fact that if the wind comes on strongly from the W while in the Somme one will be unable to leave until it moderates, as the seas with a strong wind against the ebb are dangerous. Waypoint: 50°14′.0N, 1°27′.0E, then steer east for the Baie de Somme buoy and the entrance buoys (but note warning on *Plan 5*, page 17).

Entrance
The well-buoyed channel is followed to the YBY channel division buoy E of Pte du Hourdel no matter which port is the destination. From here the channel to Le Crotoy carries about

11 Le Hourdel: the approach channel seen at LW from the G beacon.

1 m on a neap, 2 m on a medium tide and 3 m on a spring, so the best time to visit is a few days before springs (this also gives a convenient midday HW). There is over 2 m in the channel to St Valéry even at neaps, so the timing for visits here is less critical. There is plenty of water in the channel to Le Hourdel: the difficulty is to find it!

Berthing: Le Hourdel

This harbour can really only be recommended to shoal-draft craft prepared to dry. The few moorings are too light for any but the smallest yachts, and visitors' best hope is to anchor downstream from the small yacht pontoons: smooth sandy bottom. From the division buoy steer for Pte du Hourdel, leaving the G beacon which marks the spit that extends from the point well to starboard. Then steer for the harbour, keeping close in past the spit (see plan and photograph). No facilities.

Berthing: Le Crotoy

This port, whose name is pronounced as if spelt 'Crotois' (i.e. 'crotwa'), is entered by the more northerly of the two buoyed channels that lead on from the division buoy. Buoy numbers are prefixed 'C'. The red ones are low with prominent topmarks, and so easily distinguishable from the large cans in the St Valéry channel. From the last buoy steer for the fishing boat quay, pass close along it and on to leave a R conical buoy to starboard. Then steer for either of the two inner pontoons. Moor in any vacant berth as available, and confirm at the club. There are 288 berths, and those along the two inner pontoons have over 1.5 m at LW. The approach channel dries, but the harbour is a natural lagoon (helped by dredging).

Facilities

Water and electricity on the pontoons. $3\frac{1}{2}$ ton crane. Toilets and showers at the club (Club Nautique de la Baie de la Somme), open most of the day in July and August, and at daytime

12 Le Hourdel at HW.

13 Le Crotoy from the W. Pass close to the fish quay when entering marina.

HW times the rest of the year. Capitainerie tel: 22 27 81 44. Modest shopping and restaurants, rather a long walk from the berths.

Berthing: St Valéry-sur-Somme
This is very much the best and most useful port in the estuary, as well as being an outstandingly beautiful town.

From the division buoy, the buoys (which run up to No. 50) and then a few lateral beacons must be followed closely to the harbour entrance. There are submerged walls at HW at both sides of the channel approaching the town, so it is important to keep fairly closely to the fairway. As shown on the plan, there is a flashing green light on the starboard hand in the approach, and a red one at the end of the eastern wall of the harbour itself. Keep well over to the S side of the channel once the first houses of the town are abeam, crossing back to mid-channel as the red light tower comes abeam on the port side.

Continue up the harbour, past the berths for small coasters and fishing boats, and the yacht harbour comes into sight. This is of marina type, with moorings bow to pontoon and stern to buoy, but visitors usually moor to the ends of the pontoons, which have $2\frac{1}{2}$ m at LW. The capitainerie (tel: 26 22 91 64) listens on VHF Channel 9. When securing, allow for very strong stream on the ebb. Do not fail to get a key from the *guardien* (on duty only HW ± 2) as the pontoons are permanently locked. A deposit is payable for the key, returnable on departure and payment of dues, which are well below average for the region.

Facilities
The yacht club (Sport Nautique Valericain, tel: 22 26 91 64) was only completed in 1987. The imposing building contains what must be the grandest showers and toilets in any port covered by this book, and also has a restaurant and bar. Entry from the street is controlled by an electric lock, whose code is available from the harbourmaster and changed fortnightly. Water

14 St Valéry-sur-Somme: the harbour entrance.

15 St Valéry-sur-Somme: the pontoons and entrance to the canal de la Somme, which runs to Abbeville.

16 St Valéry-sur-Somme: the yacht harbour from the bridge. The yacht club is on the left, above the access ramp.

on the pontoons. 6 ton crane. Repairs (hull and engine), chandlery, charts etc from Latitude 50 near the yacht harbour.

General

Modest shops and good if rather expensive restaurants will be found in the town, 10 minutes walk from the berths. Originally called Leuconaus, the town was renamed in the 10th century after its patron, a 7th-century missionary saint. The fortifications were begun in the 9th century (the 11th-century Tour Harold survives) and rebuilt in the 13th and 14th centuries, the first occasion necessitated by the town being sacked by Richard I (of England), who removed the relics of the saint and took them to St Valéry-en-Caux. William the Conqueror's fleet originally sailed from Dives, but contrary winds forced him to put in here, and it was from here that he sailed on the final passage which resulted in the conquest of England. A memorial to him will be found in the port.

Le Tréport

Charts Nos. 2451, 2147 and 1352

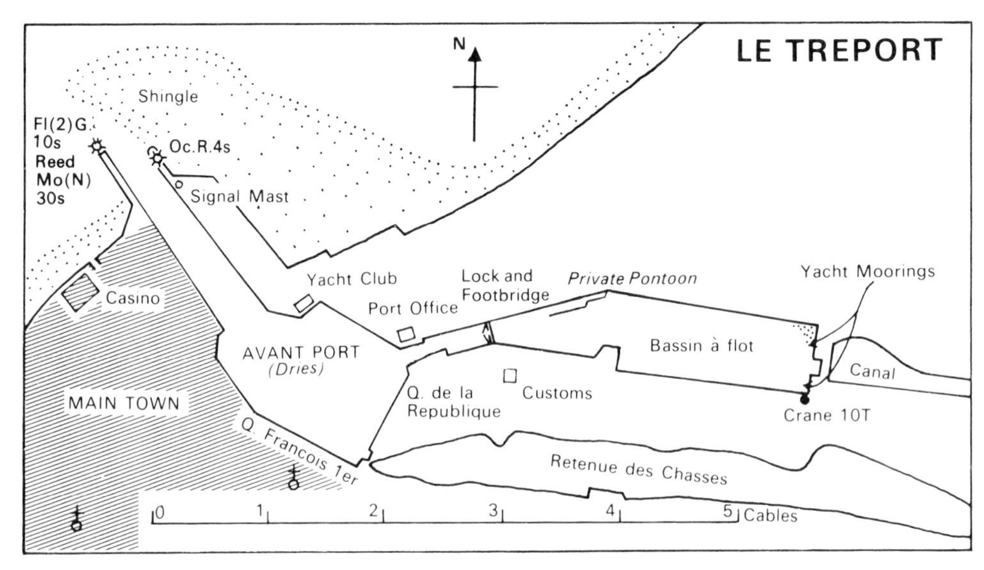

Plan 6 Le Tréport.

Lying on the border between Normandy and Picardy, Le Tréport is a pleasant little town, but unfortunately it is so far one of the few ports on this coast to have made no provision for yachts.

Tidal notes

Heights: 10.1 m MHWS, 1.3 m MLWS, 7.9 m MHWN, 3.0 m MLWN.
HW is HW Dieppe +0.01 (springs), +0.05 (neaps). The NE-going stream begins at HW Cherbourg −1, the SW-going at HW Cherbourg $+4\frac{1}{2}$. Spring rates do not exceed $1\frac{1}{2}$ knots.

Approach and entrance

With no offshore hazards of interest to a yacht, the only point to consider is timing. The outer harbour dries 2 m above chart datum in the channel to the lock, but even in good weather there is some scend, and in onshore winds this can be severe. In good weather one can safely enter 3 hours before HW, but with the least onshore breeze it is advisable to wait until $2\frac{1}{2}$ hours before. The gates close at HW, and while it is quite safe to enter after HW and stay in the outer harbour until 3 hours after, it is not wise to consider drying against the wall except in very settled fine weather, as the bottom is hard and severe pounding can be experienced. Much better to press on to Dieppe, 14 miles to the SW. Waypoint: 50°05′.0N, 1°22′.0E, then steer 170° (mag) for the pierheads.

When approaching it is advisable to contact port control on Channel 12, as the entrance is narrow. Coming from the east, it is important to note the shingle spit extending NW from the east pierhead. Keep $\frac{1}{4}$ mile off the pierheads and continue SW until the light on the E pier is almost in line with the light on the W pierhead. From here it is safe to steer for the W

17 Le Tréport: the entrance, showing the lighthouse on the western breakwater.

pierhead, keeping the E light just open of the (much larger) W light. Once round the W pierhead proceed down the centre of the channel into the Avant-Port. Note that the depths given above apply only after the annual dredging in May. Visitors arriving earlier than this could find less water, and should only approach in the hour before HW or after taking advice.

Berthing

If one has arrived in the Avant-Port too early for the lock gates to be open, it may be possible to pick up a mooring, or alternatively one may tie up alongside the NE wall, near the port office (see plan). The lock gates open at approximately $1\frac{1}{2}$ hours before HW, according to the level of the tide, and close exactly at HW. During that time the swing bridge opens on request: in theory the signal is three blasts on the horn, but in practice this is seldom necessary, as a good lookout is kept, at least during daylight hours. Once the bridge opens, pass straight through the Arrière-Port, and berth in the Bassin à Flot. The long sides of this basin are reserved for the considerable cargo vessels which use the port, and yachts are usually directed to berth at the E end of the basin, often alongside a fishing boat. Beware shoal water in the NE corner of the basin (see plan), and sound carefully before deciding on a mooring, bearing in mind that the water level can drop by as much as 1 m between the closure of the lock and its next opening. The photograph shows what *can* happen. It is sometimes possible to berth at the W end, which is more comfortable and nearer the town. Note that the pontoon in the Bassin à Flot is owned by a local yacht hire and sailing school firm. When I spoke to a member of it in 1987 he did not seem particularly disposed to be helpful to visiting yachtsmen.

In 1991, works were in progress to convert the *Retenue des Chasses* into a second basin, but there still appeared to be no plans for improving the accommodation for visiting yachts. However it is possible that when the new basin (mainly for fishermen) is opened, visitors will

18 Le Tréport. The harbour/lock office is the white building to the right of the hotel on the far left. The new basin will be up the channel on the right.

19 The new lock gates at Le Tréport leak more slowly than the old ones, making this sort of embarrassing occurrence less frequent!

be berthed there rather than in the commercial basin, so local advice should be taken and the Capitainerie (Channel 12 or tel: 35 86 17 91) contacted if possible.

Facilities

Not many! 10 ton crane in the basin. Fuel near the port office, water near the yacht club (both marked on plan). No toilets or showers (I confess I have never visited the yacht club, which may have them, but it is a long way from the usual berth). For repairs try InterMer Services, 6 quai de la Republique (see plan), tel: 35 50 26 42.

General

The town is some distance from the E end of the basin, but it has good shops in a setting of some charm. The place has a long history, largely consisting of being burnt down by the English (1296, 1339, 1413 by Henry V, 1513 and 1545). In the battle marking another unsuccessful raid in 1340, artillery was used for the first time, six years before Crécy. The 16th-century church of St Jacques, built on the ruins of its often-destroyed predecessors, is well worth a visit.

Charts Nos. 2451 and 2147

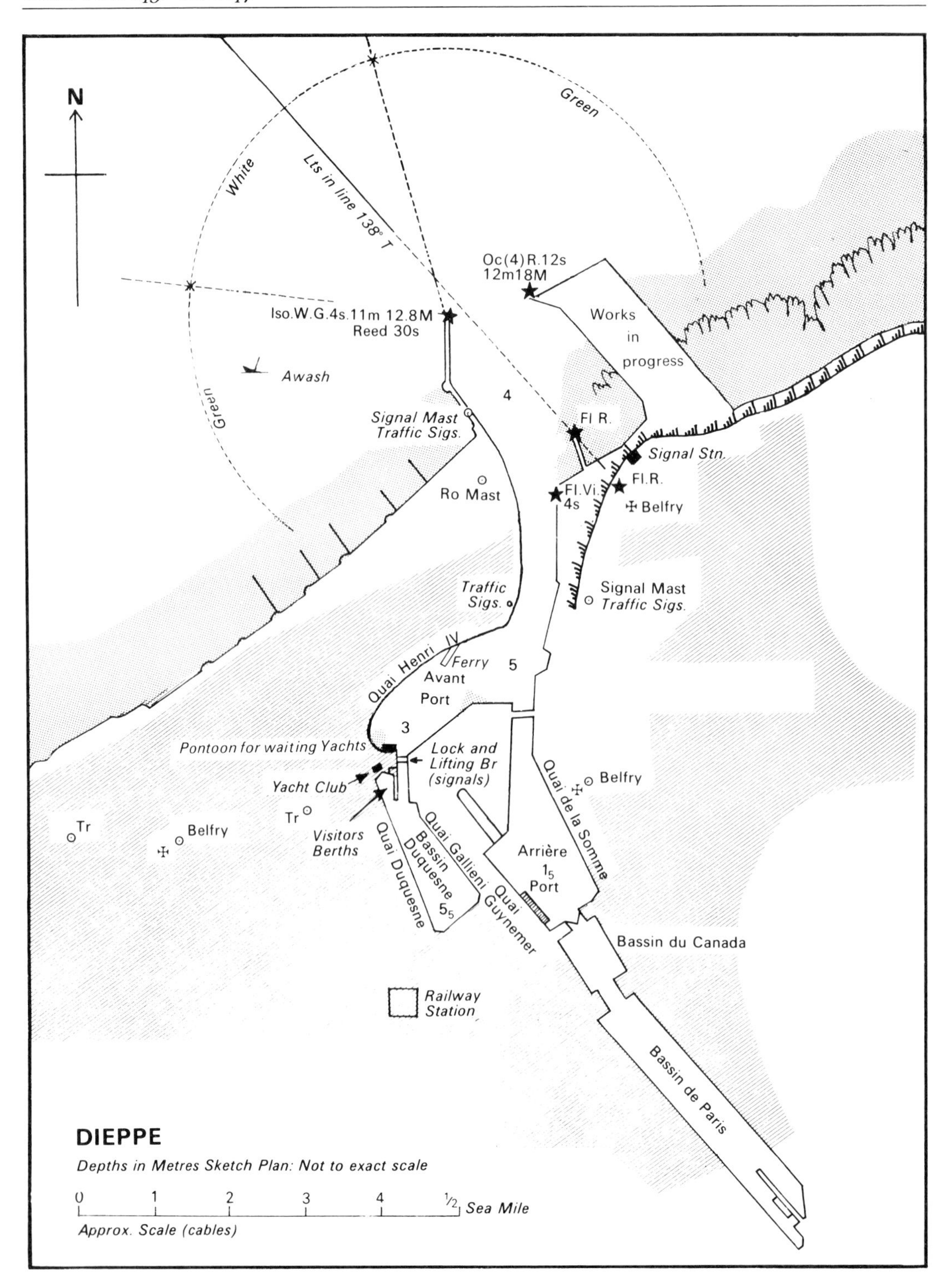

Plan 7 Dieppe.

Although the outer harbour can be uncomfortable, it is available for shelter at all tides, while the inner yacht basin is comfortable and convenient to the centre of this considerable town.

Tidal notes

Heights: 9.3 m MHWS, 0.7 m MLWS, 7.2 m MHWN, 2.5 m MLWN.
Dieppe is a principal tidal port. The E-going stream begins at HW Cherbourg −2, the W-going at HW Cherbourg +4. Maximum rates less than 2 knots.

Approach and entrance

There are no offshore hazards, and the harbour can be approached from any direction. When approaching, Notre Dame de Bon Secours, built on the cliffs above the town, is conspicuous. Waypoint: 49°57′. 0N, 1°04′. 0E, then steer 140° (mag) for the pierheads.

Once off the pierheads, the traffic signals must be strictly observed. They are as follows:

Lights	Red White Red	Green White Green	Green White Red
Meaning	No entry	No departure	No entry or departure

To enter against the signals is strictly forbidden, and unless a proper reason can be given ('It was rough out there' is not enough!) action may be taken. Port control listens on channel 12. Once inside, keep to starboard and follow that wall round into the Avant-Port, where the visitors' pontoon will be found at the west end, beyond the bridge. In its present position it is reasonably sheltered, but there is still a lot of movement from scend (especially in N winds)

20 Dieppe: entrance to the outer harbour.

and wash from passing traffic, so heavy fenders are an asset. Much better if possible to arrive while the inner basin is open, and jill around until the bridge opens.

Berthing

The lock into the Bassin Duquesne opens 2 hours before HW, and closes between 1.05 hours after (low neaps) and 1.25 hours after (high springs). The bridge will open two or three times during the open period: signal two blasts if necessary. One green light permits entry to the basin, one red departure, red and green together no passage. Turn sharp to starboard at the end of the entrance channel to enter the part of the basin reserved for yachts. Note: in 1989 the pontoon for waiting yachts was extended in length, and it was hoped to fit a ramp to the top of the harbour wall to replace the ladders.

Facilities

The yacht club was moved in 1989, and is now in the old Seajet building on the harbour wall just W of the lock. Pleasant bar and palatial showers and loos. There is a travel lift, and water and electricity are available, although for water the hose has to be borrowed from the club and a stand-pipe brought and set up, so it is advisable to fill up if the hose is seen to be in use. Diesel in cans from Marchand, 100 m NW from the clubhouse on quai Duquesne: they will lend cans. For 500 litres or more (which can be shared) the club will arrange delivery by road tanker alongside in the basin or, near HW, in the Avant-Port. Chandlery from Thalassa-

21 Dieppe: yacht moorings in Bassin Duquesne. The Yacht Club is in the large building to the left of the lock and lifting bridge.

Dieppe, 2 quai de la Cale, tel: 35 82 16 08, who also repair diesel engines of all makes. They will be found by walking ENE from the bridge over the lock until opposite the sealink ferry berth. Repairs to radios and all types of electronic equipment from Radio Maritime, 6 quai du Carénage, tel: 35 84 22 63. They will send a technician to any port along the coast as far as Fécamp. The club (Cercle de la Voile de Dieppe) will advise on repairs etc, and are always friendly and helpful, tel: 35 84 32 99. Radiotelephone on Channel 24, tel: 35 70 50 50.

General

Excellent restaurants will be found along the quai Duquesne, just opposite the basin, and also along quai Henri IV, the latter being rather more expensive. All possible shopping in town, beginning a short walk W from quai Duquesne. The church of St Jacques, begun by Henry II of England and finished in the 14th century, should not be missed, nor should the museum in the chateau half way up the cliffs. Named after the still surviving English word 'deep', Dieppe has been a port at least since 1030, when a charter bound the town to deliver 5,000 salted herrings every year to the Abbey of St Catherine-les-Rouen. It was occupied by the English from 1420 to 1435, and burnt down by an Anglo-Dutch fleet in 1694, and was of course the scene of the Dieppe Raid of 1942, one of the first 'combined operations', in which over 4,000 of the 6,000 land forces put ashore were casualties.

St Valéry-en-Caux

Chart No. 2451

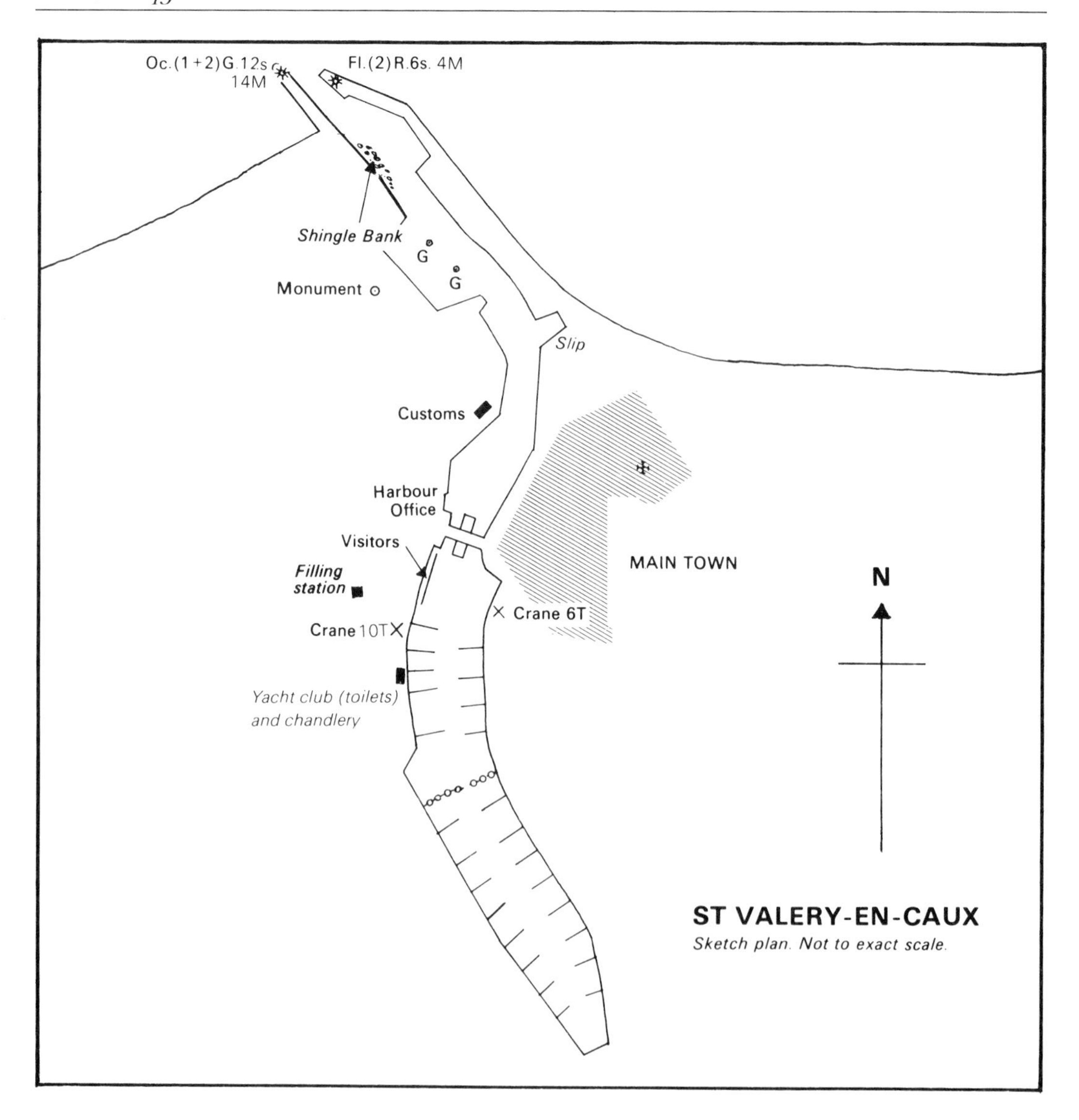

Plan 8 St Valéry-en-Caux.

One of the most active yachting centres in E Normandy, St Valéry has excellent facilities for visitors, and although the harbour is tidal it does have a long open period compared with those further N.

Tidal notes

Heights: 8.9 m MHWS, 1.0 m MLWS, 7.1 m MHWN, 2.5 m MLWN.

HW is HW Dieppe – 0.18. The E-going stream begins at HW Cherbourg $-1\frac{1}{2}$, and reaches a maximum of 2.6 knots (springs) at HW Cherbourg $+\frac{1}{2}$. The W-going stream begins at HW Cherbourg $+3\frac{1}{2}$ and reaches a maximum of 2.1 knots at HW Cherbourg $+5\frac{1}{2}$.

Approach

There are no offshore hazards. Landmarks include a red and white radio mast just E of the town, and the nuclear power station at Port Sussette 3 miles to its west. Viewed from the east, there is also a conspicuous white vertical stripe in the cliff which lies just W of the town. Especially when approached from the west, the town is invisible until it is almost abeam, as it lies well back in a gap in the cliffs. However, the lighthouse on the W pierhead can usually be seen: it is white with a green top. Waypoint: 49°53′.5N, 0°42′.5E, then steer S for the pierheads.

Entrance

The western mole extends further out to sea than the eastern one, to give craft that are making harbour some protection against the prevailing westerlies. This, however, produces bad turbulence on the more rare occasions when there is a NE wind. Wind from between N and E over force 5 causes severe sea conditions, and entry should not be attempted at such times. To act as a wave-breaker, there is a slope on the E mole which takes the sting out of the sea by absorbing and smoothing the waves. Unfortunately it has the effect of collecting a

22 St Valéry-en-Caux. Keep further to port than the yacht shown entering until past the wave-break gap on the port side.

big bank of shingle on the western side of the entrance which it is most important to avoid. The approach to the harbour is 150° (mag) which is when the lighthouse on the western mole and the light structure on the eastern mole are in line. When abeam of the lighthouse on the western mole it is of great importance to close the eastern mole and take a course parallel to it. Between the eastern light structure and the mole proper there are three posts with red tops which mark the ramp. They should be left close to port as the shingle bank lies opposite them.

After successfully negotiating the entrance and the short channel leading to the outer harbour, visitors arriving outside opening hours will generally find a mooring available to pick up while waiting for the lock gates to open. The outer harbour should only be entered 3 hours either side of HW, and the lock gates open $2\frac{1}{4}$ hours either side, except at extreme neaps when this is reduced to 2 hours either side. The wait is therefore unlikely to be a long one. During the time the gates are open the bridge opens for 5 minutes on every hour and half-hour (except between 1200 and 1300), so the sounding of horns at other times is useless and unpopular. A limited service is operated at night (June 15–Sept 15 only) with only two bridge openings, $\frac{1}{2}$ hour before and $\frac{1}{4}$ hour after HW. A green light at the bridge allows entry, a red light departure; red and green means no passage.

The entrance channel carries 2 m of water at half-tide, so entrance times must be adjusted to the circumstances, and in strong onshore winds it is wiser to postpone entry until $1\frac{1}{2}$ hours before HW, by which time the depth in the channel is 4 m or more.

Berthing

On entering the inner harbour, a pontoon will be seen immediately to starboard after passing through the lock. This is the Ponton d'Acceuil, and visitors should tie up here temporarily

23 St Valéry-en-Caux: the yacht basin looking towards the lifting bridge and lock. The visitors' pontoon is on the left of the picture parallel to the wall.

and enquire at the harbour office (see plan) for a berth. Note that, as shown on the plan, the wet basin is divided in half by a sunken beam which joins a series of concrete supports originally intended for a bridge. Do not attempt to go beyond this barrier without examining it at LW (the level falls while the gates are shut) or at least taking reliable local advice. Port Office VHF Channel 9 or tel: 35 97 01 30.

Facilities

Water and electricity on pontoons. Showers and toilets at yacht club (Centre de Voile de St Valéry-en-Caux), open all year. 6 ton and 8 ton cranes. The excellent boatyard of Nautic 76 has all chandlery, charts etc and can undertake all manner of repairs. I have used their services in the past and found them to be quick, efficient and reasonable in their charges, tel: 35 97 04 22. Diesel from the filling station shown on the plan (Nautic will lend cans). Small slip in outer harbour.

General

Shopping here is good and close to the berths, and there are several restaurants of all standards. The town's history goes back as far as 620, when St Valéry came from the Somme to preach to the pagan inhabitants. Richard the Lionheart brought his relics here in 1197 (having sacked St Valéry-sur-Somme to get them). The town was occupied by the English from 1422 to 1432, and much fought over before becoming permanently French. It was sacked during the religious wars (1589), and to make matters worse the port was almost closed by a shingle bar. However, repairs began in 1612, and by 1804 the port was prosperous enough to rate a bombardment from the British navy. The record goes on into modern times: in 1940 General Rommel destroyed the eastern part of the town by gunfire when the 51st Highland Division refused to surrender. Today it is a pleasant and peaceful place, no doubt a reaction against its warlike past.

Fécamp

Charts Nos. 2451 and 1352

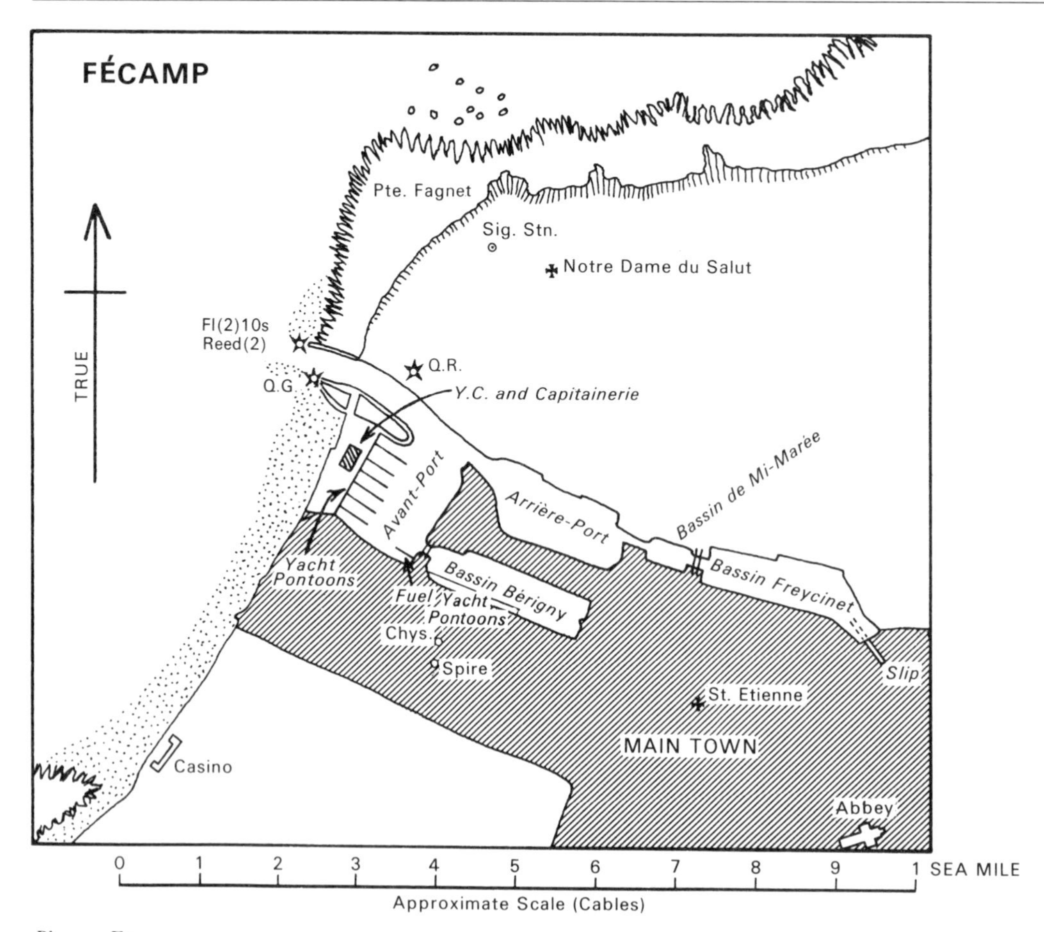

Plan 9 Fécamp.

With the exception of Boulogne, Fécamp provides the nearest all-tide yacht harbour to England in the eastern half of our area. With its comfortable marina and good facilities, only 66 miles from Brighton Marina and less than 90 from the Solent, it is a popular landfall for visitors wishing to cruise the Seine and Calvados area, and has a special tradition of friendship with British yachtsmen.

Tidal notes

Heights: 7.9 m MHWS, 0.8 m MLWS, 6.6 m MHWN, 2.6 m MLWN.

HW is HW Le Havre +0.49 (springs), +0.32 (neaps). LW is LW Le Havre +0.05 (springs), +0.20 (neaps). The NE-going stream begins at HW Cherbourg $-1\frac{1}{2}$, and reaches a maximum of 2.5 knots (springs) at HW Cherbourg +1. The SW-going stream begins at HW Cherbourg +4 and reaches a maximum of 2.0 knots at HW Cherbourg $-5\frac{1}{2}$.

24 Fécamp: the entrance and Pte Fagnet.

Approach

There are no offshore hazards, and approaching coastally Pte Fagnet, topped by its signal station and church, is conspicuous from both directions. On passage, the powerful radio beacon on Cap d'Antifer, TI(– ··) on 291.9 kHz, is useful. Waypoints: from the east, 49°47'.0N, 0°22'.0E, then steer SW until pierheads open up or pierhead lights bear SE when approach can be begun. From N or W, 49°46'.0N, 0°21'.0E, then steer 95° (mag) for the entrance.

Entrance

The entrance can be rough in winds of force 5 or more from between SW and NW, as the bottom shelves steeply, but with sufficient water entry is safe in anything short of a full gale. The approach and channel between the piers is kept dredged to 1.5 m, so for a yacht of average draft entry is safe in fine weather at any time except perhaps within 1½ hours of LWS. In rough weather, however, it is wise to time one's entry for 2 hours either side of HW (1 hour if the sea is very bad). If waiting outside it is wiser to heave-to or jill around, as the holding is poor.

The best line for entry is to approach the pierheads on a course of about 85° (mag). When close in, keep more towards the S pierhead, particularly if entering well before HW, when there is a strong northerly set across the entrance.

Traffic signals are shown from a mast on the south jetty, and must be observed. Three red lights from the signal mast means no passage: G over W over G allows passage with permission. A single W means harbour open. Port control operates on VHF Channel 9.

Once between the piers, keep to the centre of the channel as far as traffic will allow, and if under sail beware of strong gusts from unexpected directions. Take the first large opening on the starboard hand into the Avant-Port, which is the yacht harbour.

25 Fécamp: the entrance and Avant-Port from Notre Dame du Salut.

26 Fécamp: yacht pontoons in the Avant-Port. The yacht club and Capitainerie share the conspicuous building on the skyline.

Berthing

The Avant-Port at Fécamp is completely given over to yachts, and provides first-class pontoon moorings with all facilities. The visitors' pontoon is the fourth one on the starboard hand (marked 'C'), which provides 20 or more places in the outer half which is reserved for visitors. Failing a vacancy here, tie up where there is a gap and report to the Capitainerie in the large building above the pontoons, where a berth will be allotted. This is seldom necessary, however, as the harbourmaster is very active, and usually signals visitors to a suitable berth. Care should be taken when mooring, as considerable scend can develop in the harbour in winds from the western quadrant. For this reason, and also because it is cheaper, visitors planning a long stay, or leaving their boat, are advised to arrange to lock into the Bassin Bérigny, where one can lie alongside in perfect shelter. For stays of over 48 hours in the Avant-Port the third day is free.

Facilities

Water and electricity on the pontoons. Showers and toilets in the Capitainerie building (which also contains the club) tel: 35 28 13 58. Fuel from fuelling pontoon (see plan): for service apply to the Capitainerie, operating times 0900–1100 and 1400–1800, closed Tuesdays and Thursdays. Under normal circumstances they prefer not to open up the pumps for less than 50 litres, as small quantities can be bought in cans and taken aboard by hand, but if there are special problems they will always help. Cranes to 38 tons, slip. Two excellent chandlers: Chantiers Moré, who have a small wooden shop NE of the Capitainerie, but their main workshops are on the quai de Verdun, on the S side of the Bassin Freycinet (see plan), tel: 35 28 28 15; and Alain Denis at 21 quai de la Vicomté overlooking the yacht basin, tel: 35 28 30 34. Radio-Maritime, a sub-office of the main Dieppe branch also on quai de la Vicomté, can do electronic and electrical repairs, and there are several mechanics: ask at the Capitainerie. Sail repairs have to be sent to Le Havre, but can still be returned in a couple of days.

General

A reasonable selection of small shops will be found within 500 m of the berths, but the main shopping centre is a considerable walk, being up beyond the Benedictine museum, recognisable by its slender spire, and about a mile from the berths. There are, however, several good restaurants down by the harbour, and as long as my old friends the Benavides family continue to run the Hotel du Progrès on quai Vicomté overlooking the Avant-Port, I am sure it will go on providing good value and a friendly welcome.

Visitors to Fécamp should not miss the Benedictine museum. When I first visited the town in 1946 the liqueur was still actually made there, and a lot of the equipment then in use can still be seen. One of the most fascinating exhibits is the black museum of 'forged' Benedictine bottles from all over the world. The name Fécamp derives from Fiscamnum, a romanised celtic word, and the abbey was founded in 662, and was already ancient when Robert of Normandy presented his son William, the Conqueror to be, to his barons when he was a boy of seven.

Like so many Norman towns, Fécamp was much fought over during the Hundred Years War, being finally regained for France by the Governor of Dieppe in 1449. Prince Charles, later Charles II, also landed here after escaping from England after the battle of Worcester. But of course the whole world will remember Fécamp above all as the town where, in 1510, Bernard Vincelli developed his great elixir – Benedictine.

Le Havre

Charts Nos. 2613, 2146 and 2990

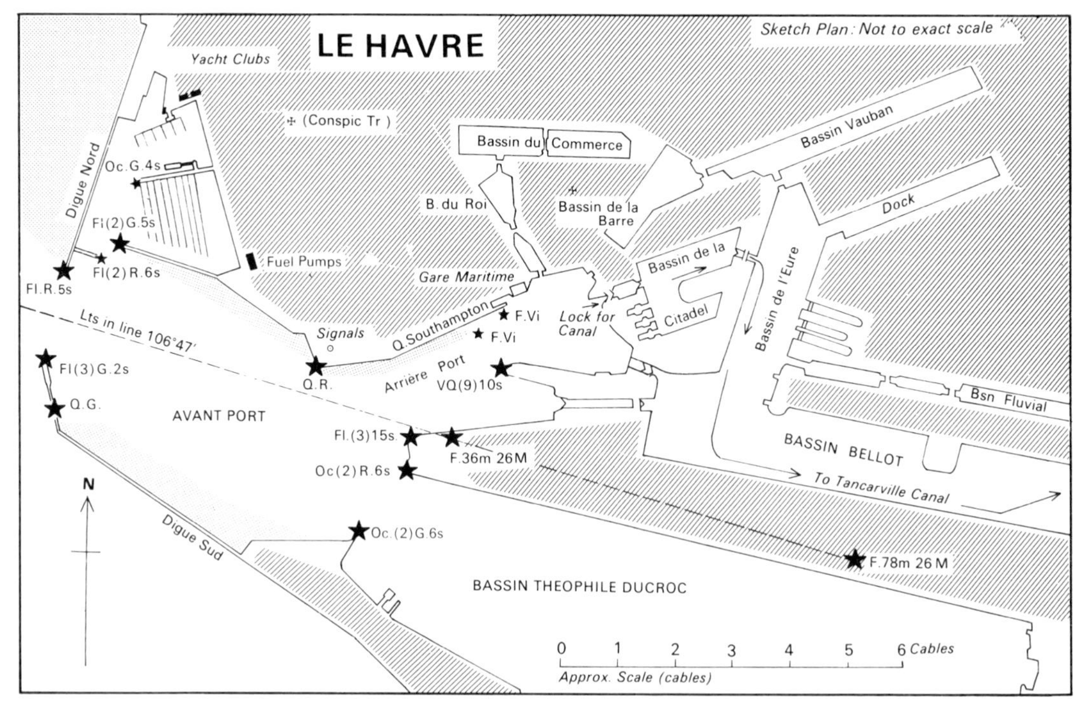

Plan 10 Le Havre.

A busy major commercial and passenger port, Le Havre also offers good accommodation for visiting yachts which is accessible at all states of the tide. It is not, however, a place at which to plan to do major shopping.

Tidal notes

Heights: 7.9 m MHWS, 1.2 m MLWS, 6.6 m MHWN, 3.0 m MLWN.

There is a distinct stand of the tide around HW at Le Havre, and this is experienced in many of the neighbouring ports to the S and W. At springs at Le Havre, for instance, the tide remains above 90% of its full height from HW $-2\frac{1}{4}$ to HW $+1\frac{1}{2}$, a total of $3\frac{3}{4}$ hours, compared with only 2 hours at Dieppe. In the offing west of the harbour entrance the tide runs W from HW Le Havre $+4\frac{1}{2}$, turns S at HW $+6$, E at HW $-2\frac{1}{2}$ and N at HW -1. The tide runs strongly into the Chenal de Rouen from the sea from HW -4 to -1, and runs out strongly from HW $+2$ to $+6$.

Approach and entrance

As with most major ports, yachts should keep out of the fairway as far as possible, and approaching from the north or NW the best approach is from close off Cap de la Hève, from where one may safely steer for a position just N of buoy LH 16 (the most easterly of the line

27 Le Havre: entrance from the last port buoy of approach. The Thermique Centrale chimneys are clearly visible.

of red buoys marking the north of the channel) and from there to pass close S of the northern pierhead. From the south, it is advisable to cross the fairway from LH 15 to LH 16, and then proceed as above. Remember that commercial vessels using the main channel have absolute priority and must not in any way be impeded. If in doubt (for instance in bad visibility) call port control on Channel 12. The fairway should be crossed at right angles and at reasonable speed, using power if necessary. Waypoints: from north of the main channel 49°30′.5N, 0°02′.0E, from south of the main channel 49°29′.0N, 0°02′.0E, then see text. Once clear of the northern pierhead turn NE to round the new short breakwater that juts out from the Digue Nord (Fl(2)R 6s), then leave the longer breakwater that protects the yacht harbour (Fl(2)G 5s) and turn E into the main yacht basin.

Berthing
The nearest of the eight pontoons is reserved on both its sides for visitors (see plan). When securing, remember that quite a scend can develop in strong winds from between SW and NW. At crowded periods, if no visitors' berth is free take any berth and contact the marina office either on foot or via VHF Channel 9.

Facilities
These are comprehensive, as would be expected from a major yachting centre. Water and electricity on the pontoons. Toilets and showers (7 franc *jeton* from the harbour office or SNH bar) at the Sport Nautique du Havre club. This is the more easterly of the two club buildings, and it is a friendly little club with bar, open 1700–2200 weekdays except Monday, and all day at weekends, the toilet block being open 0800–2030 every day. The other club, Société des Régates du Havre, is large, hospitable but rather grand. A high standard of dress is expected, including ties in the evening. It has a first-class restaurant, which is not cheap but excellent

value, and during the high season there is a secondary club-house at Sainte Adresse (near Cap de la Hève) with its own restaurant and magnificent views of the estuary. Well worth a visit. Chandlery, charts etc will be found at Acastillage Diffusion, 120 rue Augustin Normand (tel: 35 43 43 62, fax: 35 21 66 07). This road lies two blocks inland from and parallel to boulevard Clemenceau, the main road running down the east side of the yacht harbour. The other services are close by in the same street: engine repairs from ADMT at number 116 (tel: 35 43 00 41), and sail repairs from Delta Voiles at number 114, tel: 35 43 16 70. All three share the same fax. Another chandler is Marine Plus, further south along the boulevard Clemenceau, and another sailmaker Voilerie de l'Estuaire, 42 rue St-Jacques, tel: 35 43 33 34. 16 ton travel lift, 6 ton crane. Fuel from SE corner of harbour (see plan): capitainerie tel: 35 21 23 95.

General

I should perhaps point out that, though in the general text I have used the English convention, in France the name is spelt 'le Havre' and appears in alphabetical lists under H. (This applies to all towns beginning with the definite article.) The name derives from the chapel of Notre-Dame de Grace, a 15th-century landmark, and in full is 'Havre de Grace'. The main shopping centre is a long way: strike E from just N of the yacht clubs along Avenue Foch and it is a mile or so in that direction. There is however a group of small shops adequate for ordinary supplies in the road between bd Clemenceau and rue Augustin Normand (see above).

The harbour was important in the 11th to 14th centuries, but then was choked by sandbanks like so many Norman harbours. Even so it was from here that the fleet sailed that was to put Henry VII on the English throne. Francis I of France began the works that were to create the modern port. The English under Warwick took the port during the religious wars in 1562, but had to surrender a year later. After this the town increased in prosperity, in spite of a bombardment by the English in 1694, another by Lord Rodney in 1759, and a third in 1804, when the Royal Navy were blockading Napoleon's invasion forces. Close by is Harfleur, the scene of the great speech in *Henry V*, and still featuring a gothic church from that period.

The Tancarville Canal

The Seine Estuary can be rough and dangerous in westerly gales, so there may be occasions when yachts or motor cruisers may wish to use this short cut from Le Havre to the Seine via Honfleur and Tancarville. Local advice should be taken, and sailing boats will need to have their masts lowered, but this is no problem if they are continuing to Paris or beyond. The lock for small craft is at the east end of the Arrière-Port, beyond the quai Southampton where the ferries moor (see plan). Bridges open on presentation, but subject to traffic, and the 15 miles from the yacht harbour to the Seine at Tancarville has several of them and can be tedious – recommended only to dodge really bad weather. The Capitainerie will advise.

Passage Notes: The Seine Estuary

Charts Nos. 2146, 2990 and 2994

Although there is no longer, at least officially, a *mascaret* (bore) in the Seine, the flood stream can still be very fierce, with spring rates up to 4½ knots off Honfleur and 6½ knots at La Roque, 8 miles further upstream.

As with all passages on tidal rivers, achievement of a quick and successful run depends upon starting at exactly the right state of the tide. On passage to Rouen, one should aim to be off Honfleur about 4 hours before HW Le Havre, from where, by maintaining something over 5 knots through the water, Rouen can be reached on a single flood tide.

As always, the downward trip is more difficult. The ebb can only be carried for about 4 hours before the new flood is met, when one is best advised to pick up the next practicable mooring and wait for the stream to slacken before continuing. The main force of the flood only lasts for 3–4 hours, so by this method it is usually easy to reach Honfleur or Le Havre in one day, riding down on two successive ebbs. The ideal time to leave Rouen is 10 hours after LW Le Havre, i.e. 4½ hours after HW there.

Note that Honfleur is useless as a port of call on the way up to Rouen, as by the time he can leave the harbour, the yachtsman will have missed the best of the flood. To visit Honfleur in its own right (and nobody should miss it!), departure from either Le Havre or Deauville 2–3 hours before HW Le Havre will ensure arrival at a convenient time to lock straight in to the inner harbour. From Deauville, care must be taken to clear the W end of the Ratelets shoal, and thereafter keep N of the Digue du Ratier, marked at its W end by a beacon tower (VQ) and subsequently by unlit posts. Similarly, coming from Le Havre, the W end of the Basse du Nord shoal must be cleared: this is achieved by keeping W of No. 6 buoy (VQR).

The prolonged HW means that passages between Honfleur and Deauville can easily be made on a single HW, leaving the port of departure at first opening of the gates. From Le Havre to Honfleur, avoid the temptation to leave too early, especially near springs. This can result in difficulties in being swept up the estuary north of the Basse du Nord, or in entering the narrow entrance of Honfleur with a strong cross-current. 2½ hours before HW Le Havre is quite early enough.

The River Seine and Rouen

Charts Nos. 2994 and 2880

This book is written for the coastal cruising sailor, and I will therefore not cover this area from the point of view of readers intending to continue to Paris or beyond: they will need one of the excellent pilots covering the waterways they intend to visit. However, Rouen, the ancient capital of Normandy and a most beautiful city, is well worth a visit as part of a Normandy cruise, and it is possible for a sailing vessel to berth below the bridges, and thus to make such a visit without lowering her mast(s). However, in high season use of the downstream berth may be restricted to 48 hours or less: telephone Rouen Port on 35 52 54 00 or call on VHF Channel 73 to check.

Tidal notes

Depths are not important for a yachtsman in a deep-water channel: what matters is the times of the fair and foul streams. The following table gives the times of streams at various points between the entrance and Rouen. The figures are in hours and minutes to be *added* to the time of *low* water at Le Havre. LW Le Havre is 5 hours before HW at springs, increasing to $5\frac{1}{2}$ hours before at mean neaps and up to 6 hours before at extreme neaps.

	FLOOD STREAM BEGINS *(Hours after LW Le Havre)*			EBB STREAM BEGINS *(Hours after LW Le Havre)*		
PLACE	SPRINGS	MID-TIDES	NEAPS	SPRINGS	MID-TIDES	NEAPS
La Roque	2.40	2.30	2.05	7.00	6.50	6.10
Quillebeuf	3.03	2.45	2.30	7.10	7.00	6.20
Villequier	4.00	3.40	3.25	7.40	7.30	6.40
Caudebec	4.15	3.50	3.35	8.00	7.50	7.00
La Mailleraye	4.30	4.15	4.00	8.30	8.20	8.10
Duclair	5.15	5.05	4.45	9.00	9.00	9.25
La Bouille	5.50	5.45	5.40	10.00	10.00	10.00
Rouen	6.25	6.40	6.15	10.50	10.40	10.40

Maximum flood streams (springs) are 4.5 knots at Honfleur, 6.5 at La Roque, 5.0 at Courval, diminishing to 3 knots in the higher reaches. Ebb rates do not exceed 2 knots except below Courval, reaching 4 knots at La Roque and $2\frac{1}{2}$ at Honfleur.

Passages up and down river

As mentioned earlier, the upriver passage should be timed so as to be off Honfleur 4 hours before HW Le Havre. Except for those coming in from a sea passage of some length, this will almost certainly involve a departure from Le Havre yacht harbour, as Deauville and Honfleur do not open early enough to permit this timing. Le Havre to Honfleur is 9 miles, so the average yacht will probably do well by leaving the former at 6 hours before HW.

From Honfleur to the Bassin St Gervais in Rouen is 60 nautical miles, and the ebb stream begins 10 hours 40 minutes after *low* water Le Havre. As the passage has started between 1 and 2 hours after LW (see above under *Tidal notes*) the vessel will have 8 or 9 hours of fair tide to make the 60 miles, an average of say 6.7 knots. For a boat able to make 5 knots through the water the stream will supply the rest except at neaps, when it may be better to leave half an hour earlier.

Pleasure craft are prohibited from navigating the Seine above the longitude of Cap du Hode (0° 20.5′E) after dark, so departure times must be planned to take this into account. However, there are places where it is possible to moor. These are given in the next section.

Getting down a river is always harder than getting up it, and the Seine is no exception. The ebb begins at 10 hours and 50 minutes after LW Le Havre, but I advise taking advantage of the gentle streams near Rouen by starting an hour or so earlier than that, say 10 hours after. When the ebb stream begins it will be carried for about 4 hours, after which the flood will begin. Except for fast motor boats or at low neap tides, the best thing to do at this point is pick up the nearest mooring and wait for the stream to pass its peak and slacken to below 2 knots before continuing. It should then be possible to reach Honfleur (too late to enter, but see special note under that heading) or Le Havre on the second ebb.

Berthing: River Seine

Figures in brackets below refer to distance in kilometres from Paris. These figures are useful as they are displayed on tide gauges and beacons all along the river. From downstream upwards, possible mooring places are as follows:

Tancarville (338). Just above the bridge on the port side. Moor between waiting barges, or between piles if unoccupied (but be ready to slip if a barge arrives).
Quillebeuf (331). There are some mooring buoys here.
Caudebec-en-Caux (310). A small pontoon may have space for a short stay.
Duclair (278). There is a pontoon with room for three visitors.

Anchoring is not recommended, certainly not overnight unless an anchor watch is set, owing to uncertain holding and strong streams. However, it must of course be resorted to in emergency, and as long as a good watch is kept it is always safe outside the fairway where this is buoyed. La Mailleraye (303) is a useful place as there is an area too shallow for large vessels. Small craft must always manoeuvre to leave commercial traffic free passage. Rouen port control listens on Channel 73.

Berthing: Rouen

Masted yachts berth on a pontoon in the Bassin St Gervais, the basin on the port side before the bridge. Stay limited to two days in high season. Motor cruisers may prefer to pass under four bridges (keeping to the N side of Ile Lacroix) and moor on the N bank of the island to one of the two pontoons reserved for yachts. Space for about 25 boats.

Facilities

Cranes 3–25 tons. Water and electricity on Ile Lacroix pontoons. Chandlery, repairs from Villetard, Ile Lacroix, tel: 35 88 00 00. Electrical and electronic repairs Radio-Maritime, 77 quai du Havre, tel: 35 71 34 88.

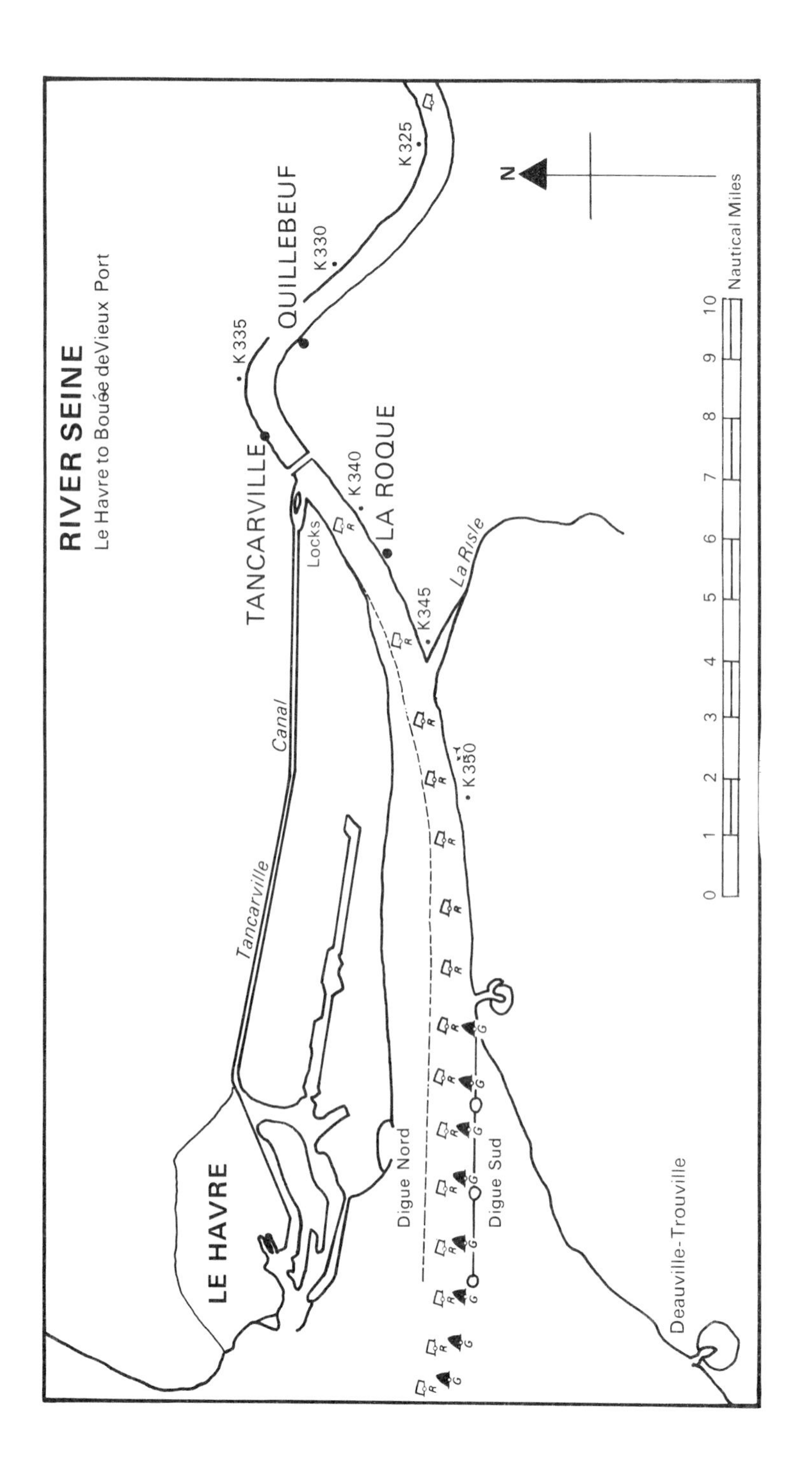

Plan 11 The River Seine from Le Havre to Rouen with the Tancarville Canal. Numbers preceded by capital K indicate distance in kilometres from Paris. These are shown on posts on the river bank.

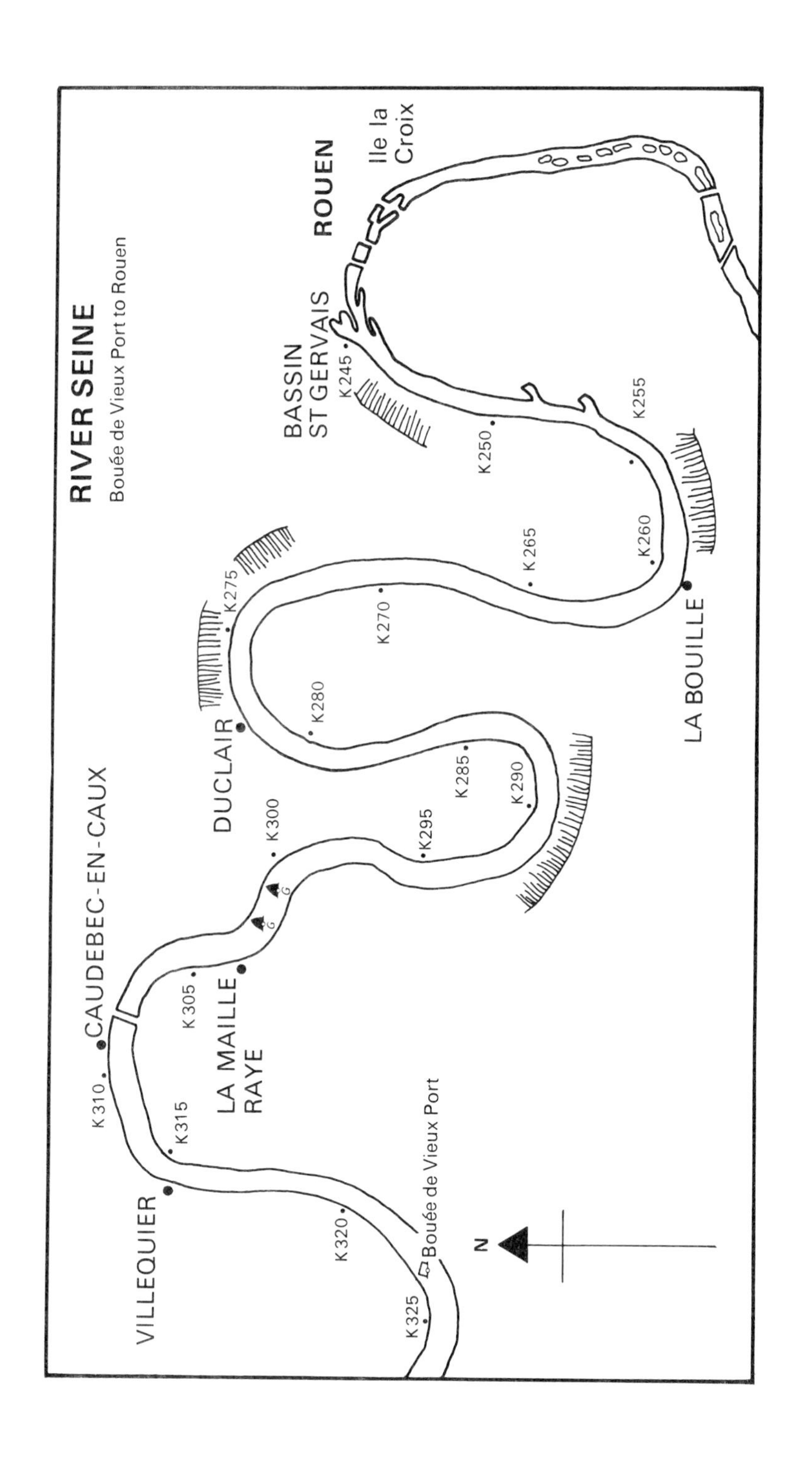

RIVER SEINE
Bouée de Vieux Port to Rouen
ROUEN
Ile la Croix
BASSIN ST GERVAIS
K245
K250
K255
K260
K265
K270
K275
K280
K285
K290
K295
K300
K305
K310
K315
K320
K325
LA BOUILLE
DUCLAIR
CAUDEBEC-EN-CAUX
LA MAILLE RAYE
VILLEQUIER
Bouée de Vieux Port
N
G
G

Plan 11 (cont.)

28 Yachts lying on the pontoon in the Bassin St Gervais, Rouen.

General

It is a fair old walk into the city from St Gervais, probably a couple of miles. All the shops and restaurants of a major city, and do not miss the cathedral (13th to 16th century) or the splendid modern church of Jeanne d'Arc. The Tour Jeanne d'Arc where she was imprisoned before her execution also survives, and there are other important buildings. William the Conqueror died here, and Arthur of Brittany was murdered on the orders of King John, so the connection with English history goes back a long time, as so often in Normandy.

Honfleur

Charts Nos. 2613, 2146 and 2994

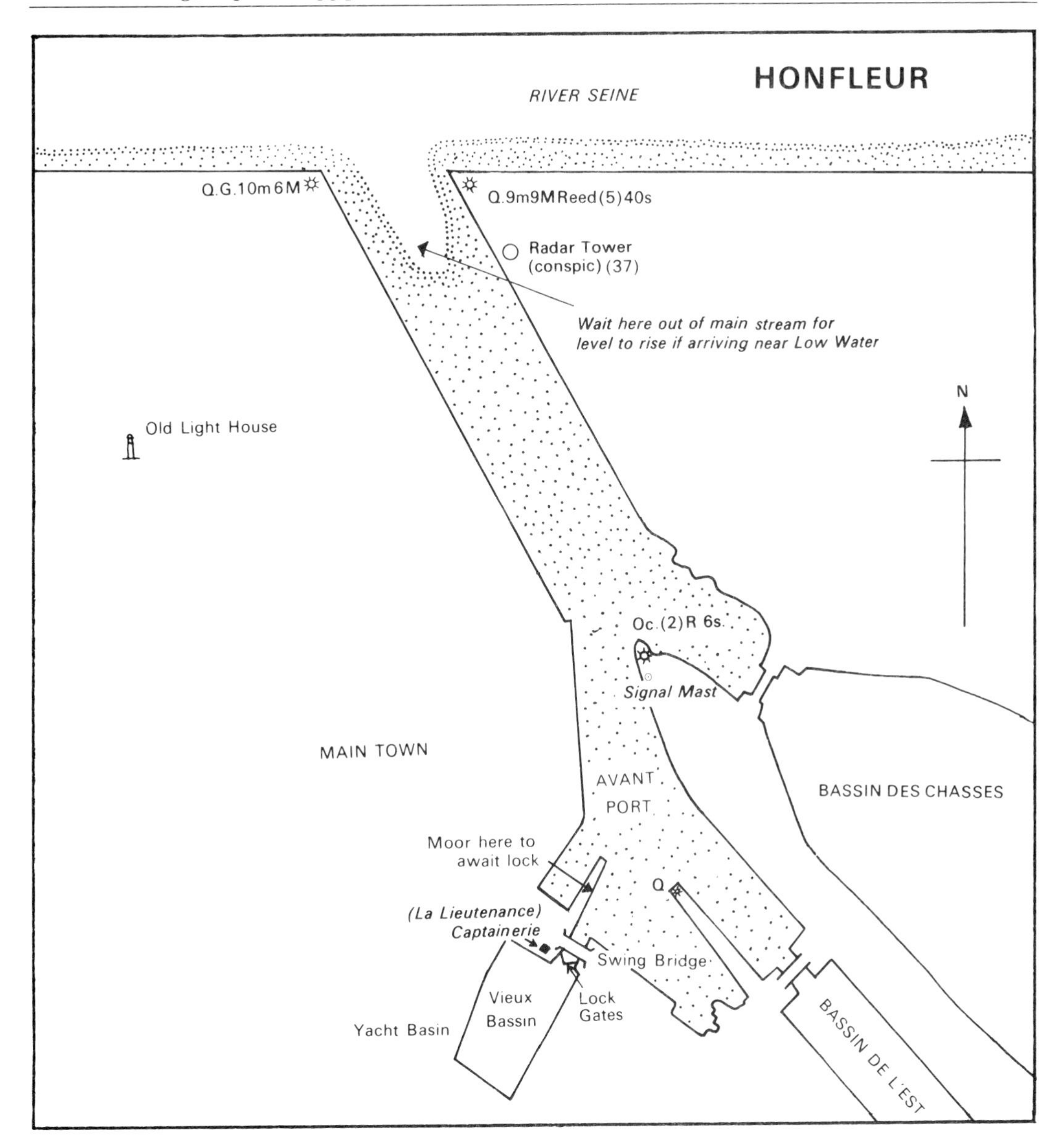

Plan 12 Honfleur.

This delightful harbour near the mouth of the Seine is sometimes overcrowded, but I would always try to cram in somehow, as it has a unique atmosphere and a charm of its own. What effect the new works (see page 52) will have remains to be seen.

Tidal notes

See also under 'Seine estuary' and 'River Seine' in the preceding section.

Heights: 8.1 m MHWS, 6.8 m MHWN.
There is a stand of HW from HW Le Havre $-1\frac{1}{2}$ to $+1\frac{1}{2}$ at springs, $-1\frac{1}{2}$ to $+1$ at neaps. Stream in the river outside reaches 4.5 knots E-going at LW Le Havre +3, and 2.5 knots W-going at LW Le Havre +10 (spring rates).

Approach and entrance

The vast majority will be approaching from down river, in which case there should be few problems. The well-buoyed channel is followed as far as starboard buoy 19, and almost at once the narrow harbour entrance opens up on the starboard hand. If the flood is still strong, one must take care not to be swept past the entrance, at night keeping the Oc(2) R light at the inner end of the entrance channel midway between the entrance lights (QG and Q) until safely in the channel. There is a lighthouse on the Falaise des Fonds, about a mile W of the entrance, showing Fl(3) WRG. 12s, but this is of little help in my experience. By day, the entrance can be recognised for miles by the elegant white radar tower, with an observation gallery projecting northwards near the top, which stands on the east side of the entrance channel.

Notes on the timing of the approach from Le Havre or Deauville will be found under 'Passage Notes: The Seine Estuary' on page 43. If it is decided to spend a night at Honfleur after making the passage down the Seine, however, a few additional notes may be useful. Coming down the river on the full ebb, the radar tower becomes an invaluable mark, as the entrance is invisible from the east until you are almost past it, and if you overshoot it can take a long time to claw your way back up against the tide, which runs very strongly. The entrance channel dries at LWS, but fortunately there is plenty of water – at least 2 m – extending far enough in to bring one out of the tidal stream of the Seine, into a gentle ebb stream from the harbour. In these circumstances, press boldly up the middle of the channel (there are

29 Honfleur: entrance channel showing radar tower.

30 Honfleur: the Avant-Port is to the right of the signal mast.

31 Honfleur: entrance to the yacht basin is just behind the mole. The Lieutenance is at the right of the picture.

obstructions near the edges) and put her aground on soft mud, where you may lie comfortably until the new flood enables you first to enter the Avant-Port, and later the Vieux Bassin. In spite of constant plans to dredge it, the Avant-Port also dries almost wholly at LWS. In the winter of 1991–92, work is beginning to install lock gates at the entrance to the main harbour. These will be completed by 1993 (for the season if all goes well) and the plans show 2 m in the approach at LWS.

Berthing

To await the opening of the lock or bridge, the best place to lie is close to the bridge, on the E side of the mole which projects from the shore just W of the bridge (see plan). However, if arriving after the lock has closed with a view to taking the ground, only the northern half of the mole is safe, as there is a concrete sill near the bridge. Even here, the ground slopes steeply away from the mole, so bilge-keelers take up an awkward angle. The lock opens from 1 hour before to 2 hours after high water, and the bridge opens at −1, HW, +1, and +2, except at night (2100–0600) when the +2 opening is omitted. On entering the wet basin, moor as directed, normally alongside on pontoons on the W wall of the basin. Port office listens on VHF Channel 73, tel: 31 89 20 02.

Facilities

Water on the pontoons. No fuel except from garages. Other facilities are much better in Le Havre, but there is a boat builder, Ateliers et Chantiers Maritimes on Jetée Est, capable of hull repairs, especially wood, tel: 31 89 13 71. Electric and electronic repairs Radio-Maritime, 12 place Hamelin, tel: 31 89 05 17. Motor repairs by Gérard Hue, quai Carnot, tel: 31 89 38 54, and some chandlery at Aubraye, 7 rue de la Ville. Cranes: 3 and 16 tons.

32 Honfleur: yachts in the Vieux-Bassin.

General

Honfleur is a haunt of artists, and the basin (which is right in the heart of the ancient town) is surrounded by art shops and galleries. Of the thousands of pictures on sale, a high proportion are of the harbour. Excellent shops and restaurants can be found within 100 m of the berths, and this is a good place to do some major stocking up. Dominated by the 16th-century tower of the Lieutenance, the harbour is one of the most beautiful and individual in Normandy, and should not be missed.

First mentioned in the 11th century, Honfleur was occupied by the English from 1419 to 1450. From its port sailed many famous discoverers, including Samuel de Champlain who left Honfleur in 1608 to found Quebec. Of the many ancient monuments worth visiting I would pick out the church of St Catherine, just west of the Lieutenance, built in the late 15th and 16th centuries by shipwrights, entirely from wood. An unusual feature is its separate bell-tower. There is a small maritime museum overlooking the basin, and the 15th and 16th-century church of St Leonard, with its main door in the flamboyant style of that period, is also worth seeing (the octagonal tower is a later addition).

Passage Notes: Baie de la Seine, Le Havre to Barfleur

In normal circumstances, once one has distentangled oneself from the banks near the mouth of the Seine, this area presents few problems. The Villerville banks are not well marked, and approaching Deauville on a rising tide one should beware of being swept E of the town: it should never be allowed to bear less than 180° (mag). To the west, it is important to remember the considerable distance that the Plateau de Calvados extends offshore: from 4 miles E of Courseulles almost to Arromanches the 2 m line lies nearly 2 miles off the beach. Further W, between Port-en-Bessin and Grandcamp the remains of the Mulberry harbour must be borne in mind. They lie more than ½ mile offshore, and almost cover at high springs.

From here to Barfleur there are no problems except in strong NE winds, when the E coast of Cotentin becomes a long and bleak lee shore, and the banks of Cardonnet and Marcouf create very unpleasant seas, especially near LW. In such conditions it is best if possible to keep to weather of the Iles St Marcouf: coming from Grandcamp this will mean a rough passage in the first hour, but overall a much more comfortable passage will be bought by that sacrifice.

If caught in a full NE gale, it is in fact safer to take shelter in the lee of Ile Tatihou and anchor as close in as draft and tidal coefficient allow rather than attempt to enter St Vaast harbour.

Charts Nos. 1349, 2146 and 2613

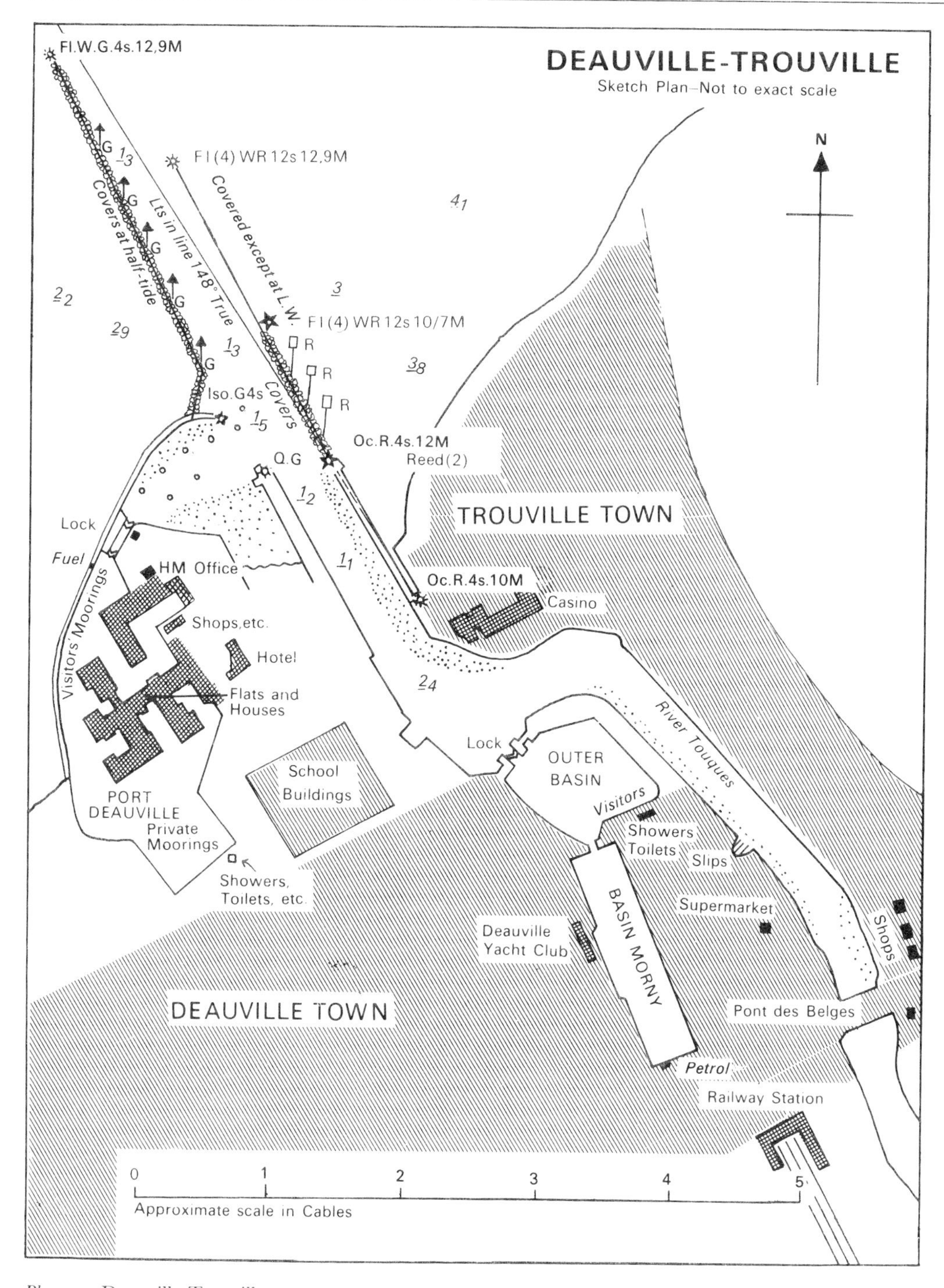

Plan 13 Deauville-Trouville.

Deauville-Trouville

Deauville, one of the great Victorian watering places, has survived into a dignified old age, still magnificent if a little shabby in places. It has two yacht harbours, both tidal although Port Deauville is closed for only 4 hours each tide. The twin towns offer every possible facility, including more restaurants to the square mile than anywhere I have ever been, some grand and expensive catering for the wealthy visitors who still come every season, but others (off the main boulevards) where modest prices and good value can be found.

Tidal notes
Heights: 7.8 m MHWS, 1.1 m MLWS, 6.4 m MHWN, 2.8 m MLWN.
HW is HW Le Havre −0.33 (springs), −0.13 (neaps). LW is LW Le Havre −0.10 (springs), −0.02 (neaps). The W-going stream begins at HW Cherbourg +3½, the E-going HW Cherbourg −2. Rates less than 1 knot.

Approach
The approach channel dries, being kept in summer at a level 2 m above chart datum, which means it has a depth of 2½ m at half-tide. The approach should be from due N through to W but not from E of N because of the Banc du Ratier. The most conspicuous building is the casino at Trouville. There is an E cardinal buoy (VQ(3) 5s), which it is desirable to identify if possible. This buoy lies 2½ miles from the harbour entrance and is almost in transit with the

33 Deauville: the W outer light at right of picture. Follow the starboard beacons and turn to starboard before the inner entrance for Port Deauville, straight on for the Vieux Port.

leading marks. It is very helpful to be able to pass it close abeam and to starboard and thus to establish position and course.

From this position, one can steer straight for the pierheads on about 160° (mag). A W cardinal buoy ('Trouville SW', VQ(9) 10s) will be seen about $\frac{3}{4}$ mile to starboard about a mile before the pierheads are reached. Coming from the west, if an offing of around $1\frac{1}{2}$ miles is maintained, course may be altered for the entrance when this buoy is reached. Waypoint: 49°23'.3N, 0°03'.7E then steer 155° (mag) for the entrance.

At night there are no problems. The white sectors of the two outer lights provide a safe angle of approach, and when closer in the leading lights (Oc R 4s) will be visible, and provide a safe line through the outer pierheads. It should be noted, however, that the front light is obscured from anywhere on the NE side of the line of the eastern breakwater, and the rear one can not be seen from much W of the line, so the two are seen together only when close to the line.

The approach and entrance is not hazardous even for a stranger and at night, provided weather is reasonable. With strong winds between W and N, however, the place is best avoided except by those with local knowledge. In such conditions the approach should be made during the period from 2 hours before to HW, but in good weather and with moderate draft the harbour is available at all times except about $2\frac{1}{2}$ hours either side of LW.

The approach course is only critical close in and near LW, when the sunken extension of the E pier becomes a hazard, but as long as the last part of the approach is made along the line of the inner piers (or leading lights at night), there are no problems. Keep outside the posts marking the shoals off the end of the curved outer W breakwater.

34 Deauville: the division of the channels (near low water). (*Photo Jack H. Coote.*)

Entrance and berthing

At this point, if not before, the choice has to be made between the two harbours: Port Deauville or the old harbour of Trouville-Deauville. The advantage of the former is that the gates are open for longer, being shut only 2 hours either side of LW. At 2 hours after LWS there is only 1.3 m in the approach channel, increasing to 2.2 m 2 hours after LWN, so most of the time if you can get in at all you can go straight in to Port Deauville. The old harbour, on the other hand, opens for periods varying from $4\frac{1}{2}$ hours to much less or even not at all (see below) but it is more convenient for yacht club, shopping and other services. Berthing charges in the two basins are nowadays almost exactly the same.

Port Deauville

To enter turn to starboard round the outer west breakwater, leaving green beacons and buoys to starboard, red to port. The harbour has a full two-gated lock, and can be entered whenever the rise of tide is over 4 m. Visitors' moorings are on the starboard side on pontoons, the first part with no pontoons being kept for large sail training vessels and the like. Diesel (see plan). There are some (very expensive) shops in the port complex, otherwise it is a half-mile walk to town. Sailmaker (Top Marine) on quai des Marchands next to the Harbour Office (see plan).

Deauville-Trouville Old Harbour

Locally referred to as 'Le Vieux Port' to distinguish it from Port Deauville, the basin is entered by keeping straight on past the entrance to Port Deauville and continuing 2 cables to the dock gates. It is wise to keep rather over to the W side of the channel between the piers. Visitors' moorings are shown on the plan.

35 Deauville: Old Yacht Harbour.

In theory the gates open for between $2\frac{3}{4}$ hours (say HW −1 to +2.40) at extreme neaps to $5\frac{1}{2}$ hours (say HW −2 to +$3\frac{1}{2}$) at extreme springs. The yacht club (Deauville Yacht Club, tel: 31 88 38 19, VHF channel 73) supplies a list of opening times. However, opening is now automatically controlled and depends on actual water heights, and wind and barometric conditions can shorten neap openings considerably, and exceptionally have been known to prevent the gates from opening at all on a particular tide. Certainly around severe neaps (say co-efficients under 40) one should take no risks and arrive at or just before HW. Berth alongside where shown on the plan, two or more deep if necessary.

Facilities

Water at the berths. Electricity only on the yacht club moorings, one of which may be free: ask at club. Petrol is available by hose at the S end of Bassin Morny. Diesel can be bought there but must be carried aboard in cans. There is a diesel station in Port Deauville (see plan): this may be used by boats staying in the Old Port. 6 ton crane, 50 ton slip. Toilets beside visitors' berths (see plan) and at yacht club (Deauville Yacht Club) which is large and friendly. Dues are payable at the small white hut just across the narrows separating the two inner basins. Unfortunately the swing bridge seems permanently open now: a lot of walking can be saved by putting the dinghy in the water and crossing this small gap for the payment hut, yacht club etc.

General

There is a good small supermarket only 250 m from the berths, on the road running S nearest the river. They will deliver to boats. The nearest specialist shops (butcher, baker etc) are just over the Pont des Belges in Trouville (see plan). Major shops and restaurants in Deauville centre (SW from Deauville YC) or Trouville (N along the river from the bridge).

Named after a Viking called Thorolf, Thorolfivilla became Trouville. A fishing village until the 1830s, it quickly became a popular bathing resort and expanded rapidly. The Casino was opened, and soon after that the much more grandiose town of Deauville began to spring up on the other bank of the river. A rival Casino was built, Deauville races began in 1864, inaugurated by the Duc de Morny the year before his death. The two towns enjoyed a more or less friendly rivalry which persists today, although their prosperity came to its peak years ago, probably in the nineties of the last century, when Oscar Wilde might have been observed doffing his hat to the then Prince of Wales as he arrived at the racecourse to watch the Deauville Cup.

Charts Nos. 2146 and 2613

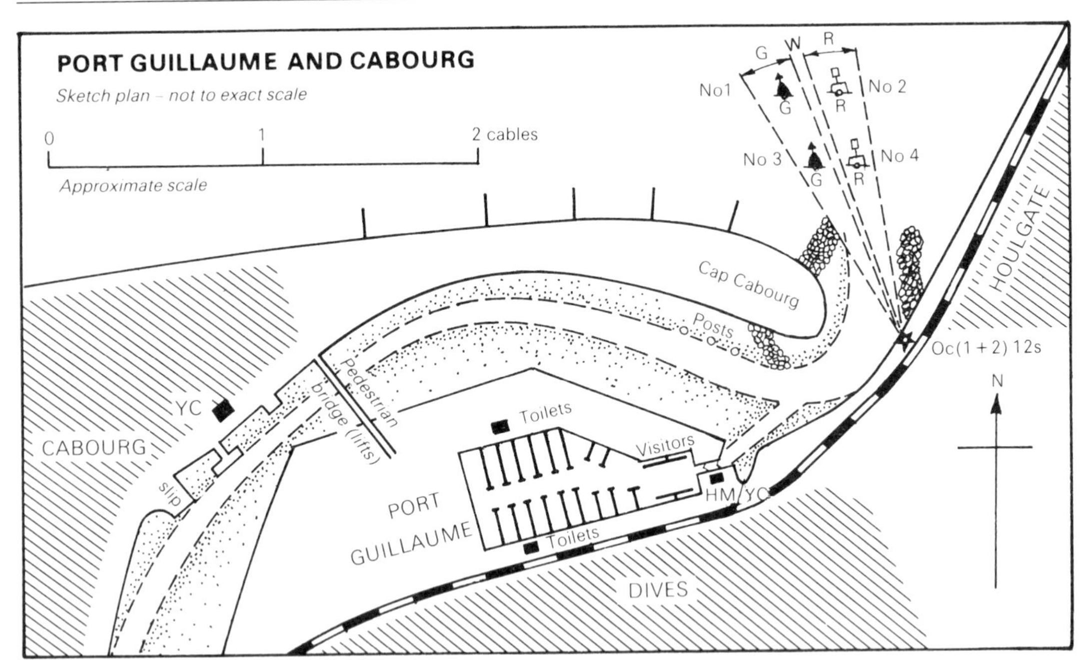

Plan 14 River Dives with Cabourg.

Once a great port, this river mouth is now once more regaining importance at least as a yachting centre with the opening of the new Port Guillaume marina.

Tidal notes

Heights: 7.5 m MHWS, 0.9 m MLWS, 6.1 m MHWN, 2.4 m MLWN.

French tide tables give HW as HW Le Havre −0.57 (springs), no figure for neaps, but I estimate the neaps difference to be about HW −0.30.

Approach and entrance

Coming either from east or west, the entrance can be identified by the gap between Houlgate and Cabourg. Steer towards this gap from between NNW and N until the channel buoys are identified; then pass between them and approach the south shore closely, then turning west for Port Guillaume. The approaches dry 3 m, so although the locks operate three hours either side of HW, most boats will be best advised to approach and leave within $1\frac{1}{2}$ hours of HW, and even then conditions are rough in strong onshore winds. The entrance is a full-scale lock with two gates, and in 1991 the intention was to use them both, though there is a tendency on this coast to open both on a good tide and only close them when the level begins to fall.

Berthing and facilities

The pontoon immediately to starboard after locking in is reserved for visitors (see plan) and no doubt they will moor two or more abreast when necessary. There are toilets and showers

36 Dives: the entrance to Port Guillaume.

37 Dives: the river mouth seen from Port Guillaume entrance.

on both sides of the basin, water and electricity on the pontoons, a 16 ton travel lift and a fuel berth opposite the visitors' pontoon. Shopping in the village was not extensive in early 1991, but will probably expand rapidly as the new yacht harbour and its associated apartments fill up. Berthing fees, inevitably for a brand new development, were the highest on the coast in 1991 (Fr 126 for 10 m in high season) but not ridiculous. The basin has 2.5 metres: any vessel worried by that would be unlikely to have fancied the approaches! Capitainerie tel: 31 24 48 00.

Cabourg

Boats capable of drying can proceed up the river to Cabourg: there is a good 3 m in the channel at springs, though less than 1½ m at a low neap. If making more than a HW flying visit, best ring the HM at the yacht club (31 91 28 89) to make sure there will be space to dry alongside the jetty or a mooring available. A keel boat can lie alongside with suitable precautions: the bottom elsewhere is flat, mud and pebbles. The club is charming with an unusual clinker-built bar, and provides water, toilets and showers. There is a good bathing beach north of the town.

General

It was here that William of Normandy established his position as independent of the French king, when in 1059 he defeated a French army at the Dives bridge. The bridge collapsed under the weight of the retreating French, and William spurred forward and killed the Duc de Berry with his own hand. On the far bank King Henri watched and soon after allowed Normandy her independence.

Seven years later William assembled his invasion fleet of 400 fighting ships and 1,000 transports, lying in the port for a month while his 50,000 men camped along the river banks. The figures come from contemporary chronicles and can probably safely be divided by four, but it is hard now to imagine a great fleet lying in the Dives. However, this is the usual Normandy tale of silting: the river was much deeper then, and indeed there are now green fields where the Conqueror's fleet once lay.

Ouistreham

Charts Nos. 1349 and 2613

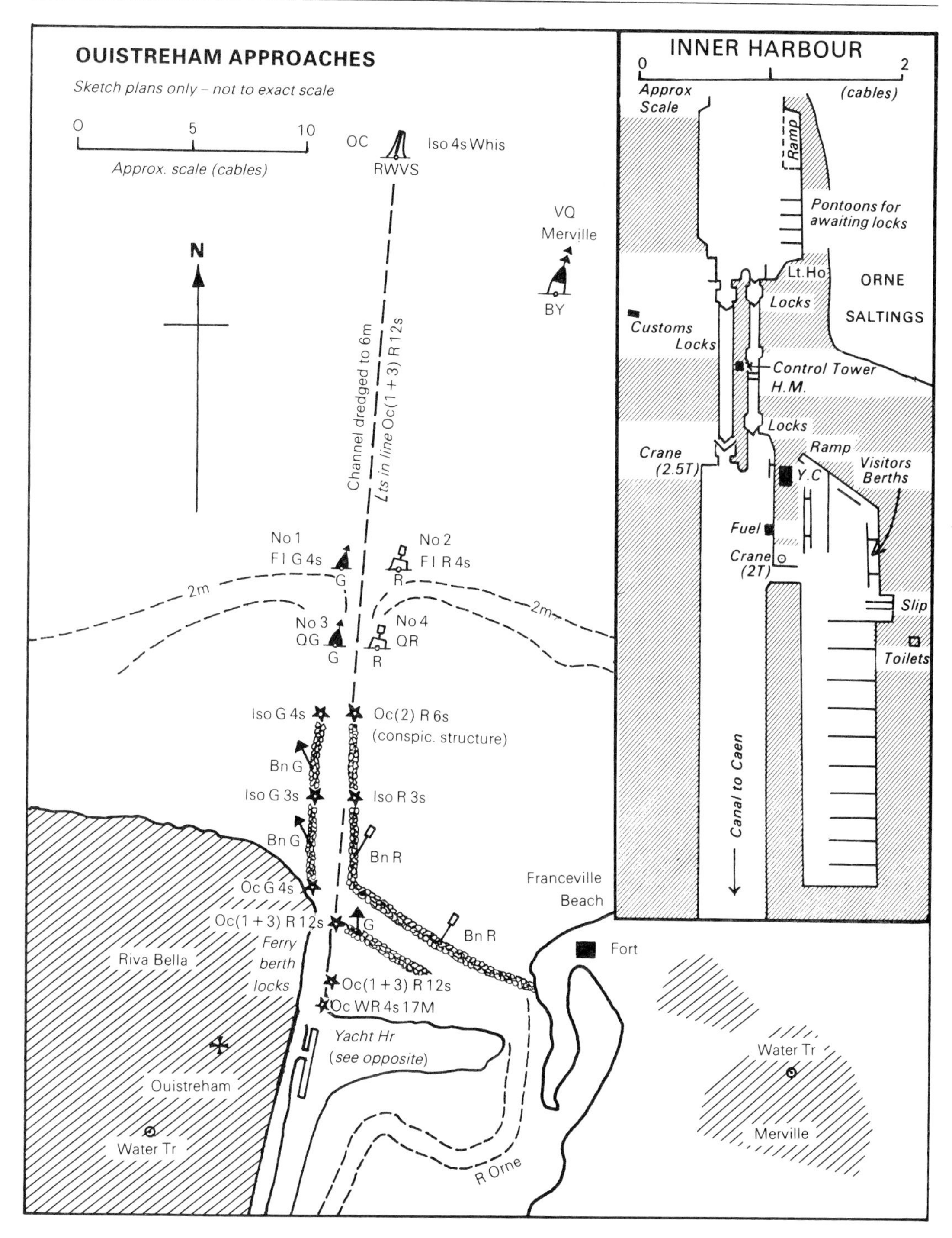

Plan 15 Ouistreham: approaches and inner harbour.

Although not itself a very interesting place, Ouistreham is important as the only all-tide harbour between Le Havre and Cherbourg, and is also the base from which Caen may be visited.

Tidal notes

Heights: 7.7 m MHWS, 1.0 m MLWS, 6.4 m MHWN, 2.8 m MLWN.

HW is HW Le Havre −0.19 (springs), −0.08 (neaps). LW is LW Le Havre −0.11 (springs), −0.05 (neaps). The E-going stream begins at HW Cherbourg −3½, and attains 1.8 knots (springs) at HW Cherbourg −1½. The W-going stream begins at HW Cherbourg +3 and attains 1.7 knots (springs) at HW Cherbourg +5½.

Approach and entrance

The sands dry for more than a mile off the entrance, so boats approaching along the shore should maintain a good offing. Waypoint: 49°20′.0N, 0°14′.5W. Once the 'OC' offing buoy (RW vertical stripes, Iso 4s) is identified, steer 190° (mag) until the first channel buoys (Nos. 1 and 2) are seen. Pass between these and the next pair. The conspicuous structure ahead is now left to port, after which red buoys and beacons are left to port and greens to starboard, keeping more or less straight on until the lock gates are reached. The main lighthouse (Oc WR 4s) is a good landmark by day.

The channel is dredged to 6 m as far as the Avant-Port, and therefore available to yachts at any time although it can be rough near LW springs in strong onshore winds. The lock into the canal, where the yacht basin is to be found, operates from 2 hours before to 3 hours after HW except in July and August, when the times are extended to 3 hours before to 4 hours after except during periods of drought when the water level in the canal falls. The lock will operate at the beginning and end of this period, and as often between as traffic warrants. It

38 Ouistreham: moorings and the control tower. Small lock to the left of the control tower, large lock to the right. The after leading light is to the left of the lighthouse.

is wise to arrive at least half an hour before the end of the period, as the locks fill slowly. If arriving outside operating times, there are (rather inadequate) pontoons outside the locks on the E side where it may be possible to moor and wait. These can be very crowded with boats moored five or six deep without springs. I have seen one entire trot drift forward and ram the other when the tide turned. Beware of severe scend in strong onshore winds.

Allowance should be made for a steady downstream current through the lock basins: this can catch out the unwary, particularly when locking in from the canal when one is carried in faster than one expects and there can be problems in stopping. There are also swirls in the area just downstream from the locks. The signal permitting entry is a green light over white over green with another white light beside this group. Harbour and lock control listen on VHF Channel 68, manned only during opening hours.

Berthing

Once through the lock, the entrance to the yacht harbour will be seen about a cable southwards on the port side. Visitors' berths are clearly marked, being the ones straight ahead or to port as one enters. Moor alongside, often two deep in busy periods. Beware of severe scend in strong onshore winds.

Facilities

Water and electricity on the pontoons. Toilets below yacht club and also as marked on plan. Fuel in canal (see plan): arrange at club in person or via VHF Channel 9. The pumps are normally manned for half an hour before each outward locking. 8 ton slip. Drying slip and grid in outer harbour: ask at lock office and inspect at LW before using. Chandlers include Riva Marine at the yacht harbour, who can advise on repairs and all needs. Sailmakers BM sails, also at the yacht basin and Cheret Voiles, 42 ave de la Redoute, tel: 31 96 88 59. Ferries to Portsmouth. There is a 50 ton slip a mile up the canal towards Caen on the E side which

39 The Bassin St Pierre marina is almost in the centre of Caen and is reached via the canal from Ouistreham.

will haul out boats for a short time at reasonable cost: run by JPL Marine, tel: 31 96 29 92. They can also repair GRP or metal hulls.

General

There are two or three restaurants on the square just W of the locks, and one or two small shops can be found a little beyond. The main shopping centre is a good 2.5 km from the yacht berths, centred around the Avenue de la Mer in Riva Bella, the resort part of the town NW from the locks. The old part of the town is clustered around the church, which was built between the 11th and 12th centuries in Romanesque style. Nearby is a 15th-century tithe barn and other interesting buildings. Ask for the church or rue de la Grève.

The Canal and Caen

The authorities are not keen to open the bridges for individual yachts, but there is at least one free run each way along the canal every day, during which the bridges open without charge. This is normally morning for Caen–Ouistreham, and afternoon for Ouistreham–Caen. Enquire at the lock office for timings (also available at the yacht club). Apart from the daily run, it is sometimes possible to travel the canal with a commercial vessel: the lock office will advise. The passage of the canal (7 nautical miles) is straightforward: continue for four bridges, and turn to starboard after the fourth into the Bassin St Pierre, a marina right in the centre of Caen. This historic city was terribly damaged during the war (I know, as I visited it for the first time in 1946) but many beautiful buildings survived, and it is well worth a visit. The marina is cheap, and there is a modern toilet block. Water and electricity on the pontoons, all possible shopping and every grade of restaurant close by. Also the railway station with frequent trains to Bayeux, where the famous tapestry may be seen, looking as though it was finished last week. Altogether readers will deduce that I consider the detour well worth while if time allows!

Courseulles-sur-Mer

Charts Nos. 1349 and 2613

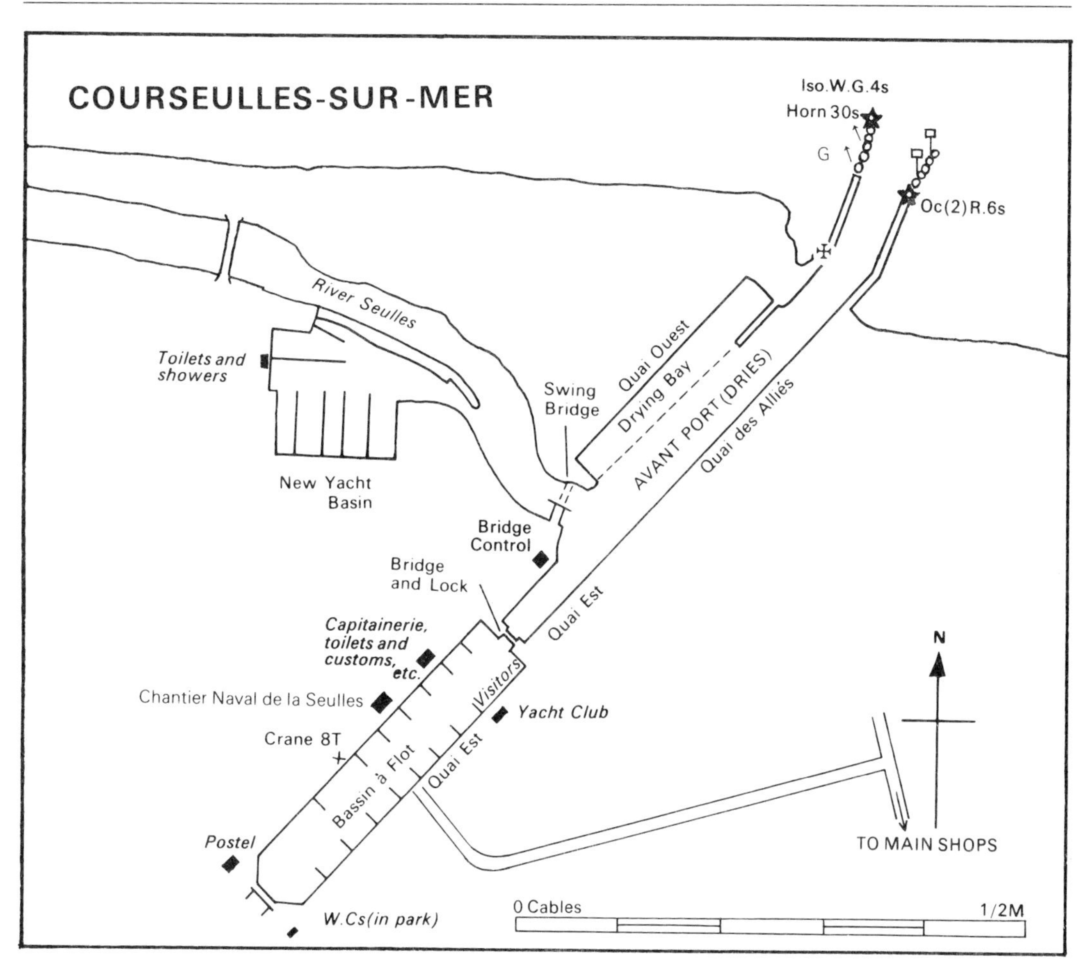

Plan 16 Courseulles-sur-Mer.

Courseulles is a pleasant small town with a tidal harbour available 2 hours either side of HW. A comfortable, quiet place in which to spend a couple of days.

Tidal notes

Heights: 7.1 m MHWS, 0.9 m MLWS, 5.6 m MHWN, 1.8 m MLWN.

HW is HW Le Havre −0.29. LW is LW Le Havre −0.21. These are spring figures: neap differences have not been issued but are probably 10 minutes less at HW and 5 minutes less at LW. Note that for many years most tide tables gave incorrect differences for this port, and some may still be wrong. The E-going stream begins at HW Cherbourg $-3\frac{3}{4}$ and attains 1.7 knots (springs) at HW Cherbourg −1. The W-going stream begins at HW Cherbourg +3 and attains 1.6 knots (springs) at HW Cherbourg +5.

Approach and entrances

The identification of Courseulles from offshore is much aided by the spires of the churches of Langrune, St Aubine and Bernieres. These are marked on the chart, and from seaward appear to stand in a straight line at exactly regular intervals. The harbour entrance will be found an identical distance to the westward as that between either pair of adjacent churches. Note that although there is a church at Courseulles, and it is marked on the chart, it is quite invisible from any distance to seaward.

In daytime, do not expect to use Pte de Ver lighthouse, 2½ miles W of Courseulles, as a landmark. Although the light is 42 m above sea level, it is totally inconspicuous as the height is provided by the land, and the tower itself is squat, undistinguished, and stands among other buildings. In poor visibility, however, the radio beacon is useful. This has a range of 20 miles, and transmits ÉR (.._.. ._.) on 291.9 kHz. At night, the light (Fl(3) 15s) is visible for 26 miles. Waypoint: 49°22′.0N, 0°26′.5W, then 200° (mag) for the entrance.

The entrance channel dries nearly 3 m, and keel boats should only attempt to enter within 2 hours of HW, although shallow-draft boats can sneak in 2½ hours before HW in good weather. At night, approach with the white sector of the WG light off the W pier in line with the Oc(2) R 6s light on the E pierhead: leave the former to starboard, and then steer for the latter and leave it to port. Keep close in to the E pier until past the wooden section, as the W side is shoal. In daylight, the large black dolphin off the end of the W pier is now the most conspicuous mark, and will probably be identified before the white light tower on the E one. Having identified these, approach on a course of about 205° (mag) until close in, when you should keep to the port (E) side of the channel until the end of the wooden part of the E pier, after which the best water is to be found in the middle. Once inside, the lock gates for the old basin will be found dead ahead.

40 Courseulles: harbour entrance.

41 Courseulles: the entrance channel looking towards the lock.

42 Courseulles: halfway up the channel. There are temporary moorings outside the lock.

The new basin lies up a channel on the starboard side, through a swing bridge. This lies just beyond the drying ramp on the NW side of the channel.

Berthing
The lock gates open from HW −2 to HW +2. The basin inside the lock is more convenient than the new basin, and in any case visitors are not normally allowed to use the latter. In the basin, small craft berth on the nearest pontoon on the port side, or better speak to port control on VHF channel 9 and ask for directions. Berths are mainly bow to pontoon and stern to buoy: look out for current while manoeuvring, as this is sometimes quite strong.

Facilities
Water on the pontoons, good showers and toilets in the Capitainerie. There is a useful chandler and shipyard (see plan): Chantier Naval de la Seulles, who can do hull and motor repairs and have good stocks of charts as well as chandlery. They are only a short walk from the berths, tel: 31 37 42 34. The yacht club (Société des Régates de Courseulles) is open in July and August every day except Tuesdays from 1100 to 1300 and 1600 to 2000, and at the same times but weekends only for the rest of the year. It welcomes visitors. Tel: 31 37 47 42.

General
There are restaurants and bars overlooking the yacht basin, but the best shopping will be found by walking up the rue du Bassin, which runs SE and then E from the middle of the SE side of the basin, and then turning right into the rue de la Mer. It is perhaps 500 m. Typical shops of a small market town. The ancient chateau is well worth a visit: the road leading SE from the SW end of the basin goes straight to it. It dates back to the 8th century,

43 Courseulles: the yacht basin taken from the bridge. The lock is at the centre of the picture.

and was already old when it was stormed by Henry V of England. Sadly, it was burnt down in the bombardment of 6th June 1944, but it has been lovingly restored.

Courseulles has its share of mediaeval history, but it is best known for having been at the site of Juno Beach, and for its claim to have been the first French port liberated on D-day. Eight days later, on 14th June 1944, it was the chosen landing place for Charles de Gaulle's return to France after his wartime exile in England.

Arromanches

Some $6\frac{1}{2}$ miles W of the entrance of Courseulles lies the remains of the Mulberry harbour at Arromanches. These invasion harbours were created by sinking what were in effect block-ships – caissons 60 m long and varying from 7.5 to 18 m in height. The remains of the harbour are clearly visible, and the entrance is marked by a pair of (very small) red and green buoys. These buoys will be found just W of the only caisson with a clearly visible superstructure. It is possible to enter the harbour area and anchor in 9 m 2 cables S of the entrance buoys with reasonable shelter in good weather. Better shelter will be found closer in towards the village, but it is wise to view the harbour at LW before going in too far. Care should be taken to avoid fouling any of the numerous pot-buoys when anchoring. The harbour offers a perfectly viable overnight anchorage in settled weather, or with suitable tides it can provide a pleasant day of picnicking and sightseeing, leaving Courseulles on a morning tide and continuing to Port-en-Bessin on an evening one or *vice versa*. The invasion museum in the village should be visited.

Port-en-Bessin

Chart No. 2613

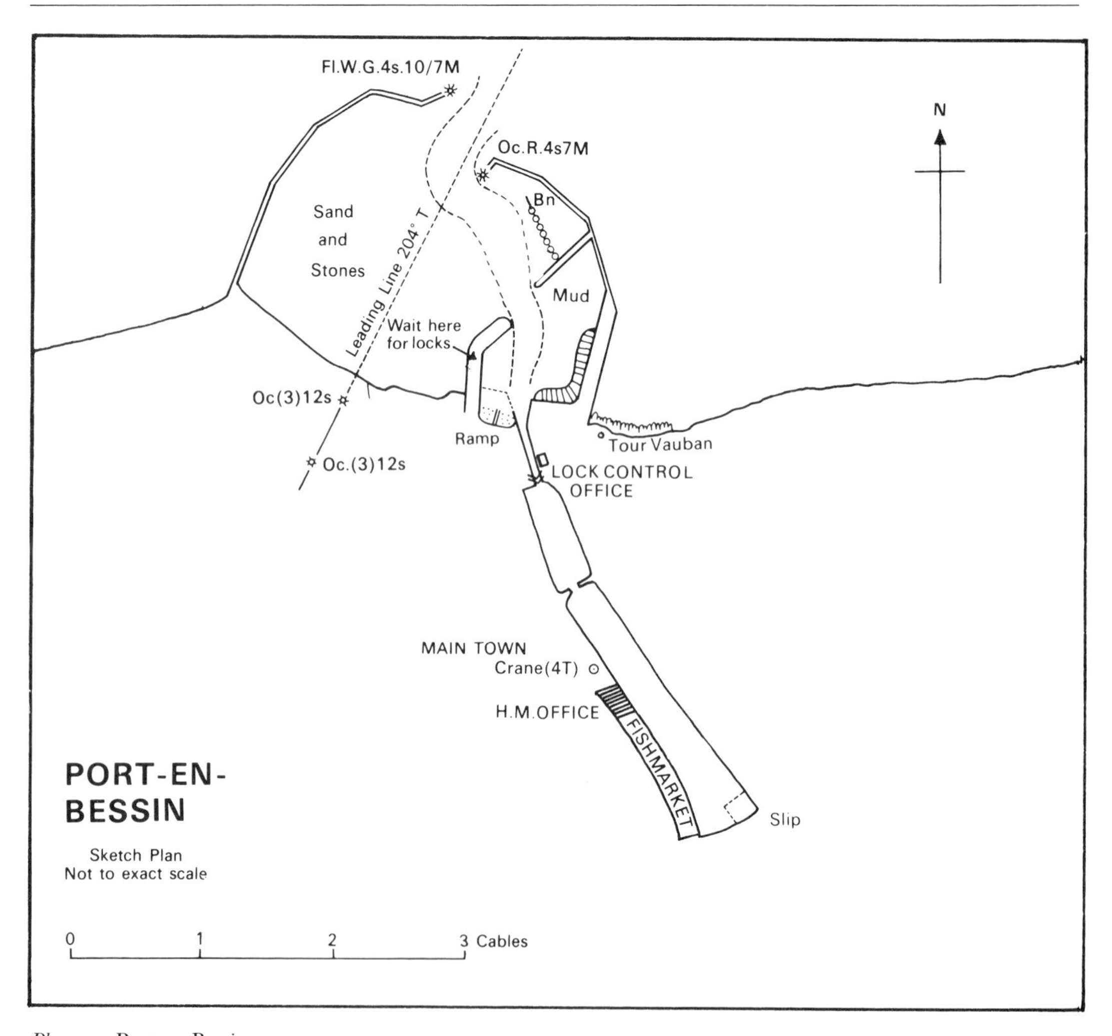

Plan 17 Port-en-Bessin.

The last Norman harbour east of the Cotentin to stand out against the encroaching flood of *plaisance*, Port-en-Bessin remains a traditional fishing harbour and makes no provision for yachts at all. The harbourmaster is keen to see more of them visit his port; some of its regular users are less so, and instances of unfriendly receptions have been reported. However, the town is a pleasant one with excellent shopping and restaurants, and the considerate visitor should experience no problems.

Tidal notes

Heights: 7.2 m MHWS, 1.1 m MLWS, 6.0 m MHWN, 2.7 m MLWN.

HW is HW Le Havre −0.43 (springs), −0.39 (neaps). LW is LW Le Havre −0.46 (springs), −0.39 (neaps). The E-going stream begins at HW Cherbourg $-3\frac{1}{4}$ and attains 1.4 knots (springs) at HW Cherbourg −1. The W-going stream begins at HW Cherbourg +3 and attains 1.3 knots (springs) at HW Cherbourg +6.

Approach and entrance

There are no offshore hazards. The outer harbour dries up to 2 m, so the average yacht can enter up to 3 hours before HW in good weather, but the entrance is rough in winds from between N and NE, and in these conditions it is safer to enter within 2 hours of HW up to force 6, I hour either side in force 7, and avoid the harbour altogether above that. Waypoint: 49°22′.5N, 0°45′.5W, then steer south for the pierheads. Yachts should not obstruct fishing vessels passing between either pair of pierheads, as they often have very little room for manoeuvre. The best place to wait for the bridge to open is shown on the plan: keep to the northern half of the inner section of the mole to avoid the drying slip at its S end: the extent of this is marked by a painted strip on the top of the wall. In poor visibility the approach can be made easier by the radio beacon (BS − ··· ···) on 313.5 kHz, range 5 miles.

Berthing

It is possible to take the ground in the outer harbour in settled fine weather, as the bottom is smooth, flat mud, but in strong winds there is a dangerous swell. The dock gates open 2 hours either side of HW, and during that time the bridge opens for 5 minutes after the gates open, for 5 minutes on each hour, and for the last 5 minutes before closing. During this period the bridge control office listens on VHF Channel 18, and it is preferable to speak to them and ask for instructions on berthing. Otherwise berth alongside the wall or a fishing boat as

44 Port-en-Bessin: harbour entrance.

45 Port-en-Bessin.

46 Port-en-Bessin: a trawler leaving the inner basin.

opportunity offers, and immediately report to the harbour office (see plan) for confirmation or fresh instructions. The small length of wall marked '*plaisance*' is of little use to the average visitor, as it is usually full of local, very small craft, and in any case the steep outward slope makes it unusable by most yachts.

Note that the harbour can be very noisy and disturbed when HW is in the middle of the night, as fishing boats enter and then manoeuvre for several hours, moving one by one to the fish quay to unload and then back to their berths. If alongside, bear in mind that the level can fall by at least a metre after the lock gates are closed.

Facilities

Water from taps on E quay. Two boatyards at the S end of the basins can carry out repairs in wood and GRP. 4 ton fixed and 6 ton mobile crane. Motor repairs Francoise Digne on the W side of the basin or Gaubert (diesel specialist) at the S end. Electric and electronic repairs from LK Electronique (W side of the inner basin near the S end) or Radio-Ocean, 3 quai Letourneur, tel: 31 21 72 90. Some chandlery from Hutrel, 5 rue Lefournier, one street inland from the W side of the N inner basin. Radiotelephone (tel: 21 31 44 00) on VHF Channel 3.

General

Good shops (excellent fish) along the W side of the N basin. Restaurants of all standards in the town. Buses to Bayeux leave several times a day: the journey takes only about 10 minutes and a visit is well worth while. Port-en-Bessin has been a port for many years: Bishop Odo, half-brother of the Conqueror, fitted out 40 vessels here as his contribution to the invasion fleet. The Tour Vauban, just E of the harbour entrance, was built in 1694 to protect it (against the English, of course!) and is in an extraordinary state of preservation for its age.

Chart No. 2613

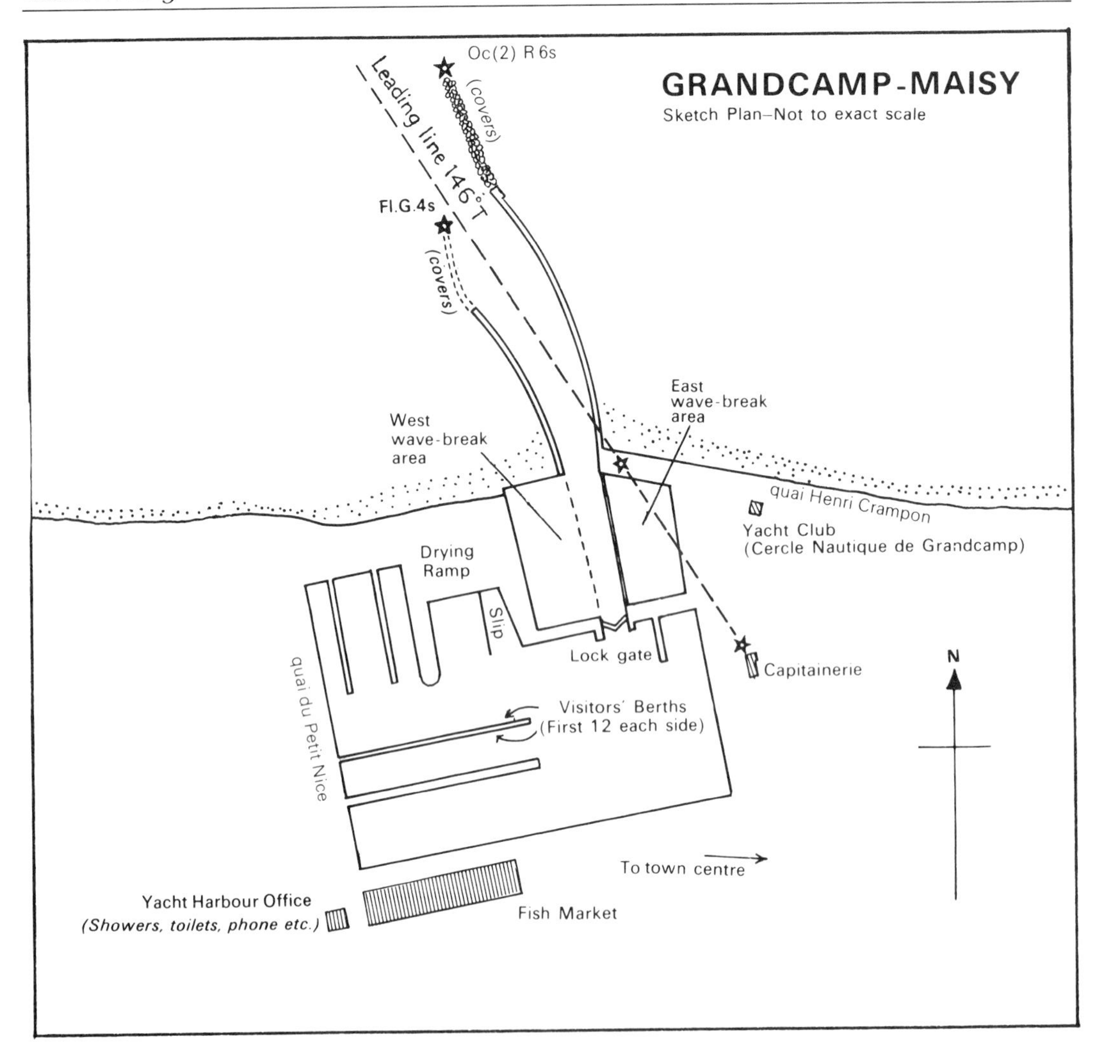

Plan 18 Grandcamp-Maisy.

Just E of the great bay formed by the estuaries of the Vire and the Carentan rivers, Grandchamp is a useful small port with good yacht facilities, although in 1987 it was struggling against an invasion of Japanese weed.

Tidal notes
For some reason which I have never discovered, no French (or therefore English) tide table gives differences for Grandcamp. However, interpolating betwen Port-en-Bessin and St Vaast gives a figure for HW Grandcamp of Le Havre −0.50, without much difference between springs and neaps, and readers are unlikely to encounter any problems using this approxi-

mation. Streams in the offing are affected by the estuary nearby, but the NW-going stream begins at HW Cherbourg +3½ and attains 1.2 knots (springs) at HW Cherbourg +6. The E-going stream begins at HW Cherbourg −2 and attains 1.2 knots (springs) at HW Cherbourg.

Approach and entrance

The harbour is approached across the Roches de Grandcamp, which look most alarming as shown on the Admiralty chart, with jagged hatching everywhere. In fact the whole area could be used as a roller-skating rink at LWS, being a sheet of almost perfectly smooth, flat rock. This dries about 2 m, so taking the mean level as 3.7 m (an interpolation erring on the side of safety) there is 1.7 m over the shallowest part at half-tide. For most yachts it is therefore safe to approach 2½ hours either side of HW, unless a big swell is running when the margin should be reduced to 2 hours or less.

At night, two synchronised quick-flashing leading lights make identification and entry easy; during the day one may safely steer in on any course between SE and SW. The town cannot be mistaken, owing to the estuary to its west. On arrival, keep near the middle of the channel between the lights, and the lock gates into the inner harbour will be found straight ahead. It is important to note that the outer extension of the W breakwater covers and is not on the line of the visible part of the breakwater, so it is important to leave the western light structure well to starboard, and then keep parallel with the E pier. There is nowhere very comfortable to wait in the outer harbour, but if the approach has been timed as advised, the gates will be open and one can proceed straight into the inner basin. Within the pierheads, fishing boats have right of way over yachts, as they often have very little room to manoeuvre. The Harbour Office listens on VHF Channel 9. Waypoint: 49°25′.0N, 1°03′.0W, then steer south for the entrance.

47 Grandcamp-Maisy: harbour entrance from seaward.

48 Grandcamp-Maisy: entrance looking towards the inner basin.

49 Grandcamp-Maisy: yacht moorings in inner basin.

Berthing

The lock gates open from about $2\frac{3}{4}$ hours before to 3 hours after local HW, but in fact by a curious coincidence the tidal rhythm is such that the lock keepers are able to use the tide table for Dunkerque, of all places: the gates open at LW Dunkerque and close at HW there. The existence of this freak correlation may possibly be a partial explanation of the neglect of Grandcamp in the official tide tables. Visitors berth on the outermost 12 berths on each side of the northernmost of the two main pontoons on the W side of the inner basin. Boats berth alongside the end of the pontoon, otherwise bows on and stern to buoy.

Facilities

Water and electricity on the pontoons. Toilets and showers in yacht harbour office block (see plan). Chandlery and repairs enquire Yachting '14, quai du Petit Nice, tel: 31 22 67 02. Small yacht club.

General

The shops are a fair walk to the east, but there is a fruit shop just opposite the pontoon which also does *charcuterie*, wine and bread and a few other groceries. Expensive, but useful for forgotten odds and ends. There are good restaurants near the port and all through the town, and a beach at the other end of town. Grandcamp is a thriving resort town during the holiday season, but never seems to become unduly overcrowded. It is an old town, mentioned on a map of 1082 as Grandis Campus, and in the 17th and 18th centuries was a major centre for guarding the coast against the depredations of pirates and the English. It was also a major oyster fishery, but the oysters died out and there is now just a small general fishing fleet operating from the port.

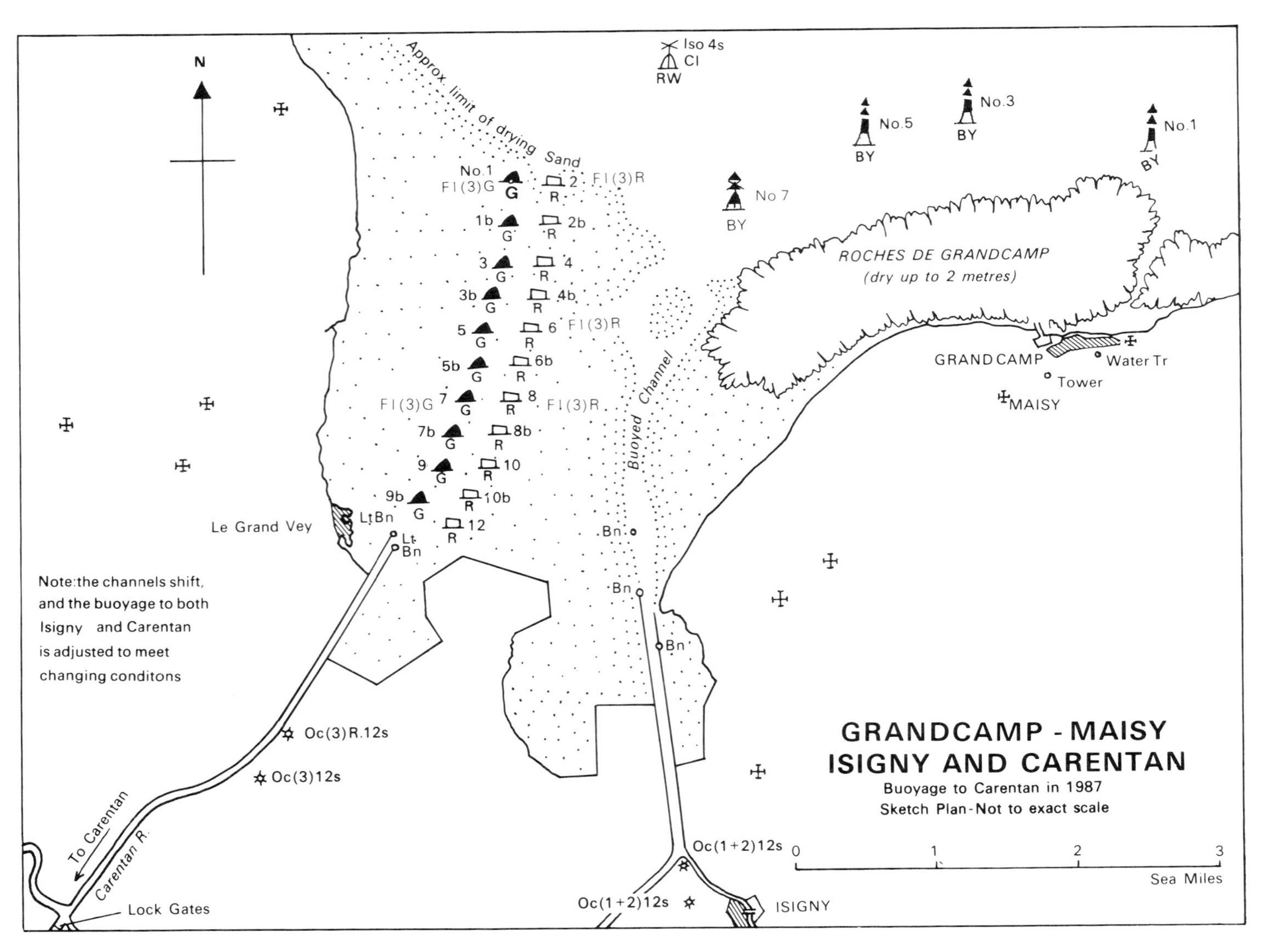

Plan 19 Grandcamp-Maisy, Isigny and Carentan.

Isigny-sur-Mer

Chart No. 2613

While Isigny is not in any sense a yachting port, it is a town of some interest which visitors who enjoy exploring shallow channels may well consider worth the trouble of visiting.

Tidal notes

HW Isigny is about 0.50 after HW Cherbourg at springs, and 1.20 after at neaps. For offshore currents see Grandcamp.

Approach and entrance

The channel carries about 3 m at MHWN, perhaps 1 m more at MHWS. Coming from the north, identify buoy CI, and steer SSE from here to buoy No 7. Coming from Grandcamp, with enough water to cross the Roches de Grandcamp it is safe to steer direct for buoy No 7. Waypoint: 49°26′.0N, 1°07′.0W, then steer for CI buoy ½ mile to the south and continue as above. Try to arrive there about 2 hours before HW Isigny. On reaching No 7, turn to steer SSW and proceed with the sounder operating. The first pair of channel buoys should soon be seen, if they were not already in sight from No 7. The channel is fairly straight and closely buoyed, and after about 4 miles it passes between two sunken breakwaters, marked by beacons. Between the last pair of buoys and the first pair of beacons keep slightly to starboard of the direct line, as a sandbank cuts in from the port side. At night there are leading lights, Oc (1 + 2) 12s. When the channel forks, keep to the port-hand limb, the River Aure, and this leads after half a mile or so to Isigny. Moor to the pontoon on the W (starboard) side, just beyond the boatbuilders' quay. One can also moor further on near the bridge, on the port hand. Berths dry at LW. Good shops.

50 Isigny-sur-Mer: the channel to Isigny lies to the left of the front leading mark.

51 Isigny: pontoon mooring on the west bank. The road bridge is at left of picture.

52 Isigny-sur-Mer: mooring against the eastern bank close to the road bridge.

Carentan

Chart No. 2613

Carentan has been revolutionised in recent years, and has developed from a dead end to an important marina, ideal for wintering a boat. The town is charming, and has a rural rather than maritime atmosphere which can make a pleasant change in the middle of a cruise. Well worth the detour involved.

Tidal notes

Like Isigny, HW Carentan Lock is about 0.50 after HW Cherbourg at springs, 1.20 after at neaps. The approach channel carries 1.5 m at HW on a low neap, 3.2 m on a good spring.

Approach

From the north, keep an offing of about 2 miles until RW buoy CI is identified. Waypoint: 49°26'.0N, 1°07'.0W, then steer for CI buoy ½ mile to the south and continue as above. From Grandcamp it is safe to leave this half a mile to starboard and proceed straight to channel buoys Nos 1 and 2. Remember that these will not be reached until a mile after CI bears N: the inviting buoys directly S of CI are those for Isigny. The first channel buoys should be reached between 2 and 1½ hours before HW Carentan Lock: to be much later than this can begin to produce problems as it is 7½ miles to the lock and once the ebb begins it soon gathers speed. The channel is straightforward, although the line may not always remain so straight

53 Carentan Lock: the yacht harbour begins only a couple of hundred yards down the canal.

and corners must never be cut. Once in the river, keep straight on to the lock, which causes little delay, being modern and efficiently run. Several buoys are lit to assist a night approach, and the bends in the canal are illuminated by street-type lighting.

Entrance and berthing

The lock operates from HW −2 to +3, day and night between 15th May and 15th September. Its telephone number is 33 71 10 85. Once through, continue to the yacht pontoons, leaving both rows of posts to port. Normally, a berth is allocated by the lock keeper and written on the passage report which is one of the papers handed over at the lock. Identifying letters are on the ends of the pontoons: even numbered berths are on the lock side of each pontoon, odd numbers on the town side. Over 50 berths are reserved for visitors, and the port captain assures me that this will be the case for the forseeable future. He can say this because there is plenty of room for hundreds more berths, and so when the number of spares falls below 50, as berths find permanent occupiers, they simply put in a new pontoon. At present the highest pontoon letter (nearest the lock) is 'M': there is plenty of room to continue pontoons to 'Z', and probably beyond. The harbour office listens from 0800 to 1800 on VHF Channel 9, tel: 33 42 24 44.

Facilities

Excellent toilets and hot showers (free, now alas a rarity) in Capitainerie building. Water and electricity on pontoons. 16 ton Travel-lift, 50 ton crane. Fuel berth at the town end of the

54 Carentan. The canal and yacht harbour from the church tower.

basin. Note that it is very much cheaper to negotiate a period berth direct with the port office than via agents based in the U.K. For all types of chandlery and repairs consult GAM Marine (tel: 33 71 17 02) or Itelec Nautic (tel: 33 42 07 83) both overlooking the yacht harbour.

General

Excellent shopping, restaurants etc in the town, some 250 m from the harbour office. It is a most attractive place, and has held the Blue Flag of Europe for its contribution to good ecological practices since 1987. Only eighteen have been awarded in France out of 400 qualifying ports. The W bank of the river is a bird sanctuary, and many interesting species will be seen on an average day. In town, the church is a point of interest, begun in the 12th century but mainly dating from the 15th: don't miss the charming little martyr nonchalantly cradling her head in her arms. The stone arches of the mediaeval covered market are another unusual feature of the town. The canal was actually built as part of a plan by Napoleon to cut a canal right through Contentin to Portbail, enabling warships to pass E to W channel without being exposed to the depredations of the English fleet.

Iles St Marcouf

Chart No. 2613

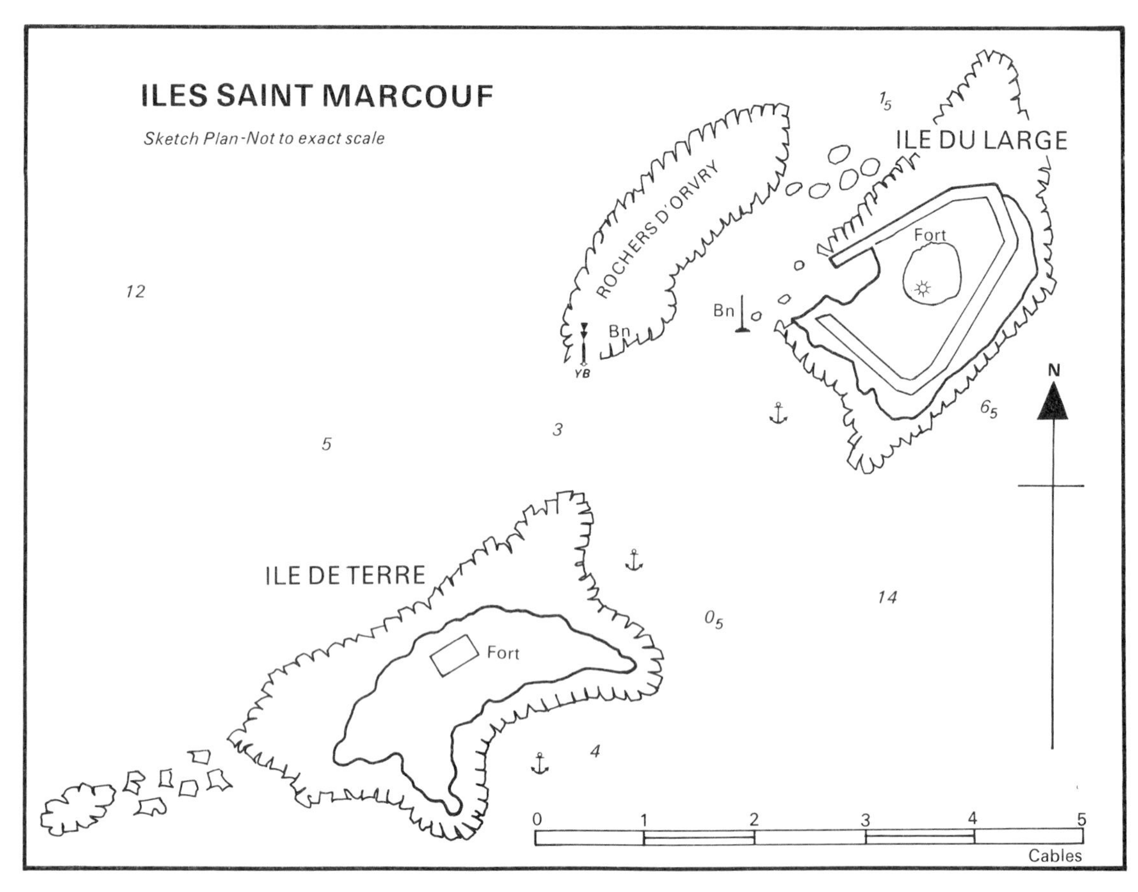

Plan 20 Iles St Marcouf. Landing on Ile de Terre is prohibited.

These small islands, fortified in the mid-17th century, were inhabited until 1914. Ile de Terre is now a bird sanctuary, and landing is prohibited, but Ile du Large is a popular weekend and holiday picnic spot.

Tidal notes

HW times approximately as for St Vaast-la-Hougue. The NW-going stream begins at HW Cherbourg $+3$ and attains 1.3 knots (springs) at HW Cherbourg $+5\frac{1}{2}$. The SE-going stream begins at HW Cherbourg $-2\frac{1}{2}$ and attains 1.3 knots (springs) at HW Cherbourg.

55 Iles St Marcouf: anchorage is between 'X' and 'X'.

56 Iles St Marcouf: beacon with rocks just awash.

Anchorage

This is about 250 m SW of the SW shore of Ile de Terre, in 4–5 m. There is good shelter from N and E, but otherwise it is rather exposed, and I would certainly not spend a night there except in very settled conditions. However, it is an interesting place to visit, preferably on a weekday outside the holiday period. It is easy to land in the small harbour on the western point of Ile du Large 2 hours either side of HW: when the reef running NE from the d'Orvry beacon is awash there is $1\frac{1}{2}$ m over the rock ledge into the harbour.

It is also possible to anchor SE of Ile de Terre, with better shelter from N or NW winds, but landing is prohibited. Note that the Banc de St Marcouf produces very heavy seas in strong NE winds.

57 Iles St Marcouf: dinghy harbour.

St Marcouf was a 6th-century saint who fled to the islands to escape admirers of his piety. The English occupied the islands in 1793 and held them until the Peace of Amiens in 1802. Napoleon I had the fort built shortly thereafter, and it was modernised by Napoleon III, but it was only used briefly as a prison.

Quinéville

Chart No. 2613

This tiny harbour lies $4\frac{1}{2}$ miles south of St Vaast, whose tidal notes also apply here. In 1987 I found 2 m in the channel an hour before HW on a 5.5 m tide at Cherbourg: there would have been 2.4 m at HW and therefore 3.2 m at MHWS and 1.9 m MHWN. Approach on a course of 275° (mag) to avoid the drying reef a mile NE of the entrance. There are two short breakwaters marked by port and starboard beacons just off their ends: beware strong cross-set while approaching the narrow entrance channel. The harbour is only suitable for boats of 9 m or less LOA, capable of drying upright. Berth according to local advice. There is a club with toilets and showers, open July and August only. The entrance is exposed and dangerous in strong onshore winds, but the creek itself is well sheltered, especially beyond the elbow.

It was from the heights above the Quinéville that the exiled James II watched the battle of La Hougue in May 1692. An army had been put together by Louis XIV to restore him to the British throne, but the French fleet under Tourville attacked a combined English and Dutch fleet without waiting for reinforcements, and were utterly defeated. Some escaped round Cotentin and south through the Alderney Race, whose southern extension is still marked on French charts as the 'Passage de la Déroute' (Channel of the Rout): the others took refuge in St Vaast and (as yet unfortified) Cherbourg, and were destroyed by English boat parties. With them disappeared James's last serious hope of returning to the British throne.

58 Quinéville entrance.

St Vaast-la-Hougue

Charts Nos. 1349 and 2613

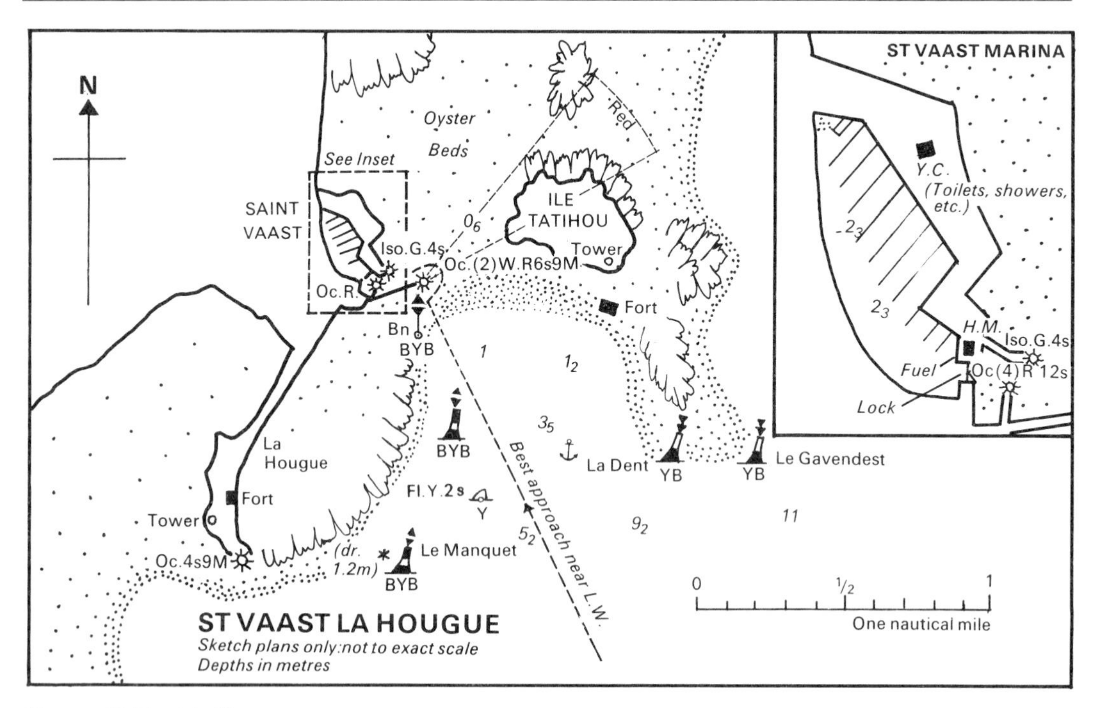

Plan 21 St Vaast-la-Hougue.

Transformed in 1982 from a sleepy little fishing port to an important yachting centre by dredging and the installation of lock gates, St Vaast now offers excellent though tidal accommodation to visiting craft, and has preserved a surprising amount of its earlier charm. The final 'st' in Vaast is mute, leaving the name to be pronounced more or less to rhyme with 'car'.

Tidal notes

Heights: 6.6 m MHWS, 0.9 m MLWS, 5.3 m MHWN, 2.3 m MLWN.

HW is HW Cherbourg +0.53 (springs), +1.06 (neaps). East of Tatihou, the S-going stream begins at HW Cherbourg $-4\frac{1}{2}$ and the N-going one at HW Cherbourg $+2\frac{1}{4}$. No figures are available for rates, but streams are relatively weak S of St Vaast, not exceeding $1\frac{1}{2}$ knots at springs, but become much stronger going N.

Approaches

Coming from the south or east, the Ile de Tatihou must be identified. This has a conspicuous tower on it, but beware of confusing it with a similar one on La Hougue, which is the promontory south of the town of St Vaast. Steer to pass a mile S of Tatihou, leaving the Gavendest and Dent S cardinal buoys to starboard, after which it is safe to steer straight for the end of the breakwater to the NW.

59 St Vaast-la-Hougue: La Dent, south of Ile Tatihou.

60 St Vaast-la-Hougue: the lock gate and the yacht harbour. (*Photo Jack H. Coote.*)

At night, bring the Oc 4s light on La Hougue into line with the Oc(1 + 3) 12s light at Morsalines, and approach on that line until the breakwater light (Oc(2) WR 6s) bears 325° (mag), when it is safe to steer for the latter.

From the north, steer to pass at least $\frac{1}{2}$ mile E of Tatihou (which is unmistakable from that quarter) until the Gavendest buoy is identified, when it can be closed. From there, steer W to leave the Dent buoy to starboard, and then NW for the breakwater. At night, this route is complicated by the lack of lights on the Gavendest and Dent buoys, and the light on Pte de Sair must be kept showing W of Barfleur light until the lights on La Hougue and Morsalines come into line, after which proceed as described in the approach from the south.

61 St Vaast-la-Hougue: lighthouse on the end of the outer breakwater. The fishing boat has just turned towards the harbour entrance.

An alternative channel coming from the north is the 'Run', most useful in strong S to SW winds, as it avoids the bad seas that are met E and S of Tatihou under such conditions. Local instructions state that the channel is confined to boats drawing no more than 1.2 m, and certainly it is for shallow draft only. The shallowest part dries to 2.5 m, so it carries 1.3 m at half tide, and it should only be used between HW -2 and $-\frac{1}{2}$, but even with these restrictions I have found it a most useful short cut.

From the large BYB Roches Dranguet beacon, steer 190° (mag) until the S cardinal Vitéqué beacon is identified. If the tide has been calculated correctly, the concrete base of this will be awash or covered, and only the post and topmarks visible. Pass close E of this, and turn onto 267° (mag). On this course the church of Quettehou will be dead ahead. It is not easy to see, being brownish and among trees below the skyline, but if it is not identified it is just as good to keep the Vitéqué beacon on a back bearing of 87° (mag). Keep on this line until the two inner light towers marking the entrance to the harbour come in line, then turn onto this transit, about 220° (mag). The two white towers have red and green tops respectively. An almost identical transit is given by the Hougue tower exactly fitting in the gap between two buildings, and this can be used instead, as it is often easier to see: there is only one gap in which the base of the tower exactly fits, and the bearing provides a check. The transit must be followed with great care, to avoid fouling the wooden oyster containers on both sides of the line. Waypoint: 49°34′.5N, 1°10′.0W gives a safe offshore point from which to steer west for the approach buoys.

Entrance and berthing

The gates are open from HW $-2\frac{1}{4}$ to $+3$ on average tides, but at extreme neaps the period of opening can be shortened by as much as $1\frac{1}{2}$ hours at each end. At half-tide there is 2 m alongside the N side of the outer mole, and if early it is permissible to moor alongside to wait: if late one may dry out alongside for a tide. The harbour office listens on VHF Channel 9. Inside there are 665 berths, of which 165 are reserved for visitors.

62 St Vaast-la-Hougue: view of entrance after rounding the end of the breakwater. (*Photo Jack H. Coote.*)

63 Yachts berthed in the marina at St Vaast. (*Photo Jack H. Coote.*)

When the gates are open, vessels entering have priority, but even so the entrance should be approached with care, as visibility is restricted. A card will be displayed from the Capitainerie (see plan: 'H.M.') showing a letter which is the identifying letter of the pontoon at which the visitor is required to berth. When maneouvring in the basin, watch out for tidal streams. These can be strong, especially near the dock gates, and can sweep a boat down onto the corner of a pontoon. The effect is most noticeable just before the gates are shut.

Facilities
Water and electricity on pontoons. Minimal toilets at Capitainerie, good ones and showers at yacht club (see plan). Fuel station just below Capitainerie, immediately to starboard on entry. Several chandlers on the quai Vauban, overlooking the harbour, two boatyards capable of repairs (Chantiers Bernard and Planque) and several marine engineers including the Garage du Port, tel: 33 54 43 64. 6 ton mobile crane. Charts from Maison de la Presse, 17 rue de Verrue.

General
Shops will be found on the street inland from the quai Vauban, and also further into town. The restaurants overlooking the basin have become rather expensive, and the ones in town offer better value. Beautiful oysters can be bought at reasonable prices on the quay. M. Gosselin in rue de Verrue is one of the last of the real old-fashioned French grocers and has a tremendous range of goods, especially wines, although no doubt the supermarkets are cheaper. The forts, designed by Vauban, were built in 1695, three years after the disaster of the Hougue battle (see under Quinéville).

I should perhaps mention that no charge is made for a visit in which the boat enters and leaves on the same tide. Once the gates have closed, however, a visitor has incurred the daily charge even if he leaves on the next tide during the same day that he arrived.

64 St Vaast-la-Hougue: view of Ile Tatihou from St Vaast.

Barfleur

Charts Nos. 1349, 1106 and 2613

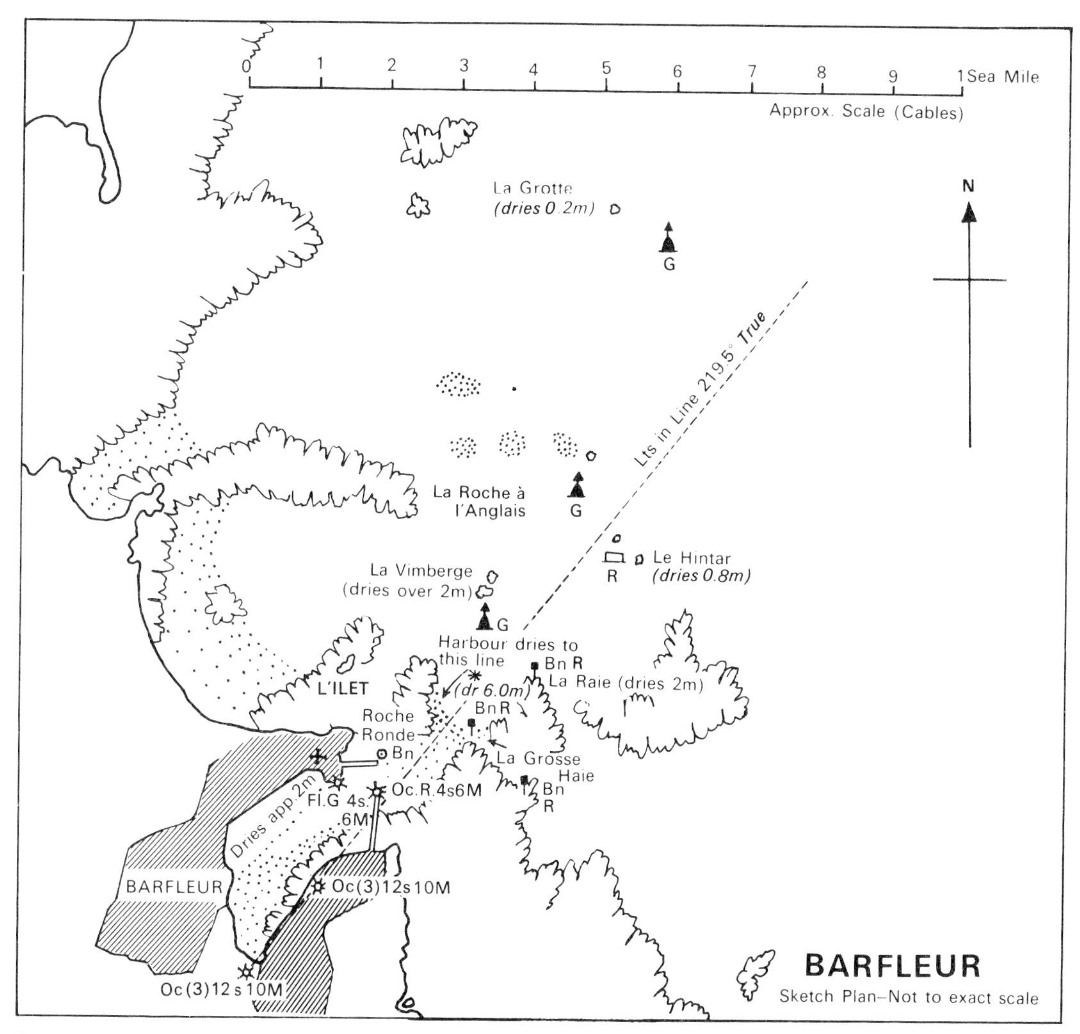

Plan 22 Barfleur.

Still a drying fishing harbour (in spite of continual plans to redevelop it), Barfleur is nevertheless popular with cruising boats, attracted by the beautiful village and traditional atmosphere.

Tidal notes

Heights: 6.5 m MHWS, 1.1 m MLWS, 5.3 m MHWN, 2.5 m MLWN.

HW is HW Cherbourg +1, LW is LW Cherbourg +0.52 (springs) to +0.41 (neaps). The N-going stream begins at HW Cherbourg $+2\frac{1}{4}$. The S-going stream begins at HW Cherbourg $-4\frac{1}{2}$. Spring rates reach 2–3 knots in the offing, and 2 miles further N the rates approach 5 knots on a mean spring ebb and exceed that speed on a mean spring flood (see 'Passage Notes: Barfleur to Cherbourg' on page 100).

Approach

If coming past Cap Barfleur, see also the Passage Notes quoted above. Approaching from the south, offshore hazards are well marked: the only problem is that to arrive at HW Barfleur (which is approximately 2 hours before HW Dover) one will have been plugging northwards against the flood stream. Coming from St Vaast (which is 9 miles) I tend to leave at HW Barfleur −1, arriving there at about HW +1 or maybe quarter of an hour later: that way the tide is slack by the time I am off Barfleur. From seaward, a valuable landmark is the immensely tall tower of the lighthouse on Cap Barfleur, which also has a radio beacon, FG (..–. ––.) on 291.9 kHz.

From either direction, keep at least 1½ miles offshore until NE of the town, which is easily recognisable by its church, which looks from seaward rather like a castle. Waypoint: 49°41′.5N, 1°14′.0W. Approaching from this direction, steer straight for the church, adjusting the course for tidal set to remain on a SW (mag) course for the town. When just under a mile from the pierheads, a green buoy, La Grotte, will be seen to starboard. This should be left about 1½ cables to starboard, when a pair of green and red buoys will be seen ahead. Pass between these (the red one is Le Hintar), and then steer for the first of two port-hand beacons, with cylinder topmarks. Pass both of these close on their starboard side, and then steer straight for the entrance. A third port-hand beacon between and to the south of the two referred to should be ignored. At night there is no problem, as the leading lights, Oc(3) 12s, lead straight through all the hazards. Follow the line until close in to the S pierhead, Oc R 4s, then steer to N of it and into the harbour. Entry at night is really easier than in daylight, as is often the

65 Barfleur: the entrance from La Roche a l'Anglais buoy.

66 Barfleur: the last port hand mark (beacon).

case in the similar North Breton harbours. Of course, if the transit on the leading lights were maintained too long, a collision with the S breakwater would result, but in fact the lights disappear behind the wall before this danger develops. Note that in daylight the approach is to the south of the S pierhead until only 50 m off: the isolated dangers are all on the N side of the channel.

For shelter from westerly winds, it is possible to enter to just inside the pierheads as much as 4 hours before or after HW: at that time there is 1.5 m of water at a top spring, and 2.2 m at neaps. One can anchor there and wait for enough water to go alongside.

Berthing

Yachts should berth along the SW half of the NW wall of the harbour. There are small ladders all along the wall, and the bottom is firm sand and fairly flat. The SW wall is mostly used by fishermen, and the SE side is shoal and foul. In strong NE winds severe scend develops in the harbour, which can cause heavy bumping as boats are taking or leaving the ground. If caught in such condition in a boat capable of drying upright, consult the harbourmaster who may be able to allot a mooring buoy where the boat will dry onto soft mud.

Facilities

Water and electricity are available, and there are toilets on the quay, but they were pretty disgusting when inspected in 1991. In July and August the harbourmaster meets yachts on arrival and allocates berths. There is a marine mechanic, M. Bouly, 68 rue St Thomas, tel: 33 54 02 66.

General

The village is a pretty one, and not too tourist-oriented. The shops are not very large or numerous, but they are adequate and conveniently close to the berths, and there are some good restaurants. Off the beaten track but well worth a visit is the Restaurant Moderne, just opposite the post office in Place Charles de Gaulle. The 17th-century church is also worth a visit.

It was on the Quilleboeuf reef only a mile north of Barfleur that in 1119 the White Ship was wrecked, with the loss of the heir to Henry I of England who would have been William III. The ship was new and fast, and not only passengers but crew had been celebrating her first voyage when, unnoticed by the drunken skipper, the tide swept her onto the reef. The prince was put aboard the only boat and got clear, but insisted on returning for his half-sister, who had been left behind, and the boat was swamped by sailors trying to climb aboard. The only survivor was one Bérold, a butcher from Rouen, who clung to a floating spar. Legend says that the skipper was clinging to the same spar, but when he heard of the prince's death he loosed his hold and sank.

No one dared tell the king: at last a young boy was sent to him to break the news. Chroniclers of the time said that Henry never smiled again. William's death resulted, years later, in the wars between Stephen and Matilda, and the final succession of Henry II, the first Plantagenet.

67 Barfleur: the harbour at high water . . .

68 . . . and low water. Note extent of drying rock by beacon outside entrance.

69 Barfleur Lighthouse.

Races arise when the tide is accelerated by a headland or promontory, and they are intensified when the fast stream thus created has to pass over a rough bottom. The Barfleur Race has both these characteristics in generous measure, and it is often a thoroughly unpleasant and dangerous piece of water. In a heavy NW blow, the seas on the ebb are ferocious, and could easily overwhelm a yacht, and in such conditions the point of the Cape should be given an offing of at least 7 miles, and even then the effects of the race will be clearly felt. In these conditions the ebb outside Barfleur will tend to draw one up into the danger, so it is important to leave before HW to get a good offing before this effect develops. A similar offing is needed in a strong SE wind on the flood. The distance off from Barfleur Light can be found in seconds with a sextant – even a cheap plastic one – and the tables in any good almanac. If by misfortune you find yourself in the race, keep the engine running, as the strong eddies and whirlpools can twist a sailing vessel round, gybing her or heaving her to unexpectedly, thus making sailing almost impossible. In calm weather it is safe to pass through the race, but the sea can get up in minutes if even a moderate breeze develops. In any strong wind it is safest to pass through the race at slack water (HW Cherbourg $-4\frac{1}{2}$ or $+2$). Obviously, conditions will be worse for a given wind strength at springs than at neaps.

The classic route from Barfleur to Cherbourg is outside the Equets and Basse du Renier N cardinal and Pierre Noire W cardinal buoys, and after passing through the race at the HW slack this gives the best tidal stream westwards. However, with BA chart 1106 or the French equivalent 6737 aboard it is safe to take the inshore passage. Make out the Equets buoy,

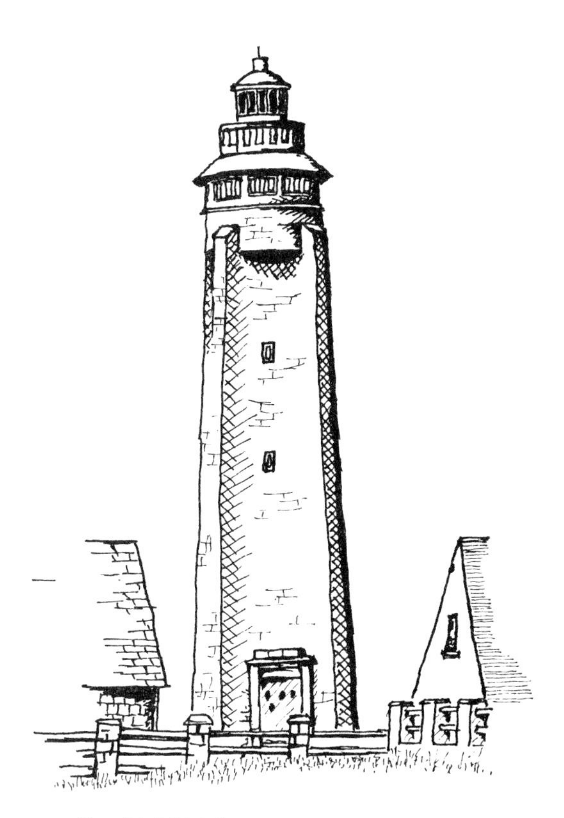

70 Cap Lévi Lighthouse.

avoiding being swept W of a line between it and the beacon off Barfleur light. From there it is safe to steer 275° (mag) until after about 4 miles soundings increase to over 20 m. At this point one can turn somewhat to port and steer to pass 2 cables N of Bieroc, the most northerly rock pinnacle N of Cap Lévi. From here a direct course may be set for the towers marking the north of Ile Pelée, which are left to port before turning into Cherbourg eastern entrance.

There is a passage still further inshore favoured by fishing boats cheating the stream, which passes south of the Trois Pierres beacon, but the navigation is very tricky and a sudden deterioration of visibility can be most embarrassing, so I do not recommend it.

Port de Lévi and Port du Becquet

Chart No. 1106

Both of these are very small fishing harbours and there is little object in staying in either, although they are both worth a visit at HW for those who like to explore every nook and cranny of the French coast. Both are drying harbours open to winds from SW through to W to NW in the case of Port de Lévi and NW to NE in the case of Port du Becquet.

Port de Lévi

There are no leading lights, but the light structure is sectored and gives fixed red, green, and white, and it is extremely important to stay in the green sector to avoid the outlying hazards. You are strongly advised not to make this entrance at night because there are numerous lobster pots and their cork floats are impossible to see.

In daytime the white marks on each side of the harbour entrance are clearly visible and entry should be effected when the white structure on the wall (on which the light is mounted) is midway between them.

Once inside take local advice if possible: on my infrequent visits there has not been much room, and the harbour is criss-crossed by the mooring lines of the permanent residents. The stream outside sets southwards from HW Cherbourg $+1\frac{1}{2}$ to $+4\frac{1}{2}$, and northwards the rest of the time, maximum rate 2 knots. No facilities: supplies from Fermanville, a mile to the east.

Port du Becquet

The entrance to this port is marked by leading lights: Dir. Oc (2 + 1) 12s in front, and Oc (2 + 1) R 12s to the rear, synchronised. The two lights are in line on 187° (True). They are clear to see when making Cherbourg harbour, particularly when swept by the tide too far to the

71 Port de Lévi: entrance to harbour.

72 Port de Lévi: Note Cap Lévi lighthouse in the background on the extreme right.

73 Port du Becquet: note beacon on left of picture, leading lights on the right.

eastward. By day the two white towers housing these lights are visible, as is a red beacon tower surmounted by a red cylinder just to the E of the entrance, named La Tournette.

There is only one possible place to lie and this is the southern side of the jetty which runs E and W. Outside the harbour the E-going stream begins at HW Cherbourg −5.00 and the W-going at HW Cherbourg +2.00, maximum rate at 2 knots. There is considerable scend with any onshore swell.

Charts Nos. 1106 and 2602

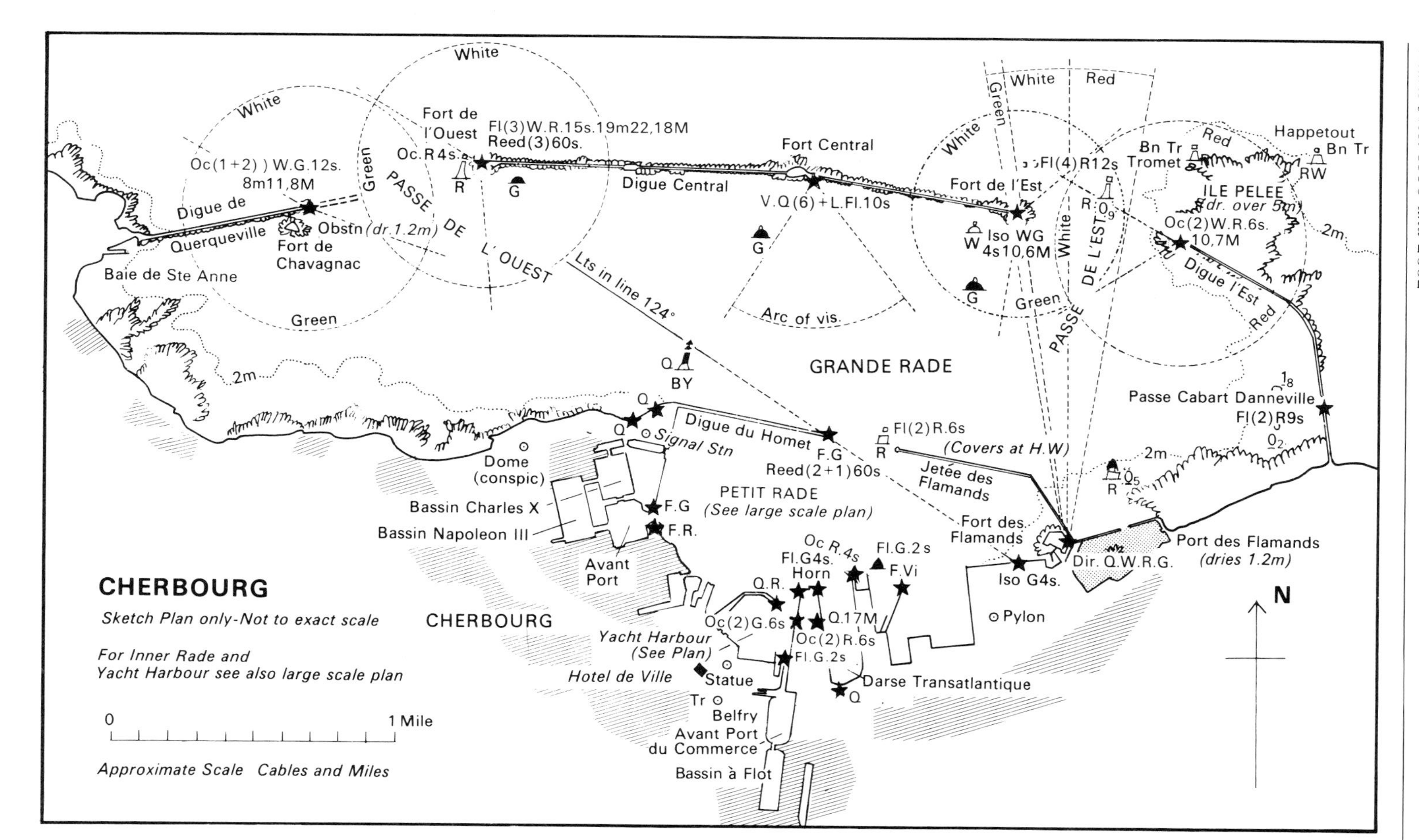

Plan 23 Cherbourg: overall plan.

74 Cherbourg: the eastern entrance showing Ile Pelée and Tromet tower.

Cherbourg is arguably the most important yachting port on the whole of the N coast of France, providing as it does a yacht harbour with nearly 800 berths, available at all states of the tide and in all weathers, and offering every possible facility for repair and service.

As well as being a yachting port, Cherbourg is of course also a commercial and fishing port, an important naval base and, geographically, for yachtsmen, it is the gateway to the Channel Islands and the coast of Brittany.

Tidal notes

Heights: 6.3 m MHWS, 1.1 m MLWS, 5.0 m MHWN, 2.5 m MLWN.

The W-going stream begins at HW Cherbourg $+3\frac{1}{4}$. The E-going stream begins at HW Cherbourg -4. At the entrances to the harbour, maximum mean spring rates in the Passe de l'Est are 1 knot NE 3 hours before HW and 0.7 knots SW 3 hours after HW; in the Passe de l'Ouest they are 1.9 knots SE 3 hours before HW and 1.3 knots NW 2–3 hours after HW. A few miles W of Cherbourg, however, the stream is almost permanently W-going within 3 miles of the shore, owing to an eddy which forms during the flood stream. This is very helpful for reaching Cap de la Hague in time for the turn of the tide there at HW Dover $-\frac{1}{2}$.

Approach

From the Nab Tower to Cherbourg entrance is about 70 sea miles, and it is worth taking some care with navigation on this passage to ensure a landfall up-tide from the entrance. The cross-current may exceed 4 knots at springs, and the last thing one wants is to find oneself, say, 7 or 8 miles E of Cherbourg E entrance with the flood stream building up towards full strength. Cherbourg is not easy to see from seaward and is often covered by haze, but the radiobeacon on Fort de l'Ouest, RB (·—· —···) on 312.6 kHz range 20 miles, and the bright lights on Cap Lévi and at both entrances at night are invaluable aids.

75 Cherbourg: the eastern entrance showing Fort de l'Est and Digue Central.

There are three entrances, but the Passe Cabart-Danneville is not much used except by fishing boats. The E and W *passes* (entrances) are both well marked, and either can be used, but small craft should avoid getting in the way of commercial traffic. The approach from the east has been covered under 'Passage Notes: Barfleur to Cherbourg', and that from the west may be found under 'Cherbourg to the Channel Islands': let me therefore finish this section by emphasising that the streams N of Cotentin are so strong that yachts sailing slowly in hazy weather have found themselves swept into the Alderney or Barfleur races without realising what was happening. It is vital to keep steering a course which allows for the tide right up to the pierheads, and resist the temptation to steer for the entrance once it is sighted. That inevitably results in being swept down-tide of it, an error from which it may take hours to recover. Waypoints: East entrance 49°41'.5N, 1°35'.5W, west entrance 49°41'.5N, 1°39'.5W. In both cases steer south, allowing for the tidal stream, for the entrance.

Entrance

The choice of which of the two main entrances to use depends on the direction of approach, or on the landfall if coming from the north. The Passe Cabart Danneville is only useful when approaching from the east and cheating a foul tide. It should only be used at half-tide or higher, when there is at least 1.7 m over the nearby shoals: stream through the *passe* can reach 5 knots at springs. Keep a sharp eye out for fishing floats.

There is no problem when using the western entrance, the only hazard being an unmarked extension, awash at an average low water, which projects about 150 m beyond the end of the Digue de Querqueville, the most westerly of the three outer breakwaters. Care must be taken with the eastern entrance, however, particularly at night: the rocks of the Ile Pelée extend nearly ½ mile N of the breakwater, and are marked only by two unlit beacon towers, Happetout to the east, and Tromet to the west. Coming from the east at night, it is therefore important to give the Ile Pelée light a good berth until the light on the Fort de l'Est changes from green to white (Iso 4s). It is then safe to steer for the Fort de l'Est, keeping in the white sector, until

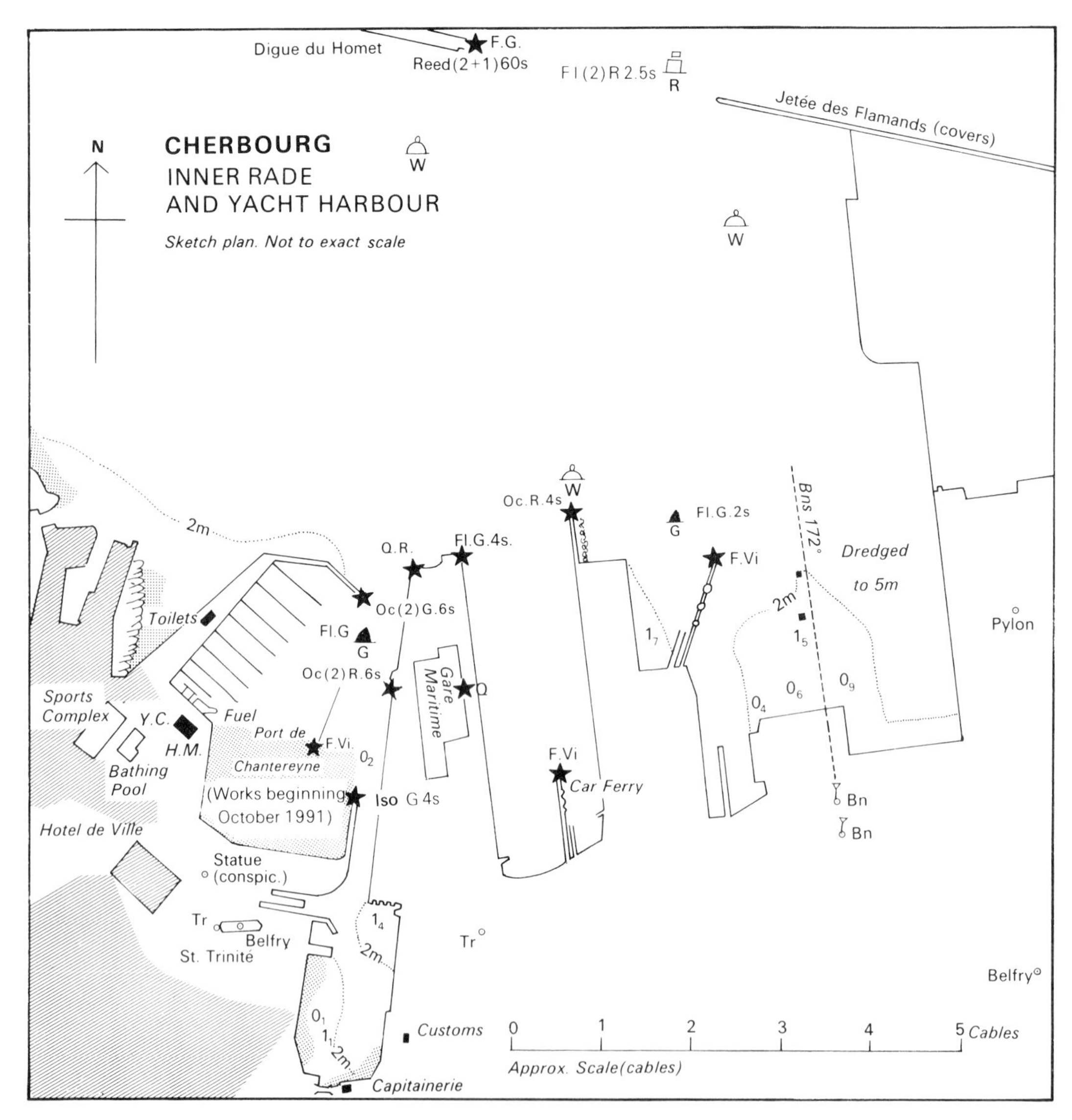

Plan 24 Cherbourg: Inner Rade and Yacht Harbour.

Ile Pelée light turns white, then turn SE into the Grande Rade. Chart 2602 will make clear what I mean.

Once inside the Grande Rade, the first thing to do is to identify the entrance to the Petite Rade, or inner harbour. This lies ESE from the western entrance, or SW from the eastern one, and is marked by a light, FG, on the end of the Digue du Homet to starboard, and a red buoy, Fl(2) R 6s, to port. The latter is just clear of the end of the Jetée des Flamands, part of which covers at high tide. Pass midway between these two marks, and from here a course of 205° (mag) leads into the yacht harbour. This lies immediately to the west of the main ferry and liner port, which is brightly lit, and indeed the plethora of lights, both navigational and shore, can be confusing until one is used to it. However, just to starboard of the brightest

76 Cherbourg: entrance to the yacht harbour from the Petite Rade.

shore lights, it should be possible to pick out the lights marking the entrance to the yacht harbour, Q R to port and Oc(2) G 6s to starboard. Once in, the yacht harbour is well lit at night.

Berthing

The second pontoon from the N end (pontoon 'G') is reserved for visitors. If possible pick up a berth there; if not, moor wherever space allows and report to the Capitainerie (see plan). They listen on VHF Channel 9 from 0800 to 2000, and the office is always manned. It may be worth calling an hour or so before arrival in high season, especially in the case of boats over 12 m LOA. In daylight hours during the season there is often a harbour official on the pontoons to indicate a berth. Mooring is alongside finger pontoons, except for large boats who use the outermost pontoon and moor bows on, stern to buoy.

In October 1991, works will begin on a new extension of the yacht harbour in the bay south of the existing pontoons. When these works are completed (target March 1993) there will be 400 new berths, and most of these will be for visitors leaving the existing pontoons for permanent residents. The new berths will involve a much shorter walk to town. The fuel quay will also be improved, with much enlarged tank capacity and separate pumps for fast and slow delivery, enabling large motor cruisers to be refuelled speedily without causing the long delays previously experienced.

Facilities

These are unrivalled in the area covered by this book, and it is therefore pleasant to record that dues as late as 1991 were, as previously, little more than average for Normandy and thus very good value for money. Water and electricity on the pontoons. Showers and toilets on the pier and also at the Capitainerie. The former are open 0900–1115 and 1400–1700 (with a

77 Cherbourg: the yacht harbour. The yacht club is on the left, with the fuelling jetty.

small annexe open 24 hours), the latter 0800–2000. Cherbourg Yacht Club is large and comfortable, with a bar and restaurant: it is closed on Mondays, tel: 33 53 02 83. Capitainerie tel: 33 53 75 16. There are numerous shops close to the yacht club/Capitainerie building, and most services can be found there. Chandlers include Cap Loisirs, Cherbourg Plaisance and Acastillage Diffusion, sailmakers Cheret Voiles (tel 33 94 15 51). Cherbourg Plaisance can also arrange all repairs. Duty-free stores available with minimal red tape from shop at the root of the main pier. Fuel from fuel station (see plan), but only within 3 hours of HW. Opening hours (with that proviso) 0800–1400 and 1500–2000. The berth is a structure of girders and wooden cross-pieces, and although improved it is still a tricky place to secure if the wind is blowing strongly onto it. It is to be hoped that the rebuilding will include the provision of a pontoon for use when refuelling.

General

Cherbourg is a big town, and one can walk a long way without ever finding a shop. The best route is to go to the statue of Napoleon on horseback (marked on the plan), take the road running straight inshore from the other side of the coast road, and bear left at the top of the little square. A little way further on, an alley, the Passage Digard, leads off to the left, just before the employment exchange. Take this alley and follow it: it becomes a tunnel and then opens out into a street full of all kinds of shops. As far as I have been able to discover, this is the nearest shopping area to the yacht harbour. As in any large French town, there are restaurants and bars everywhere!

The Port de Plaisance Chantereyne takes its name from an incident in 1142 when Matilda of Anjou was caught in a storm: as the skies cleared and land came into view, the captain turned to her with the words 'Chante, Reine, voici la terre!' The town was taken by the Duke of Gloucester for Henry V in 1418, and Henry himself rode through its streets in 1420. The French did not recover it until 1450. The modern harbour was planned by Vauban, but the main works were carried out under Napoleon, who inspected the port in 1811, though not officially completed until 1858, when Napoleon III opened the new dock in the presence of Queen Victoria.

Omonville-la-Rogue

Chart No. 1106

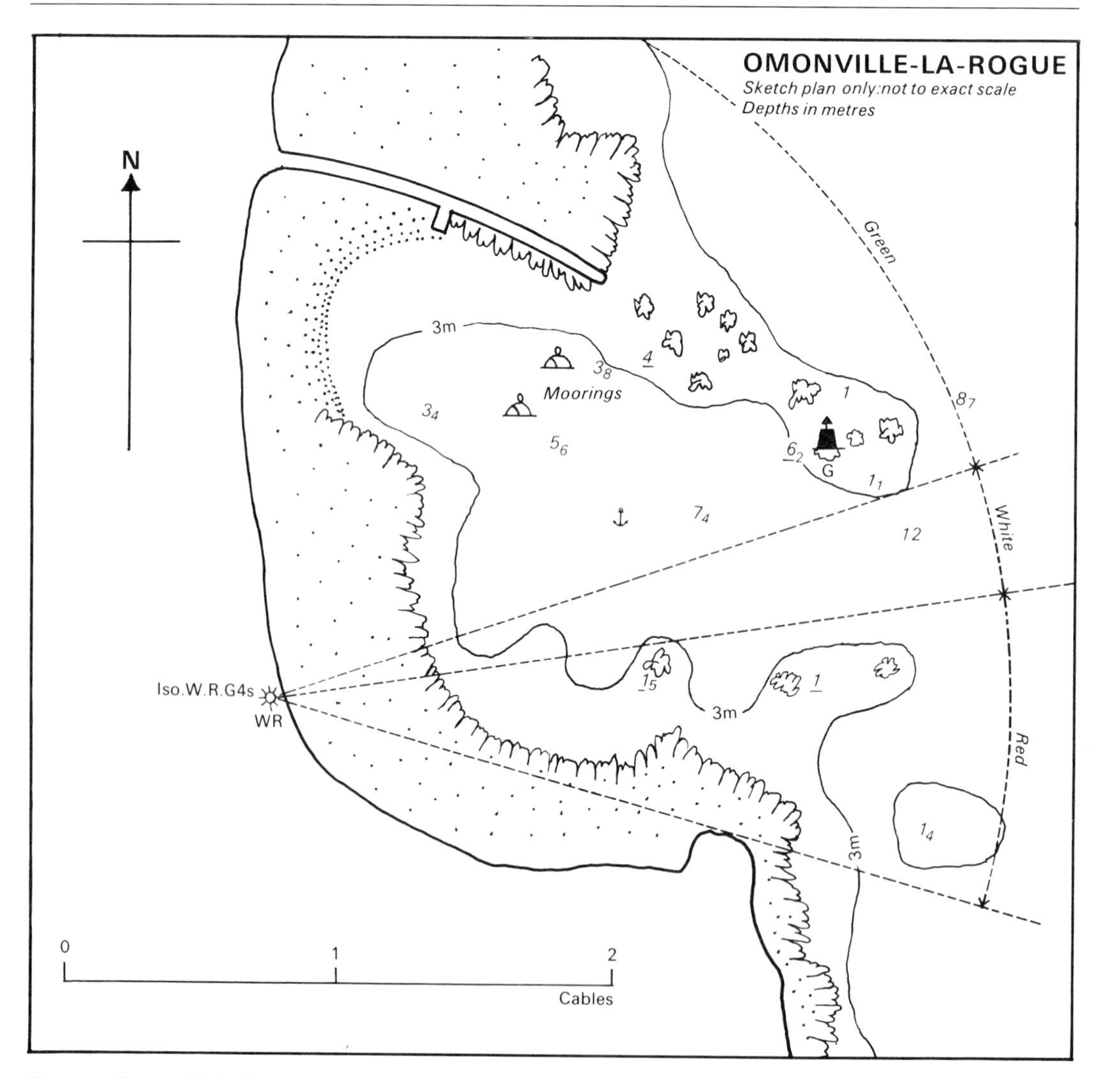

Plan 25 Omonville-la-Rogue.

This small harbour lies some 7 miles west of Cherbourg's western entrance, and provides good protection from all but winds from the eastern sector, to which it is dangerously exposed. Waypoint: from the north or east, 49°42′.4N, 1°48′.5W, then steer west for the entrance. The approach is straightforward by day, the entrance lying a cable S of Le Tunard beacon, and at night the white sector of the harbour light leads in clear of all hazards. There are two large visitors' buoys: several boats can moor to each buoy, each using their own stern anchor. There is a small snack bar overlooking the anchorage and a shop in the village, which is about half a mile from the harbour. A useful place to spend a night after passing through the Alderney Race on the last of the NE-going tide, and pretty enough in its own right.

Anse de Saint-Martin

Chart No. 1106

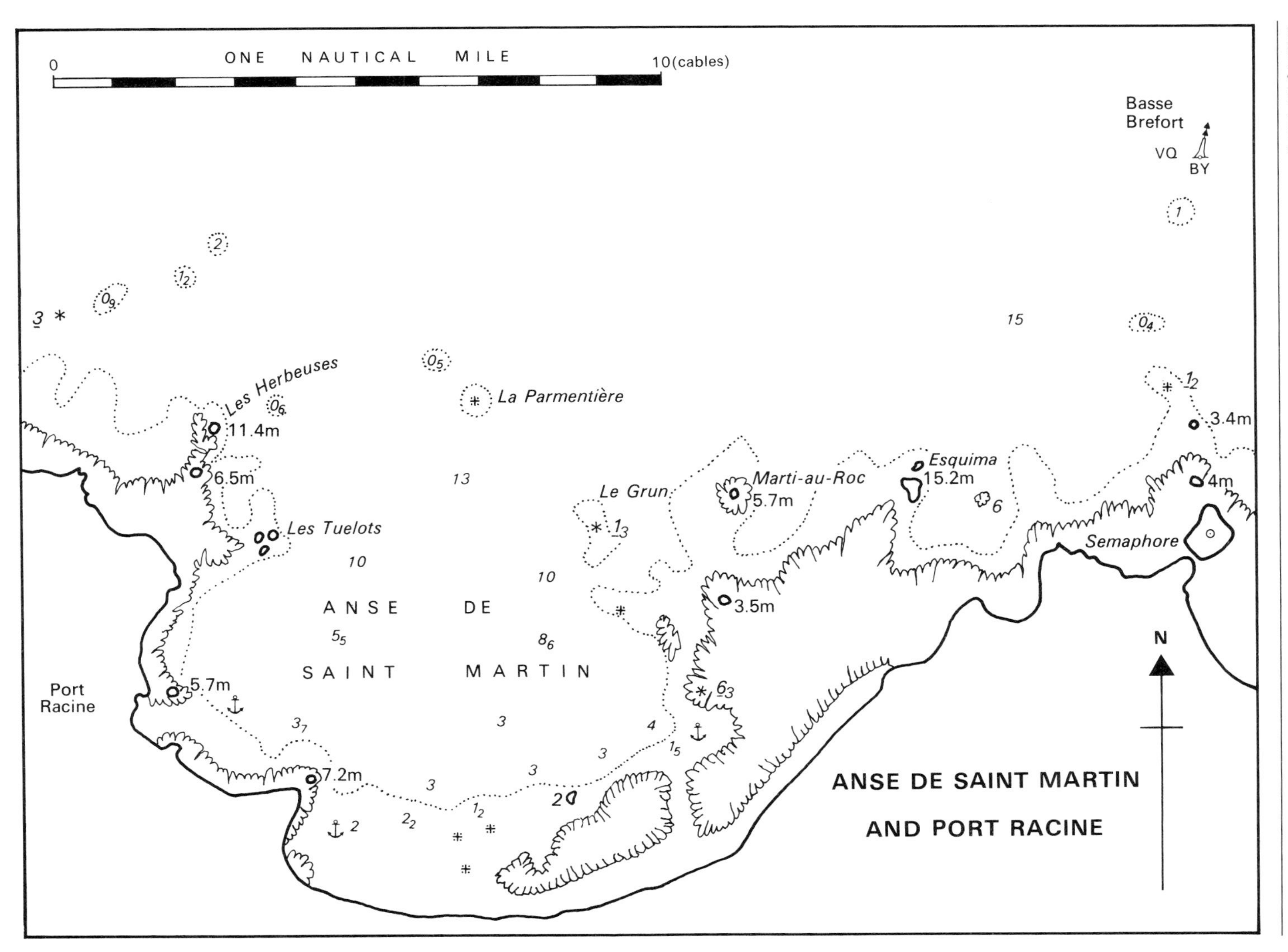

Plan 26 Anse de Saint-Martin and Port Racine.

Anse de Saint-Martin

Chart No. 1106

This is another useful anchorage for a boat that has passed through the Alderney Race on the last of the flood, or in which to spend a night before going W to catch an early morning HW slack at Cap de la Hague, lying as it does only 4 miles from the eastern end of the race.

The entrance is difficult near LWS, when La Parmentière, a rock awash at LAT, has only a metre over it. It is then necessary to identify Port Racine (which has a number of small boats moored just to its east) and approach it from a position a cable N of Marti-au-Roc, a jagged peaked rock which is the furthest NW of all the high offshore rocks at the E side of the bay, on a course of between 235° and 240° (True), say 240° to 245° (mag). This course misses Le Grun (dries 1.3 m) on the one side and La Parmentière (awash) on the other. Once inside, the bay is clear except close inshore. The best anchorage in W winds is just E of the moorings off Port Racine or in the W part of the southern bay, E of Pointe du Nez. In E winds, there is a sandy bay just S of the 6.3 m drying rock (always visible except at HWS) which lies a cable S of rock pinnacle 3.5 m high, which is itself another cable S of Marti-au-Roc, 5.7 m high. Anchor in about 1.5 m as shown on the plan.

There is always some swell in these anchorages, but they are protected from any real sea except in winds between NW and NE. No facilities.

Passage Notes: Cherbourg to the Channel Islands and West Cotentin

Apart from the few who intend merely to visit Omonville and return, most people who sail westwards from Cherbourg along the north Cotentin coast intend to visit the Channel Islands or, less probably, the west coast ports of Cotentin. In either case, the Alderney Race has to be reckoned with, and this is potentially one of the most dangerous stretches of water in Europe, and should always be treated with great respect.

Having said this, let me make it clear at once that there is no problem in navigating this area, as long as careful attention is paid to timing. If wind is with tide (and of course both must then be favourable, or no progress will be made) the overfalls and eddies that occur in the race are not dangerous, and indeed nothing could be greater fun than sailing through the race at the height of the stream with a moderate following breeze, perhaps attaining 10 knots over the ground. Even in such conditions, however, strong swirls may be encountered, and unexpected gybes are always a risk that the whole crew should be prepared for.

The problems arise in wind-over-tide conditions (or in really strong winds from any direction, when the whole area is really best avoided). It is difficult to lay down definite wind forces where the conditions become unacceptably bad, but certainly passing through the Race with the full force of a mean tide against a SW wind force 4 produced some very steep seas when I tried it recently, and I would not have cared for the experience had there been an extra force in the wind, or had it been a day or two nearer spring tides. That was motoring into the wind: sailing is made more difficult by the sudden patches of steep seas and swirls of tide: I remember on one occasion being put right about under sail and finding myself hove to.

Going SW through the Race, the prudent thing to do is to arrive north of Cap de la Hague just as the fair tide is beginning, thus getting through the worst area long before the stream, and therefore the overfalls, has reached its peak. This is facilitated by the fact that there is a W-going eddy running inshore along most of the coast from Cherbourg to Cap de la Hague during most of the E-going stream. An average yacht leaving Cherbourg 3 hours before HW Dover should therefore reach the Cap at or a little before HW Dover, when the stream is slack in the E part of the race, and just beginning to run SW on the Alderney side. With this timing the worst area of overfalls will be far behind by the time the stream reaches its maximum rate 3 hours after HW Dover. Be warned, however, that patches of tide-race conditions can be met under such circumstances almost anywhere between Cap de la Hague and Guernsey, especially near springs, and in any but good conditions, care should be taken to avoid passing over the Alderney South Banks or the Banc de la Schole, which can both produce bad seas.

It is not practicable to visit the Cotentin ports direct through the Race from Cherbourg, as one would arrive at LW and be unable to enter Carteret, the most northerly port: these harbours are best visited from St Malo on the way north. From Carteret to Cherbourg is straightforward: the 22 miles to Cap de la Hague will take the average yacht 3 hours at springs (leaving 1 hour before HW Cherbourg with an average fair stream of about 2 knots) and perhaps half an hour more at neaps, when departure should be timed at HW Cherbourg $-1\frac{1}{2}$. From St Peter Port the distance is 28 miles, but the streams are stronger, and maintaining 5 knots through the water a departure at HW St Helier $+\frac{1}{2}$ is early enough at springs (only to be undertaken in winds between S and W or light airs), HW St Helier $-\frac{1}{4}$ for neaps. Note that these timings allow for passing through the worst of the race near slack water: if the

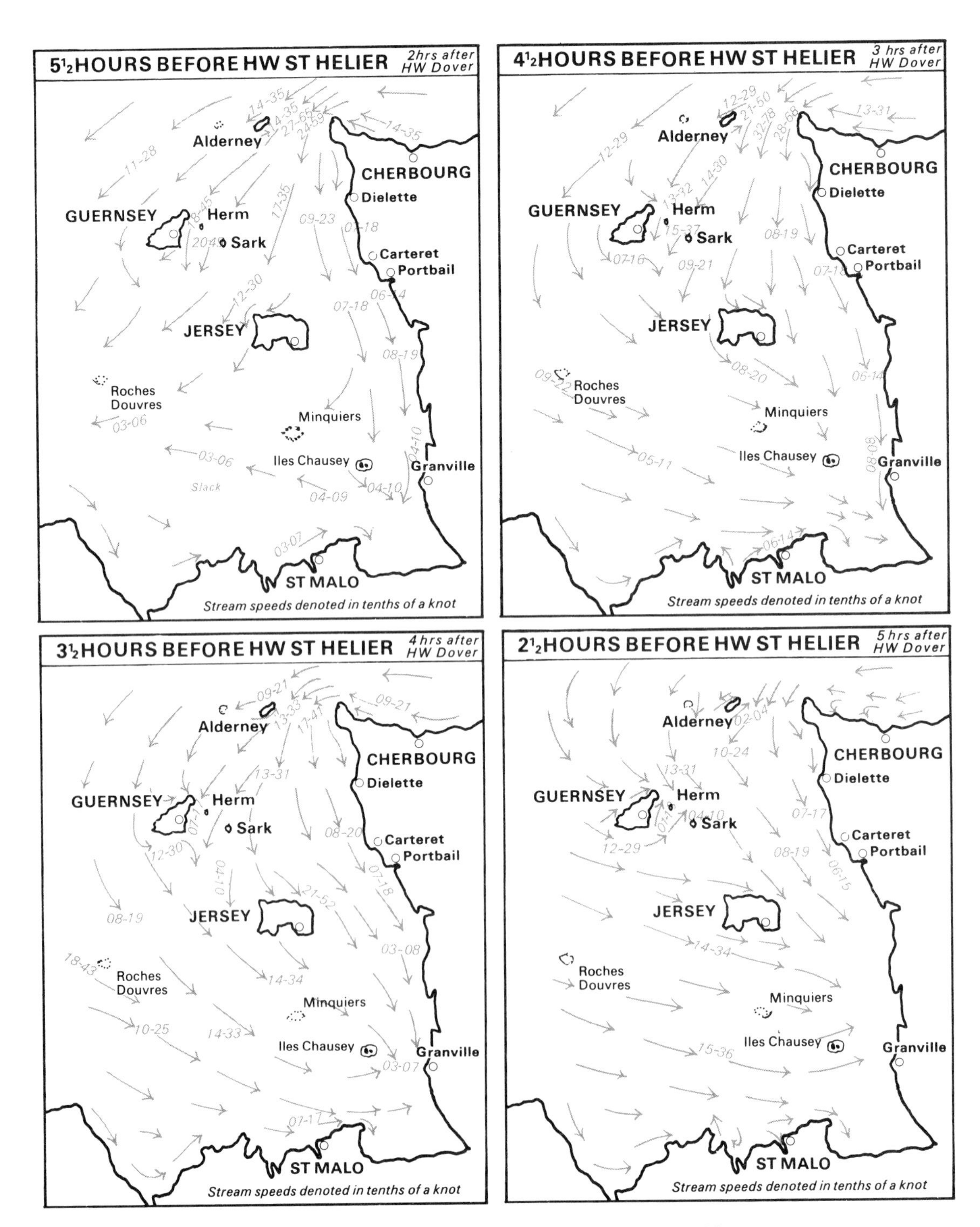

Plan 27 Tidal diagram for Channel Islands and adjacent coasts: differences on HW Dover.

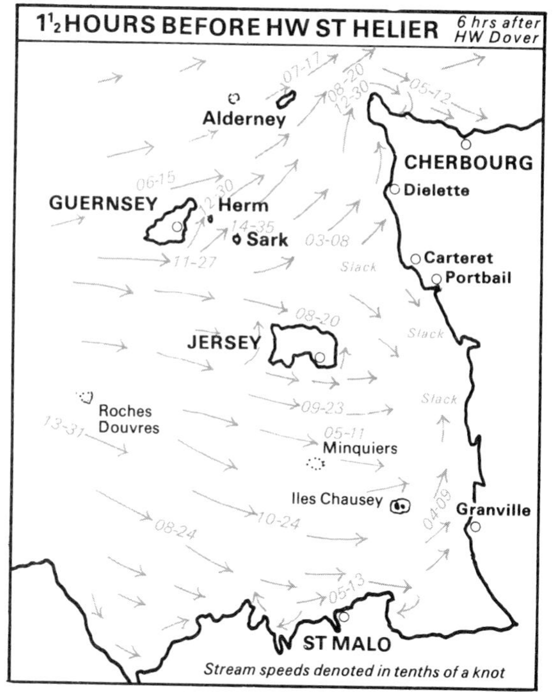
1½ HOURS BEFORE HW ST HELIER
6 hrs after HW Dover
Alderney
CHERBOURG
Dielette
GUERNSEY
Herm
Sark
Carteret
Portbail
JERSEY
Roches Douvres
Minquiers
Iles Chausey
Granville
ST MALO
Stream speeds denoted in tenths of a knot

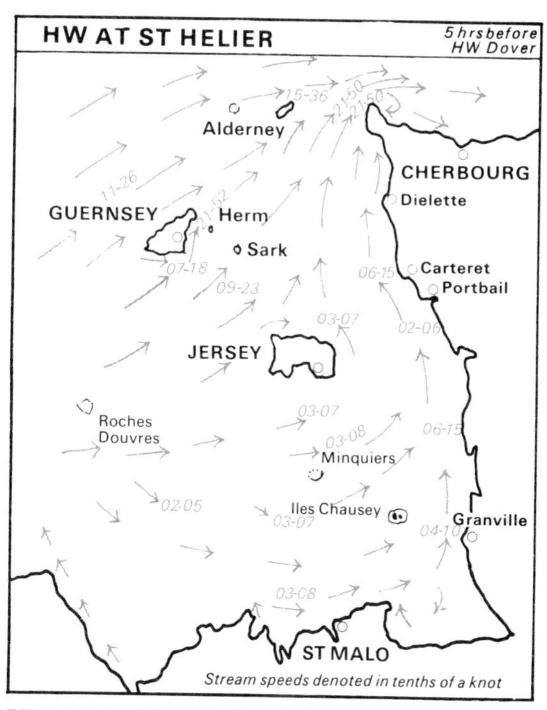
HW AT ST HELIER
5 hrs before HW Dover
Alderney
CHERBOURG
Dielette
GUERNSEY
Herm
Sark
Carteret
Portbail
JERSEY
Roches Douvres
Minquiers
Iles Chausey
Granville
ST MALO
Stream speeds denoted in tenths of a knot

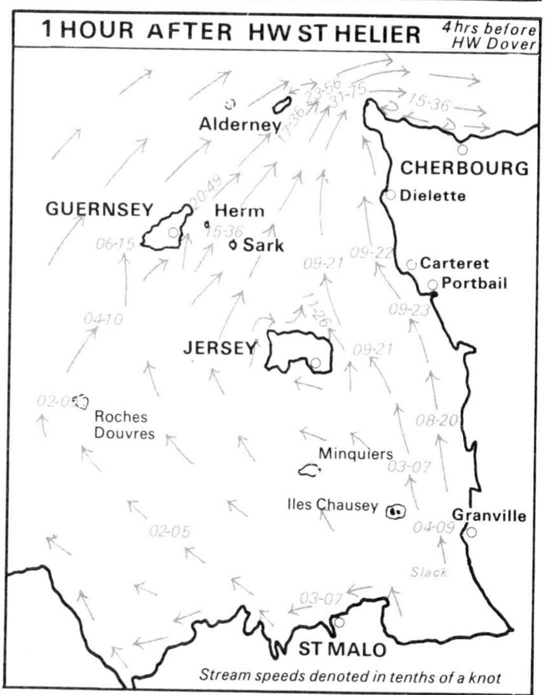
1 HOUR AFTER HW ST HELIER
4 hrs before HW Dover
Alderney
CHERBOURG
Dielette
GUERNSEY
Herm
Sark
Carteret
Portbail
JERSEY
Roches Douvres
Minquiers
Iles Chausey
Granville
ST MALO
Stream speeds denoted in tenths of a knot

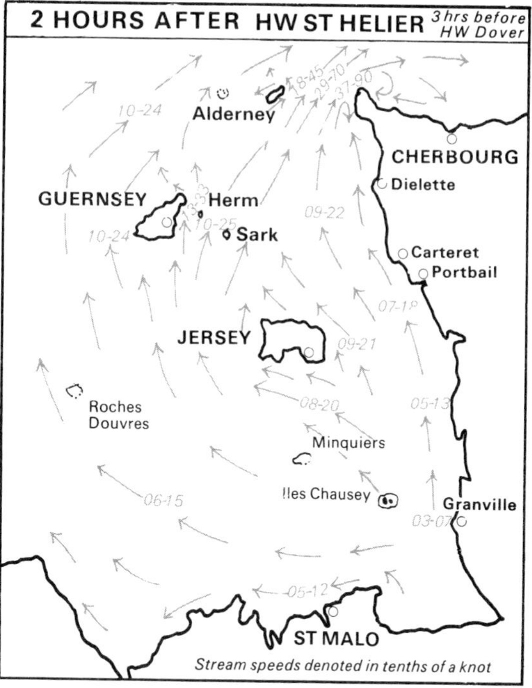
2 HOURS AFTER HW ST HELIER
3 hrs before HW Dover
Alderney
CHERBOURG
Dielette
GUERNSEY
Herm
Sark
Carteret
Portbail
JERSEY
Roches Douvres
Minquiers
Iles Chausey
Granville
ST MALO
Stream speeds denoted in tenths of a knot

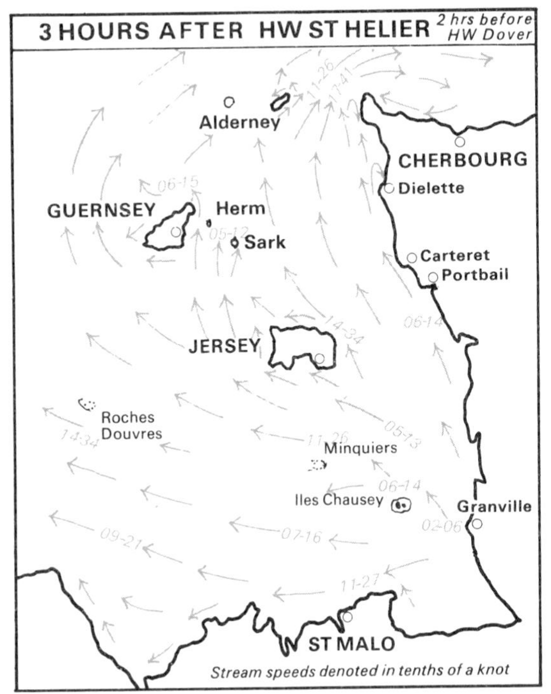
3 HOURS AFTER HW ST HELIER
2 hrs before HW Dover
Alderney
CHERBOURG
Dielette
GUERNSEY
Herm
Sark
Carteret
Portbail
JERSEY
Roches Douvres
Minquiers
Iles Chausey
Granville
ST MALO
Stream speeds denoted in tenths of a knot

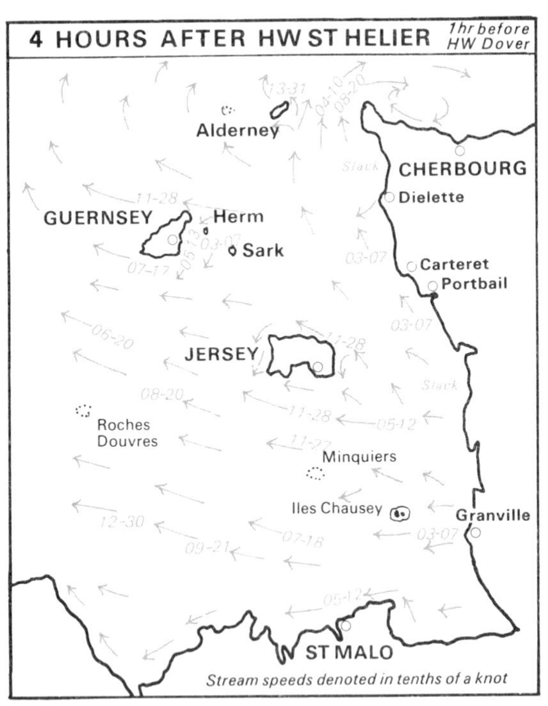
4 HOURS AFTER HW ST HELIER
1hr before HW Dover
Alderney
CHERBOURG
Dielette
GUERNSEY
Herm
Sark
Carteret
Portbail
JERSEY
Roches Douvres
Minquiers
Iles Chausey
Granville
ST MALO
Stream speeds denoted in tenths of a knot

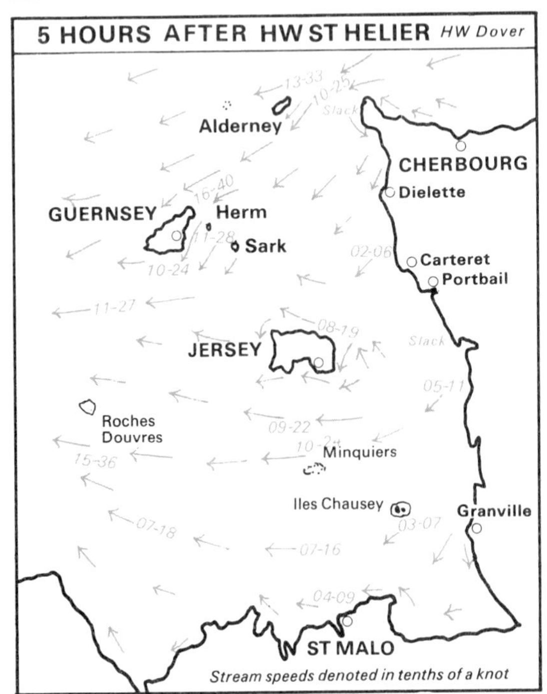
5 HOURS AFTER HW ST HELIER
HW Dover
Alderney
CHERBOURG
Dielette
GUERNSEY
Herm
Sark
Carteret
Portbail
JERSEY
Roches Douvres
Minquiers
Iles Chausey
Granville
ST MALO
Stream speeds denoted in tenths of a knot

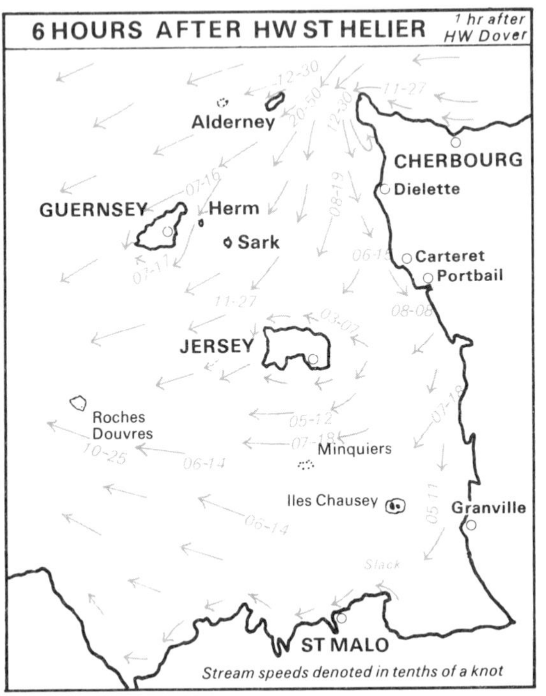
6 HOURS AFTER HW ST HELIER
1 hr after HW Dover
Alderney
CHERBOURG
Dielette
GUERNSEY
Herm
Sark
Carteret
Portbail
JERSEY
Roches Douvres
Minquiers
Iles Chausey
Granville
ST MALO
Stream speeds denoted in tenths of a knot

weather is set fair a departure can be made as early as 2 hours before HW St Helier from Guernsey, but this will mean passing through the Race while it is still running very hard. Departures from Sark should be about half an hour later than those given for St Peter Port.

On the NE-going tide, the worst of the overfalls are on the eastern side of the Race, and the aim should be to pass some 3 miles S of Alderney and then steer NE until well N of Cap de la Hague before turning E and SE. However, if the recommended timings have been used and arrival is near slack water this is less important. Coming from Carteret, keep well offshore to avoid the shoals S of Nez de Jobourg and W of Cap de la Hague. Once E of the Cap, one may buck the foul tide to Cherbourg or wait for a fair one at Anse de Saint-Martin or Omonville.

The passage to Alderney itself avoids the main part of the Race, but great care must be taken not to be swept unwillingly into it, especially near springs. Notes on the Swinge, the channel north of Alderney, will be found in the section on that island.

Charts BA 1106 and French 5636

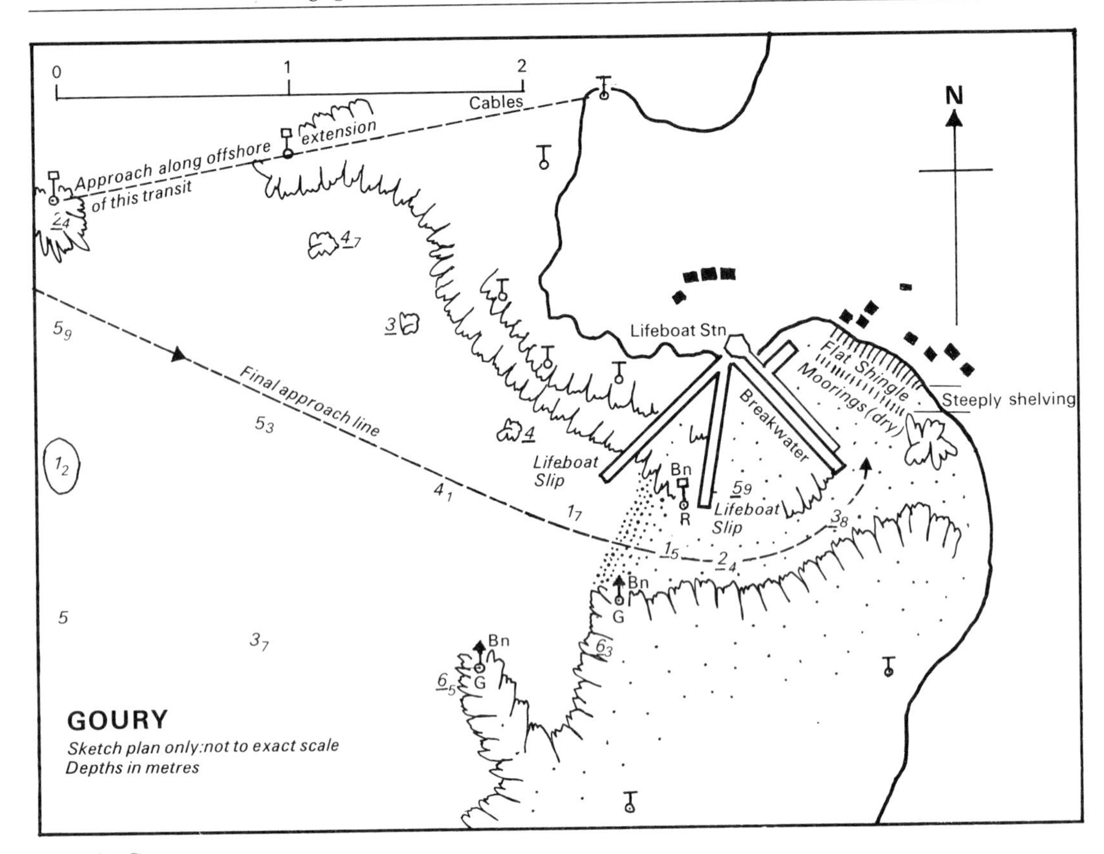

Plan 28 Goury.

Goury has always been difficult of access, a port for the experienced and intrepid who visit it for the challenge rather than for any practical value it has as a port of passage. Now that the main part of the harbour is full of private moorings, there is also a severe problem in finding a berth. I can only advise against a visit: anyone who ignores this advice should arrive in working hours and well before HW to have plenty of time to organise something by rowing ashore.

Tidal notes

Heights: 7.9 m MHWS, 1.2 m MLWS, 6.5 m MHWN, 3.5 m MLWN.

HW is HW Cherbourg −0.43 at springs, −0.59 at neaps. The N-going stream begins at HW Cherbourg $-3\frac{3}{4}$ and reaches its maximum at HW Cherbourg, with rates of 9.7 knots at mean springs in the outer race W of La Foraine beacon, and 5.6 knots in the inshore approach S and E of the Gros du Raz. The S-going stream begins at HW Cherbourg +1 close off Goury, resulting from an eddy, but the stream in the main race does not turn until after HW Cherbourg $+3\frac{1}{2}$. Maximum rates occur at HW Cherbourg −6, reaching 6.8 knots in the main race outside La Foraine, but only 1.1 knots in the inshore approach, both at mean springs. This is why the inshore channel is so much used by eastbound fishing boats which have arrived late on the tide.

Approach

Anyone who insists on attempting this harbour must carry French chart No. 5636, and should visit it in good weather and preferably near neaps. Coming from the north it is best to arrive at the slack water which occurs at HW Cherbourg $-3\frac{3}{4}$, and anchor off the harbour until there is enough water to enter, which is at about HW Cherbourg $-2\frac{3}{4}$. From the south the same timing is safest at springs, but near neaps it is safe to arrive at up to HW Cherbourg -2, allowing an immediate entry. From the north, pass close W of La Foraine YBY tower, making sure to approach it from slightly W of north. Once 100 m south of the beacon, two red beacons will be seen bearing about E (mag). Turn onto that course and keep them in line: this transit leads south of the dangerous La Magne rock (dries 4 m). Keep on the line until 200 m short of the front beacon, and then turn SE for the harbour, leaving green beacons to starboard and red to port.

Coming from the south, pass $\frac{1}{2}$ mile W of Greniquet, the first of two islets south of Goury (it is also the highest, at 9.7 m). From this position, Diotret, the second islet (4.7 m high) will be seen to the NE. Steer N until the two green beacons S of Goury come into line visible just N of this islet, then turn onto this line and keep meticulously on the transit until approaching

78 Goury: the two beacons on the right of the picture are left to starboard, and with a little more rise of tide one can enter past the pierhead.

the first beacon, when it and the second can be left close to starboard and the harbour entered. The dangerous Grios rocks lie only a cable N of this transit, so it is vital to counteract any N-going stream, hence the danger of arriving too near HW, especially near springs, when the stream is running strongly to the N.

Berthing

As stated above, a visitor must negotiate a berth alongside a boat on the trots, or perhaps bow and stern between two. It is possible (see photograph) to anchor on the shingle bank NE of the moorings. It is fairly flat, but there is a sharp slope down to the moorings pool on the one side and up to the wall on the other, so the bottom must be carefully sounded with a pole. Holding is only moderate, but that is less important as the boat will be aground for about 10 hours each tide. A stern anchor is of course necessary.

From my observations in 1987, the moorings area dries about 4 m above datum, and the shingle bank about 5 m. At low neaps the latter is therefore only available to boats of very shallow draft.

General

There are surprisingly good toilets ashore. The lifeboat museum, with souvenirs from all the ships they have attended, is famous. The official works say there is severe swell in bad weather: local advice tends to contradict this.

79 Goury: *Gully-Gully*, the bilge-keeled Fulmar we chartered for the 1987 cruise, is dried out on the upper shingle bank. Better, if possible, to make fast alongside or between boats on the moorings, as the shelter is better and the bottom safer.

Passage inside the Gros du Raz

The main light on Cap de la Hague stands on an offshore islet called the Gros du Raz, and it is possible to pass inshore of it. This is the only practicable passage between Goury and Cherbourg near springs, when the N-going stream makes it impossible for a low-powered boat to keep S of the Foraine beacon and reach the main race. It can also be used to cheat the S-going race, as the ebb stream never exceeds 2 knots even at springs. It is a highly tricky piece of pilotage, however, for experienced navigators only. French chart 5636 will be needed.

Coming from the south, keep a mile offshore until the two green beacons S of Goury come in line. Turn onto this line and keep the beacons *exactly* in line until Diotret, a rocky islet 4.7 m high, bears S (mag), about 150 m away. Now steer N (mag), checking with continual back-bearings, until the outer of the two red beacons W of Goury is in line with the inner one. Maintain this course for one more cable, then steer to pass close E of the islet on which the light is built. La Plate rock (dries 5.4 m) is usually visible either above water or by the overfalls it creates: if it is, keep halfway between it and the Gros. There is N cardinal beacon N of the islet: once past this steer north (mag) until it comes in line with the lighthouse, then keep on this transit for just over a mile into open water. If cheating the tide, however, keep on it only until La Plate BY beacon bears E (mag), then steer for the beacon on that bearing. Pass no more than 50 m S of the beacon and continue E into open water. The least sounding on this route if followed exactly is about $1\frac{1}{2}$ m, N of Le Galet: this would of course be an actual depth of over $2\frac{1}{2}$ m at MLWS. By my observations, the tide turns in this channel about an hour earlier than in the main race. I must emphasise that this is a difficult and potentially dangerous passage, and any reader attempting it does so at his own risk.

80 Just before passing inside the Gros du Raz.

Dielette

Charts Nos. 2669 and 3653

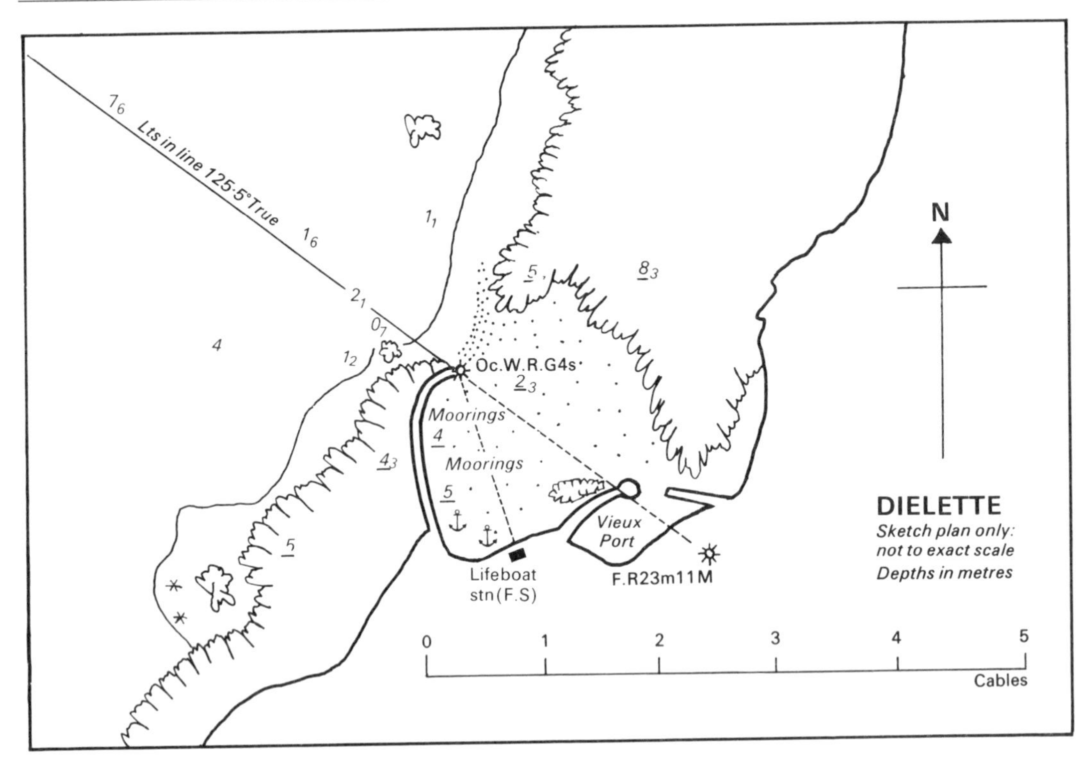

Plan 29 Dielette.

This small drying fishing harbour is criss-crossed by fishermen's mooring lines, some sunken and some floating, so great care is needed when manoeuvring.

Tidal notes

Heights: 9.7 m MHWS, 1.3 m MLWS, 7.4 m MHWN, 3.6 m MLWN.

HW is HW St Malo +0.33 (springs), +0.14 (neaps). The N-going stream begins at HW St Malo $-1\frac{1}{2}$, the S-going at HW St Malo $+4\frac{1}{2}$. Note that all West Cotentin tidal data have been given as differences on St Malo. This avoids the dangers of using a reference port in a different time zone. (If your almanac does not give St Malo tides, it is advisable to buy a table that does, but meanwhile differences for St Malo on Cherbourg are given in the St Malo entry in this book.)

Approach and entrance

In daylight the line of the white patch on the end of the W inner pierhead just open of the end of the outer breakwater leads clear of all dangers; at night a similar approach is achieved by keeping the lights in line. Keep no more than 50 m from the breakwater head to avoid the line of drying rocks which extend to within 100 m of it, but do not pass *too* close, as violent eddies occur there at certain states of the tide and wind. If entering the Vieux Port keep midway between the inner pierheads. Waypoint: 39°33′.8N, 1°53′.0W, then steer 130° (mag) for the entrance.

Berthing
It is possible to anchor in the SW corner of the outer harbour, clear of the moorings. Do not go E of the line between the lifeboat station (flag) and the outer pierhead as the beach is rocky on this side. One can also enter the Vieux Port and anchor in the western part, taking a line ashore: this provides better shelter but is shallow, about 1 m at MHWN to 3 m at MHWS. Even in here scend will be experienced with onshore swell, and if this is heavy the harbour should be avoided. In bad weather the best emergency berth is just inside the outer breakwater head, alongside or outside a fishing boat. However this should only be used in genuine emergencies as mooring alongside the pier is against port regulations, because the limited space is used by fishing boats unloading.

General
There is a small general store in the village, a hotel and a bar-restaurant. The harbour was of importance once, having been begun in the 17th century under Hervé de Bazen, a remarkable character who rose to be commander of the Gendarmes only to take holy orders and end up Bishop of Perpignan. As recently as 1911, Merk was writing 'The harbour has a

81 Dielette: visitors anchor and dry inshore from the moorings (see plan). The drying reef is visible to the right.

considerable depth of water': it was then used for carrying granite blocks quarried from the cliffs. When this trade fell away, it would seem that it was no longer worth dredging the harbour, but for boats that can dry it is a charming and unspoiled place to visit. The disused structure standing in the sea S of the entrance should be passed on its seaward side.

Carteret

Charts Nos. 2669 and 3655

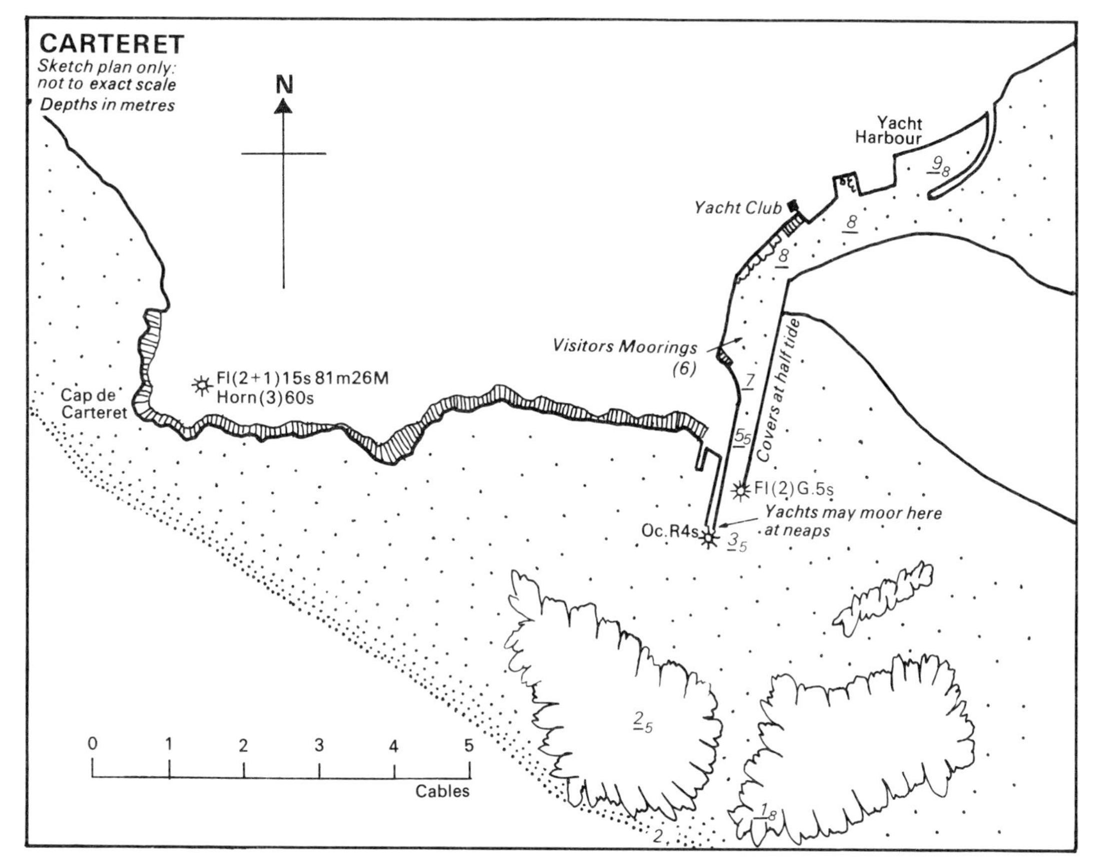

Plan 30 Carteret.

This is a pleasant holiday resort with an active fishing fleet, but on the whole it does not welcome visiting yachts. There have been plans to close off the upper harbour and develop a marina, which could one day become very large as the area of water is considerable, but in 1991 these seemed to have faded.

Tidal notes

Heights: 11.2 m MHWS, 1.5 m MLWS, 8.5 m MHWN, 4.1 m MLWN.
HW is HW St Malo +0.26. The N-going stream begins at HW St Malo $-\frac{1}{2}$, the S-going at HW St Malo +6. Spring rates exceed 3 knots in both directions.

Approach and entrance

The entrance lies about $\frac{1}{2}$ mile E of the large Cap de Carteret light (Fl(2 + 1) 15s 81 m 26 M) and there is an Oc R 4s light on the head of the main west jetty, which is left close to port when entering. Tides are almost identical in height and timing with St Helier. Waypoint: from the south or SW, 49°21′.0N, 1°47′.2W, then steer north for the jetty. The outer part of

82 Carteret. The beacon near the right of the picture marks the end of the covering east breakwater.

the entrance channel dries only 3–4 m, so with a half-tide level of over 6 m it is possible to reach the shelter of the W jetty at any time above half-tide, but to enter the inner part of the harbour, which dries 7–9 m, it is necessary to wait until near HW, and even then the upper parts remain dry at neaps. The approach is straightforward in daylight: keeping the E side of the jetty just open gives a good approach line, and warns if the boat is being swept off line by the stream.

Berthing

The ferry to Gorey berths along the inner half of the W jetty (the eastern one is a breakwater covering at half-tide, whose end is marked by a green beacon), but yachts are permitted to berth alongside the outer part at neap tides only. Otherwise proceed inwards past the fish quay and the slip: there are six visitors' moorings (which, of course, dry) each with a separate bow and stern warp. Further up still is the Petit Port, a small basin which should not be used without local advice, as the bottom is foul. Still higher is a small yacht basin which few visiting boats would be able to reach except at high springs, as it dries 9.8 m, and so has 1–1.5 m at HW on a good spring. However, it is occasionally possible to moor alongside a fisherman for a couple of tides in the lower part of the harbour if the visitors' area is full, by finding one that is not intending to go out, or who is already aground on a falling tide. I have often spent a day here on my way from Portbail to Dielette, arriving in the morning and leaving in the evening. If the tides are suitable, this works well as there is always plenty of wall free during the day because the fishermen are all at sea. Visitors mooring alongside fishing boats should

83 Carteret. It is sometimes possible to moor on the fishing quay if a boat can be found that is not intending to go out.

make sure of the intentions of their hosts before going ashore, as a British yacht was dismasted when a fishing boat attempted to leave without noticing that the yacht's halyard was made fast ashore.

Facilities and general

The Bureau de Port is open from 1100 to 1200 (no, not a misprint!) except Mondays and Sundays, between 1st April and 15th September. This is next to the yacht club (see plan) which is open 1000 to 0100 in July and August only. It is little more than a small bar, but cheerful and friendly. There are restaurants ranging up to first class overlooking the lower part of the harbour, and good small-town shopping beyond the yacht club. Buses to Valognes (the Versailles of Normandy) and Cherbourg. Daily ferry (catamaran) service to Gorey, Jersey.

Portbail

Charts Nos. 2669 and 3655

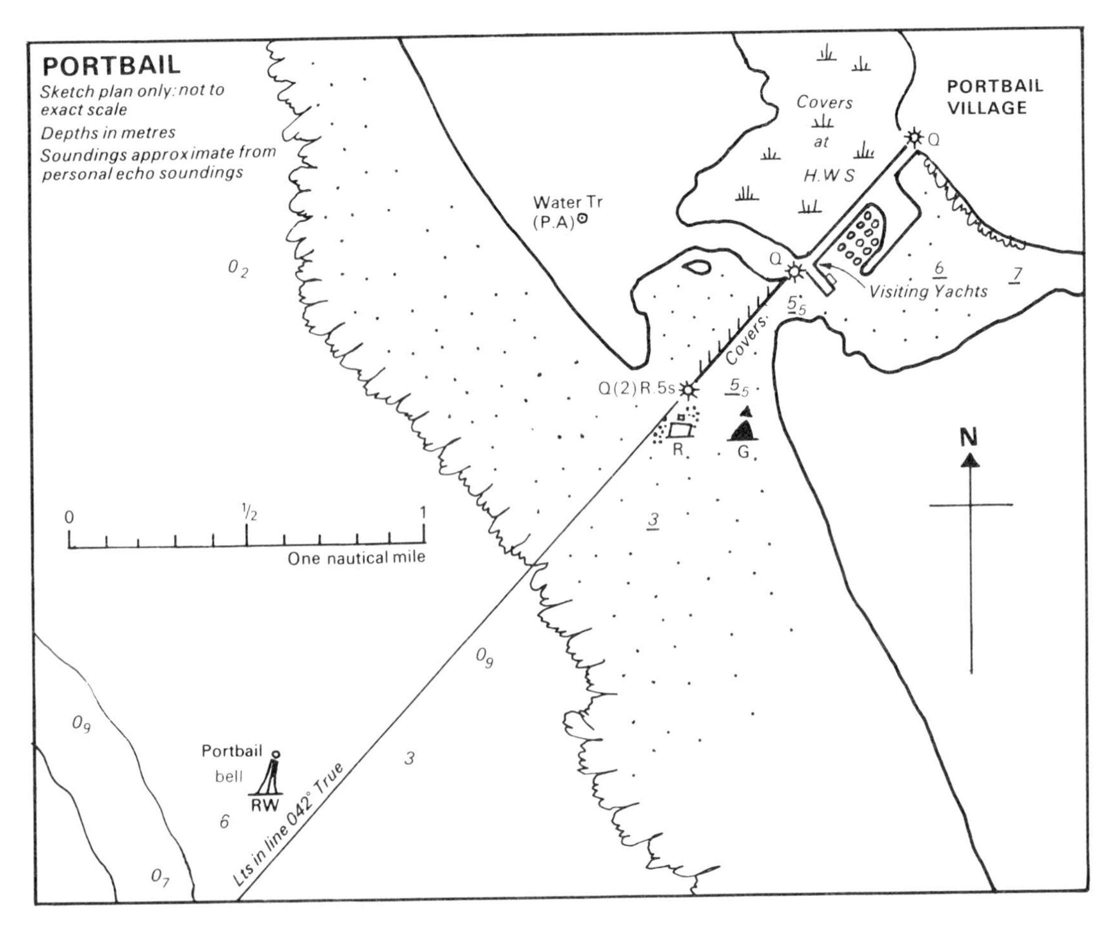

Plan 31 Portbail.

This is an interesting little harbour with room for six boats or so to dry against the wall in perfect shelter. Beyond the harbour is a huge expanse of water where it is possible to anchor and dry after checking the bottom for stones (rare): it is wise to avoid this berth in strong SW winds. Correct pronunciation, by the way, is Por-Bye. Note: only boats capable of drying upright should visit Portbail, as it is often necessary to lie up alongside other visitors.

Tidal notes

The French tables give no information; however the harbour is only 4 miles from Carteret, so the information given under that heading may be safely used. HW is probably 2 or 3 minutes earlier, and heights fractionally higher.

Approach and entrance

The tall elegant white water tower just N of the entrance is a valuable landmark, as there is little else to see until close in. There are extensive offshore shoals, but these will be well

84 Portbail: the entrance from the head of the jetty. Steering for here from the second last beacon pole gives the best water.

covered long before it is safe to approach the harbour, which according to my observations dries almost exactly 5 m along the best approach line. It is best to approach just after HW to avoid being swept in too fast by the flood, but be warned that the ebb can exceed 5 knots at springs, so do not be late. Waypoint: 49°18′.5N, 1°44′.3W, then steer NE for the entrance buoys.

From the RW offing buoy make for the red beacon marking the end of the training wall after passing midway between the two harbour entrance buoys. Note that a sandbank builds up here in winter until the entrance is dredged every May. Leave the beacon to port about 5 m off and proceed along the training wall (it submerges, but is marked by pole beacons) until abreast of the second-last pole. From here steer straight for the jetty head until 50 m off, then alter course slightly to starboard so as to leave the end of the jetty 10 m to port, then turn sharp to port and enter the basin close along the NE side of the jetty.

Berthing and facilities

The ferry berths on the pontoon attached to the NE side of the jetty: yachts berth as they can further in along the jetty. There is a small pontoon N of the ferry pontoon on the inner wall – it was planned (1991) to extend this and provide extra visitors' berths. There are also numerous moorings in the basin, and one of these can be picked up if free, although of course the boat should not be left uncrewed until it is clear that the owner cannot return on the tide

85 Portbail: visitors moor inshore of the Jersey ferry's pontoon.

in question. If going to the moorings, the best line is to cut diagonally from the jetty head to the inside of the mole and then along the moorings: a bank builds up between the deep water near the jetty and the fairly deep water where the moorings are. (Deep is of course comparative: the whole harbour dries.) The jetty moorings can be reached 1½ hours either side of HW at neaps, the buoys 1 hour either side, by a boat with a 1.5 m draft. These times extend by half an hour at each end at springs.

There is a bar 100 m to seaward of the jetty, which is open seven days a week and provides light meals (grills) and ices etc as well as drinks. All other supplies from the charming town, about half a mile to the NE across the causeway. The 'Mont Orgueil' (seen on her pontoon in the photograph above) provides a regular ferry service to Gorey, Jersey. There are two interesting churches, and some fine old buildings. A pleasant and interesting place well worth a visit.

Granville

Charts Nos. 3672, 2669 and 3659

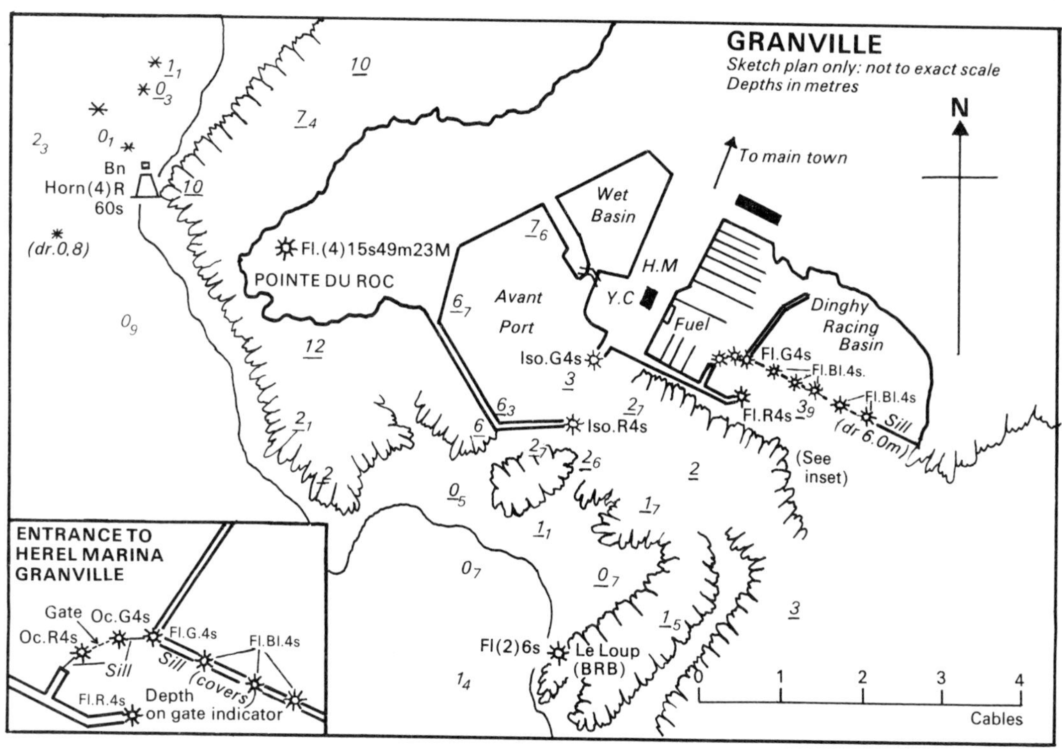

Plan 32 Granville.

By far the most important yacht harbour between Cherbourg and St Malo, Granville is easy of access in spite of having the largest tidal range of any coastal port in Europe. It provides excellent (if rather expensive) accommodation for visitors, good facilities and excellent shopping.

Tidal notes

Heights: 12.9 m MHWS, 1.5 m MLWS, 9.7 m MHWN, 4.6 m MLWN.
HW is HW St Malo +0.05, LW is LW St Malo +0.10. The N-going stream begins at HW St Malo −3. Between St Malo and Granville the tide is broadly E-going from HW St Malo $-4\frac{1}{2}$ to HW, after which it is mainly N-going for 2 hours and W-going for the remainder of the time. Streams are strong in the St Malo area but relatively weak near Granville.

Approach and entrance

The approach is straightforward, with no offshore hazards once there is enough water to enter the harbour. The Pointe du Roc, just W of the entrance, is craggy and unmistakable and its light (Fl(4) 15s) is visible for 22 miles. Pass about $\frac{1}{2}$ mile S of the point, leave Le Loup beacon (BRB, Fl(2) 6s) fairly close either side and steer for the enrtrance, which is round the

86 Granville with the Pointe du Roc lighthouse to the left, from Le Loup.

87 Granville yacht harbour at low water, showing the sill and gate.

E end of the more easterly of the two E-pointing pierheads. Waypoint: 48°49'.0N, 1°37'.0W, then steer NE for Le Loup beacon. Do not enter if there is not enough water on the illuminated indicator for your draft: if too early the Avant-Port may be used to wait for shelter for sufficient rise. The bottom is hard mud and reasonably clear, so it would be possible for a late arrival to dry out there for a tide.

The sill which protects the yacht basin dries 6 m, but it has a section drying only 5.25 m, closed by a gate 0.75 m high, thus maintaining the height at 6 m. When the water rises above the sill the gate begins to fall, and by the time there is 65 cm of water over the sill it is fully down and there is 1.4 m over the gate. An illuminated display shows the depth over the gate both outwards to boats approaching and inwards to boats in the basin: it jumps straight from 0 to 1.1 or more on a rising tide, and falls from 1.1 or more to 0 as the tide falls. It is strictly forbidden to try to cross the gate even a moment after the display has changed to zero. The gate lies between a red column (Oc R 4s) and a green one (Oc G 4s). The harbourmaster calculates that entry is possible from HW $-2\frac{3}{4}$ to HW $+3\frac{1}{2}$ for 1.4 m draft at springs: the gate is open for the same period at neaps but last-minute entry or departure is then only available to drafts of 1.1 m or less.

Berthing and facilities

Some 150 berths are reserved for visitors. These are marked, or the harbour office can be contacted on Channel 9. Fuel from the fuel berth (see plan): apply to office for service, 24 hours if necessary in July and August, otherwise 0800–1200 and 1400–1800. Travel-lift (12 tons). Water and electricity on the pontoons, showers (hot) and toilets (seatless) through the harbour office, and also a 24-hour set outside. The yacht club is open 1100–1400 and 1700 until 2100 every day during the season (mid-June to mid-September), otherwise weekends only.

There are several large chandlers, most of whom do or can arrange repairs. There is an excellent sailmaker, Voilerie Granvillaise, in the yacht harbour beside Moteur Baudouin (tel: 33 50 62 28), or further away Voilerie Augin in the Zone Industrielle, tel: 33 50 25 58. Electronic, electrical and alternator repairs from S.E.E. Nautilec, 64 rue du Port (tel: 33 50 04 96).

General

There are good shops and restaurants in the town, some 300 m from the harbour office. The old walled town has a 15th-century church, built mainly by an English general, Sir Thomas Scales, who rebuilt it on the site of an earlier church in 1439. He began the fortification of the citadel, but the Knights of Mont St Michel retook the town in 1442, and completed the walls as a defence against the English. There are many interesting buildings of the period in the old town, an aquarium near the Roc lighthouse, and even a casino. Communications include direct trains to Paris ($3\frac{1}{2}$ hours) and ferries to Jersey, Guernsey and Chausey.

Rothéneuf

Charts Nos. 2700, 3659 and 2669

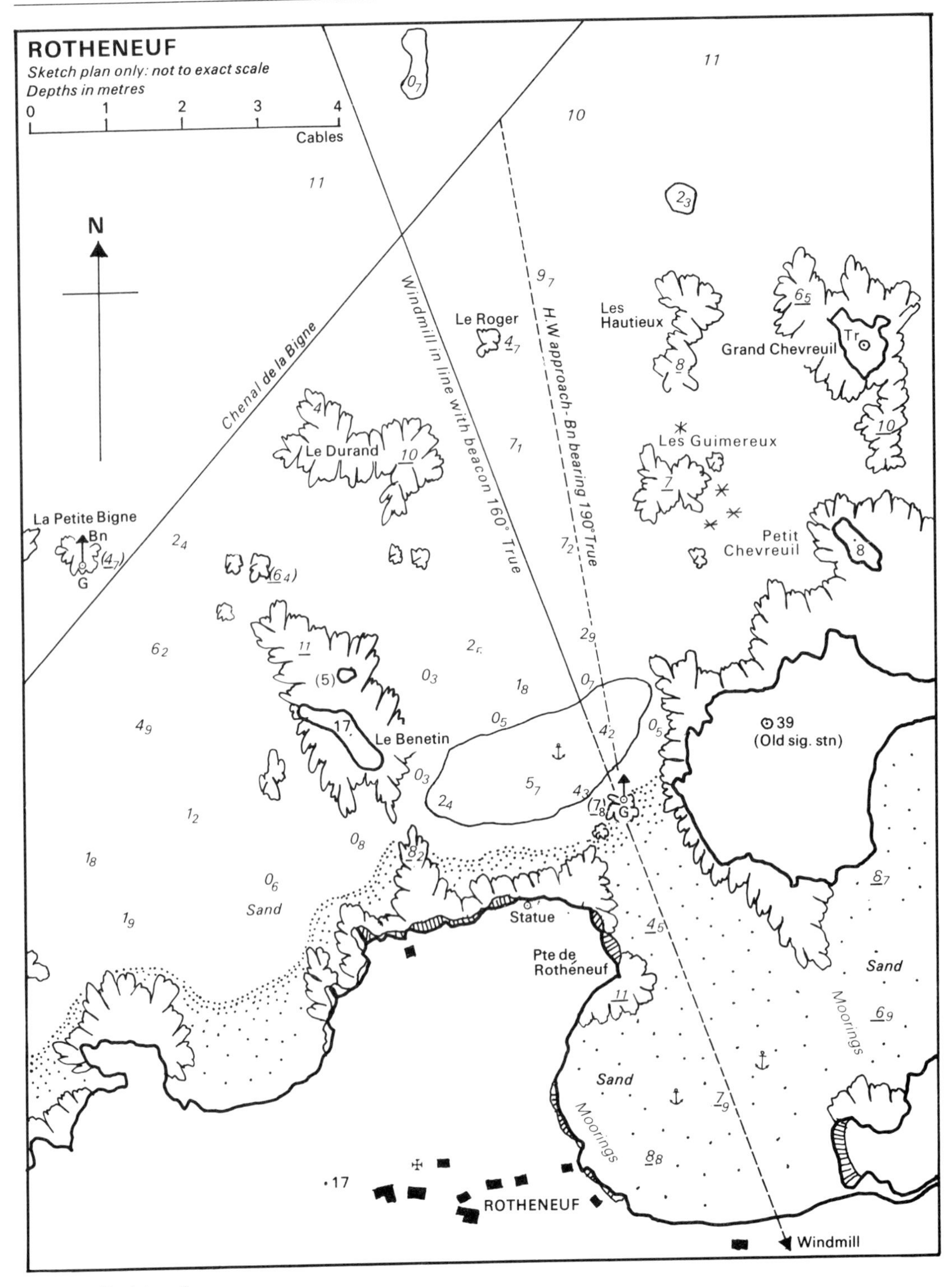

Plan 33 Rothéneuf.

Four miles east of St Malo, this is an extremely tricky place to approach, and it can be a most uncomfortable place to dry out, so it can only be recommended in fine weather and to those experienced in this kind of pilotage.

Tidal notes
No official figures are available for Rothéneuf, but any variation from the St Malo figures is very small so they may safely be used.

Approach and entrance
From the E cardinal Basse aux Chiens buoy, course should be set for La Bigne (approx 230° mag) until the beacon in the middle of Rothéneuf entrance is bearing about S. Rothéneuf should not be approached with less than 7 m rise of tide, and at that level the 4.7 m drying rock Le Roger can be ignored. Le Durand, which dries 10 m near its eastern edge, is usually visible: if it is, steer to leave its most easterly visible part 100 m to starboard (i.e. pass 100 m E of it) and then for the entrance beacon, which should be left 50 m to starboard, and so into the harbour.

On the rare occasions when the tide is over 10 m, and Le Durand is itself invisible, then it is the main danger to avoid, as the S end of Les Hautieux must have more than 2 m over it. Approach La Bigne as before, and keep on a straight line from the Basse aux Chiens buoy to the Petite Bigne beacon (keeping N rather than S of the line) until the beacon in the entrance bears 170° (True) (say 175° mag), when it may safely be approached on that bearing. The photograph, taken unfortunately in less than ideal visibility, shows the beacon and the

88 Rothéneuf: approach. The entrance beacon is centre: the photograph was taken on the transit with the windmill, but this is hard to pick out.

general line of approach: the beacon should be left about 50 m to starboard. If the mill (no sails, but a steeply pitched roof) can be identified, the beacon in line with it gives a safe approach transit, passing 50 m W of Le Roger and more than 100 m E of le Durand: it is the most conspicuous house near the skyline in the middle of the bay, just touching the topmark of the beacon in the photograph.

Berthing

Between the moorings off the village and the others in the eastern part of the bay there is plenty of room to anchor on smooth but rather hard sand. Of course the harbour dries, so it is only suitable for bilge-keelers or boats equipped with legs. Even in very calm weather, there can be enough scend to make the process of drying out and floating off extremely noisy and unpleasant, so I would not really recommend a visit except just for an hour or two around HW: however for those who do decide to stay longer, there is an excellent restaurant and one or two shops in the pleasant little town.

There is good anchorage outside the harbour entrance, about 250 m NW of the green entrance beacon, sheltered except from winds with any northerly element. This can be used as a base from which to explore the village at suitable rise of tide; but note that it is a good ¾ mile row, so a seaworthy dinghy is needed, and probably a reliable outboard. W of Pte Rothéneuf there is an aquarium exhibiting local fish, a showroom for local hand-painted Faïence pottery, and some amusing sculptures on the cliff face.

89 The moorings at Rothéneuf. Anchor as close in as possible, but be prepared for some heavy bumps if drying out.

Passage Notes: Granville to St Malo

Charts Nos. 3659 and 2700

To get a fair stream, the best time to leave Granville for St Malo is HW St Malo $+1\frac{1}{2}$. This is fine at the departure end, as there is still plenty of water over the sill at Granville, but the 20 mile passage means arrival at St Malo around LW, involving a wait of several hours before entry into the Bassin Vauban, and at springs perhaps 2 hours or more before even Bas-Sablons is available. At neaps the solution is to leave Granville as soon as the gate allows and buck the foul tide, which will not be much more than 1 knot at worst. At springs, however, there is a problem unless the boat can keep up at least 6 knots, and it is best to leave at the proper time and put up with the delay: for the impatient there is always Dinard, whose approach channel is dredged so that it dries only 1 m above chart datum.

The passage from St Malo to Granville times much better. The ideal departure is $3\frac{1}{2}$ hours before HW at St Malo, which gives a fair stream and arrival at Granville around local HW. The first outward locking from the Bassin Vauban in St Malo is not usually until 2 hours before HW St Malo, but this still allows 3 hours of fair or neutral tide, and most yachts will be able to make Granville in time to get in as long as the motor is used if necessary.

The shortest route between the two ports is by the Chenal de la Bigne. Coming from the east, pass N of La Fille N cardinal buoy (about a mile NE of the light tower on La Pierre de Herpin), and from there steer about W (mag) until the YBY Rochefort beacon tower is identified. Steer for this tower, taking care to avoid getting S of the direct line, until the Basse aux Chiens E cardinal buoy is identified a mile ESE of the beacon tower. Steer for this buoy, and from a position a cable south of it, a course of 222° (True), 228° (mag), will lead to the green La Petite Bigne beacon. The dangerous Le Durand rock is almost always visible, but the part that can be seen should be given a berth of 2 cables, as deeper but still dangerous parts of the reef extend more than a cable WNW from the highest part of the rock. Leave La Petite Bigne beacon 100 m to starboard, then pass two cables N of the rocks off Pointe de la Varde (the outermost ones do not cover), 1 cable south of the green conical Letruns and Roches aux Anglais buoys, close NW of the red can Crapauds du Bey buoy and so SW into the deep-water channel. This route carries a least depth of 1.8 m at MLWS, 4.8 at MLWN. Admiralty chart 2700 or its French equivalent must be carried: it shows a transit for the middle part of the channel, but the marks are a long way off, and this is the safest bit anyway: the approach from Basse aux Chiens buoy to the Petite Bigne beacon is the critical one, and this can be made by keeping the beacon tower on la Crolante (the islet just W of Pte de la Varde) in line with the summit of le Grand Bey, the 23 m high island 400 m W of St Malo. Even this needs pretty good visibility, though, as these marks are difficult for strangers to pick out when it is misty, but the buoys and beacons are numerous enough to make the channel navigable by anyone experienced in inshore pilotage as long as visibility is at least 1 mile.

Saint Malo

Charts Nos. 2700, 3659 and 2669

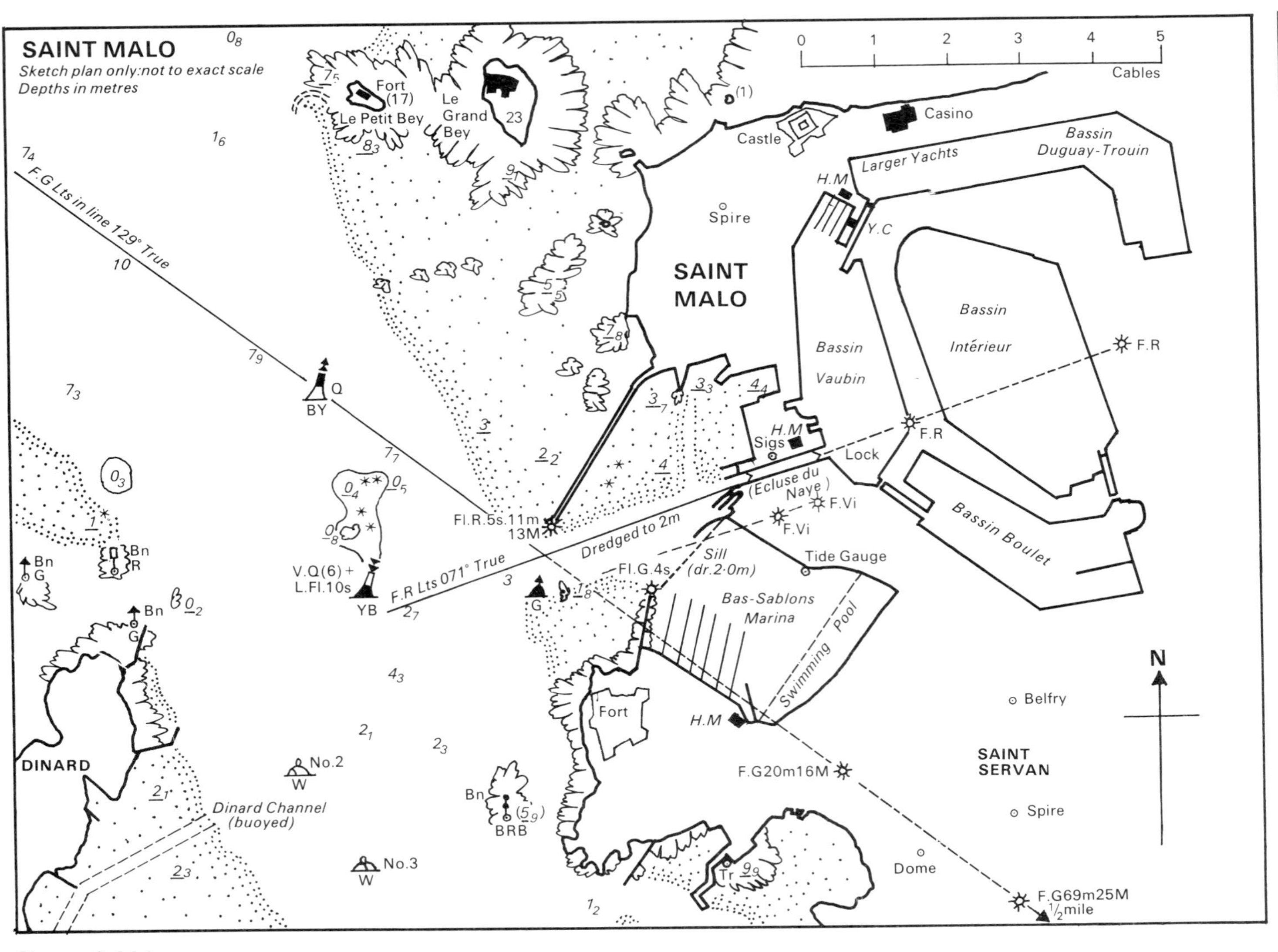

Plan 34 St Malo.

Almost totally destroyed during the war, St Malo was rebuilt within its ramparts to its original plan. This defiant gesture has proved surprisingly successful, and it is a charming town with a pleasant and friendly atmosphere.

Tidal notes

Heights: 12.2 m MHWS, 1.5 m MLWS, 9.2 m MHWN, 4.4 m MLWN.
In the offing, the E-going tide begins at HW St Malo −5, the W-going at $+\frac{1}{2}$. In the approaches the streams turn at HW and LW, but keep a careful eye out for cross-sets which can be quite strong over short stretches. For anyone whose almanac does not give tidal data for St Malo, HW St Malo is HW Cherbourg −1.46 at springs, −2.06 at neaps.

Approach and entrance

The approach via the Chenal de la Bigne has already been described. From the north there are the Petits Pointus and Grande Conchée channels; from the NW the main deep water route, the Chenal de la Petite Porte; and from the west the Chenal du Décollé. The last named is very tricky, and should not be attempted on a first visit: the others (all clearly marked on chart 2700) present no problems as long as there is visibility of 3 or 4 miles. If arriving near LWS, avoid the Plateau de la Rance 3 cables W of the N pierhead: at MLWS the rocks have as little as 0.5 m over them. Entering the outer harbour, keep a good lookout as traffic is heavy. Waypoint: 48°41′.4N, 2°07′.2W, then steer SE and enter by the Chenal de la Petite Porte.

90 St Malo: the Bas Sablons marina.

Berthing: Bas-Sablons

The yacht harbour of Bas-Sablons really attaches to the town of St Servan rather than St Malo. It is protected by a sill 2 m above chart datum, which therefore has 2.3 m over it at MLWN, and only dries 0.7 m at MLWS. A tidal gauge displays in electric lights the depth over the sill in decimetres. The harbour can therefore be entered with average draft at any time during neaps. At springs, there is about 2 metres over the sill 2 hours before or after LW. The harbour can accommodate boats of up to 18 m.

Facilities

All facilities are available including repairs and sailmaker. Diesel from fuelling berth near the root of pontoon 'I'. 12 ton Travel-lift. Toilets and showers at Capitainerie. Dues are somewhat higher than those for the Bassin Vauban. Capitainerie tel: 99 81 71 34, VHF Channel 9. Radio-telephone St Malo Radio tel: 40 22 39 04. Engine repairs Pascal Houery tel: 99 82 62 97: electronics SEE Nautilec tel: 99 82 86 48.

General

Good shops and restaurants in the little town about ½ mile from the berths, where there is also an interesting museum, housed in the 14th-century Chateau de Solidor, devoted to the history of voyages round Cape Horn. The exhibits are of the greatest interest to any student of the history of navigation.

Berthing: Bassin Vauban

This basin (and all the others at St Malo) is entered through a lock, the Ecluse du Naye, just N of the main ferry berth in the Avant-Port: it can be hard to identify when closed, especially if there is a large ship in the berth. Note that much of the Avant-Port dries.

The first opening for entry is normally HW $-2\frac{1}{2}$ hours, and the first for exit HW -2 hours: openings continue until about HW $+1\frac{1}{2}$. These times can be affected by the movements of large ships, and one should allow plenty of margin if possible. Once inside, there is a list of times for the next 2 days posted at the marina office. There are mooring buoys on the N edge of the approach channel: these can be used to wait for an opening, but they dry at LW. The lock listens on Channel 12, tel: 99 81 62 86.

Light signals are displayed at the lock as follows:

<table>
<tr><td>R:</td><td>No entry, departure permitted</td></tr>
<tr><td>G:</td><td>No departure, entry permitted.</td></tr>
<tr><td>R
G:</td><td>No entry or departure</td></tr>
<tr><td>R W or W R:</td><td>Both gates open: no entry, ships may leave.</td></tr>
<tr><td>G W or W G:</td><td>Both gates open: no departure, ships may enter.</td></tr>
<tr><td>R
G G:</td><td>No movement, large ship entering.</td></tr>
<tr><td>R R
G:</td><td>No movement, large ship leaving</td></tr>
</table>

Any other three-light signal prohibits movement except to a designated vessel. The lock keeper also has a loud hailer and speaks English, although a combination of accent and distortion can make it a little difficult to understand.

91 St Malo: The Bassin Vauban. Harbour office and facilities are in the further left of the two flat-roofed buildings.

Visitors berth where space allows and report to HM office (see plan). Boats over 12 m can lie along the E wall S of the pontoons, or it is possible to enter the Bassin Duguay-Trouin: arrange on Channel 12 or through the harbour office. HM tel: 99 56 51 91.

Facilities
Toilets and showers at Capitainerie. Water and electricity on pontoons. 1 ton manual crane.

General
The great advantage of this basin over Bas-Sablons is the close proximity of the walled town with its shops and restaurants only a couple of minutes walk from the berths. The cathedral dates from the 12th century and although the spire was destroyed in 1944 much remains of the original building. The museum of the history of the town in the 15th-century tower of the Hotel de Ville is another must, as is the aquarium just opposite. The town dates from the 12th century and was the home of many famous sailors including Jacques Cartier, discoverer of Canada.

Cruising the Channel Islands

Cruising in this beautiful archipelago needs careful planning, as the rate of tidal stream sometimes encountered can be higher than the maximum speed of the average yacht. Careful study of the tidal stream charts is therefore vitally important, and constant awareness of the danger of local cross-sets should be cultivated.

Prospective visitors should remember, however, the consoling fact that the charts make the waters look much more dangerous than they really are. This is because of the enormous tidal range, which means that mean level at St Helier, for instance, is 6.1 m, so that at half-tide a reef marked as drying 2 m will have over 4 m of water over it. One can see from this that it is most important when cruising in the area to keep a constant check on the tide level: a Jersey rock drying 10 m on a day of spring tides will be a pinnacle nearly 30 ft high at LW, while at HW it will be lurking dangerously 3 or 4 ft below the surface. But if you know that the tide level at a particular moment is, say, 8 m, then in reasonable conditions you will know that rocks drying less than 5 m can be ignored and those drying more than 8 m are visible, leaving only those between 5 and 8 m to worry about. This sort of calculation usually cuts down the problems a lot. In my experience, the Rule of Twelfths (which states that the tide rises or falls one-twelfth of its range in the first hour, two-twelfths in the second, three-twelfths in the third and fourth hours, two-twelfths in the fifth and one-twelfth in the sixth) gives sufficient accuracy for most purposes.

Notes on charts will be found in the Appendix. Good heavy ground tackle and an ample scope of cable are vital, and remember that the holding in some of the anchorages is only moderate, so always make sure the anchor is holding. I always reverse it in under power, and if it will not hold when the engine is running quarter astern, I haul it up and try again.

A good dinghy is important if the smaller anchorages are to be visited, and shopping should be carefully planned, as some of the harbours in the islands are extremely convenient for the purpose, and others very much the opposite. This is a most interesting and enjoyable cruising ground, despite the requirement for careful and accurate navigation.

One final point: anyone wishing to cruise both the Channel Islands and the W coast of Contentin will be well advised to work southwards through the islands to St Malo, then E to Granville and then N along the coast from there. The tides work out very much better for this circuit than for anyone attempting the reverse.

Passage Notes: To and from Alderney

Charts Nos. 2669, 3653 and 60

The approaches to Alderney from the east present relatively few problems, as long as adequate allowance is made for the very fast streams. 'Passage Notes: Cherbourg to the Channel Islands and West Cotentin' explain the W-going eddy which can help a yacht to reach a position N of Cap de la Hague just as the stream in the Race is beginning to run SW. If bound for Alderney, the Cap should be given a berth of at least 2 miles, after which it is wise to over-correct for the calculated effect of the stream by 10° or so: once clear N of Quenard Point, any distance wasted will be made up in a matter of minutes. The essential thing is to avoid being carried S and into the Race.

The obvious way S from Braye Harbour, Alderney, is via the Swinge, passing along the N and W coasts of Alderney, but the overfalls and heavy seas that can be encountered when using this route are often far worse than those in the Race itself, and if conditions are doubtful (say SW wind force 4 and medium tide) it is preferable to work back round Quenard Point and S into the Race. Only heavy and powerful boats should attempt the southbound passage in wind-over-tide conditions with winds above force 4.

If using the Swinge, great care must be taken to avoid Pierre au Vraic (dries 1.5 m), 2 miles WSW of the W end of Alderney. A white conical beacon just S of Tourgis in line with the N edge of Clonque Rock fort leads safely N of it.

Approaching from Guernsey or Sark, the navigation is easier and the ride usually smoother if one passes S of Alderney and then turns W round Quenard Point for Braye Harbour. This tactic is made possible by the fact that an eddy runs W along the N coast of Alderney from HW St Helier until the main stream turns 4 hours later. Thus one can leave St Peter Port at HW St Helier – $1\frac{1}{2}$, have a fair stream for the 22 miles to Quenard Point, and be carried round the point and down to Braye. Navigationally it is only necessary to steer for the Noir Putes (conspicuous S of the SW corner of Alderney), pass close S of them, the southernmost Coque Lihou and then Noire Roque (keep well in to this one to avoid the dangerous Bonit which just dries), and on to pass close to L'Etac de la Quoire. Once past this, keep its base in line with the N Coque Lihou and the high Noire Pute: this leads clear of Brinchetais Ledge. From here keep a generous half mile offshore and round the island until on the approach for the harbour.

Braye Harbour, Alderney

Charts Nos. 2845, 60, 3653 and 2669

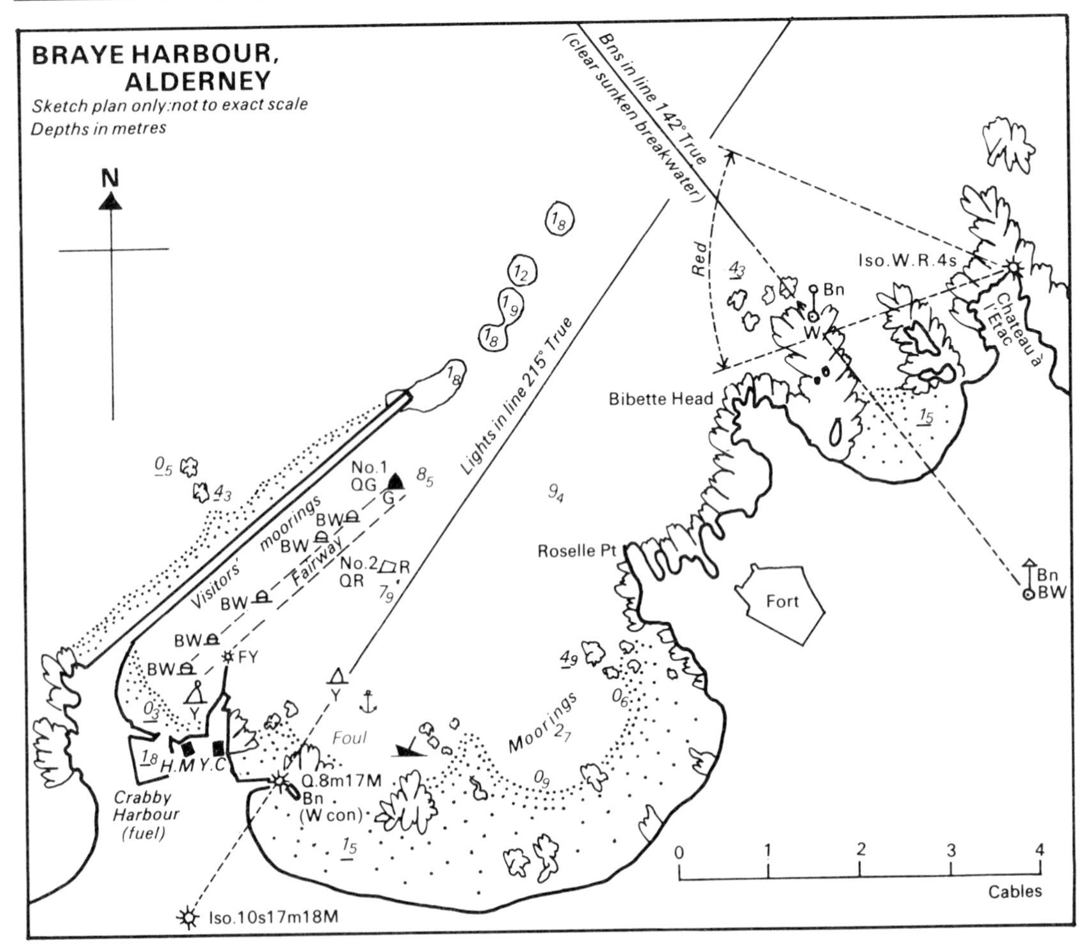

Plan 35 Braye Harbour, Alderney.

The only true harbour on Alderney, Braye has an excellent shop and several restaurants. The island's main town is $\frac{1}{2}$ mile up a steep hill.

Tidal notes

Heights: 6.3 m MHWS, 0.8 m MLWS, 4.7 m MHWN, 2.6 m MLWN.

HW is HW St Helier +0.45. LW is LW St Helier +0.25 (springs), +1.05 (neaps). The main NE-going stream begins at HW St Helier −2. The main SW-going stream at HW St Helier +4. However, in the approaches to Braye Harbour the stream runs to the E only from HW St Helier −2 to $+\frac{1}{2}$, and is W-going all the rest of the time. (See also 'Passage Notes: To and from Alderney', page 145.)

92 Braye Harbour approach. The breakwater (right) must be kept open until clear of the submerged extension.

Approach and entry

From the east, the approach is straightforward, but remember to guard against being carried too far S on the ebb. Grois Rocks are almost always visible and should be given a berth of 2 cables to avoid the Boués Brisées, but a half-mile margin from the land clears all dangers. The strategy for approach from the west is given in 'Passage Notes: To and from Alderney'. If approaching via the Swinge around LW, allowance must be made for the sunken extension to the breakwater. The shallowest patch, about 2 cables, NNE from the pierhead, has 2 m at MLWS. Waypoint: 49°45'.0N, 2°11'.0W, then steer to keep the inner side of the breakwater just open.

Berthing

Visitors lie, often two abreast, to one of 80 yellow mooring buoys, mostly between the buoyed fairway and the breakwater but some on the east side of the harbour. Owing to the gradual build-up of private moorings in the harbour there is now very little room left to anchor: the best bet is just east of the leading line as shown on the plan. Go no further S than the position shown as there is a wreck, and also an old mooring chain on the bottom. In strong NE winds the harbour is untenable, and although a boat moored alone on mooring would be unlikely to come to harm as long as her line held, a sensible skipper hearing such a forecast would leave for Hannaine Bay (see 'Other anchorages') before too late. The harbour can be choppy in strong winds from any direction, but the taxi service minimises the inconvenience: call them on Channel M (37).

93 A stormy view of Braye from up the hill. Visitors' moorings are laid along the length of the breakwater.

Facilities

Chandlery, gas, diesel and water alongside in Crabby Harbour, available for 2 m draft 3 hours either side of HW. Call Mainbrayce & Co on Channel 80 before entering: they operate from 0800 to 2400 7 days a week. They also run the taxi-launch service to and from the moorings during the same hours: call on 37, £1 per trip per head in 1991. They can do engine and hull repairs, and basic sail repair. Also electrics and electronics. Alderney Radio listens Channel 16 operates Channel 74 HM tel: 822620.

General

Bread and milk, showers and toilets at the harbour. Also small snack bar. The yacht club opens 1800–2000 on Thursday, Friday and Saturday, and 1200–1400 and 1800–2000 Sunday. The small village extends about 250 m up the road to town, where Jean's Stores will be found – a small supermarket with good selections of everything except meat. Drink from the Seaview off-licence, open 1000–2400 (Sundays 1200–1400 and 1800–2000): spirits prices are less than those in the UK, though Guernsey is cheaper. Several restaurants near the harbour, including one of my favourites anywhere, the First and Last (advisable to book, tel: 823162 or 822535). Apart from providing wonderful food, especially shellfish, at reasonable prices, the owner Rita Gillmore has for years had a knack of persuading exceptionally pretty girls to come and serve it. (As with all such observations, I can take no responsibility for post-1991 events!) All supplies in the main town (St Anne) about ½ mile to the S. It is a steepish climb to get there: the grass paths to the right of the road provide a short cut. It is a charming little town and the shopping is excellent for its size.

Other anchorages on Alderney

Some ½ mile SW of Quenard Point is the old harbour of Longy Bay, overlooked by Essex Castle. The entrance is between Raz Island, which has a conspicuous fort, on the E side, and the islet of Queslingue, nearly 50 feet high, on the W. There is a rock which dries over 1 m in the middle of the entrance, but this is a drying height above LAT, and at MLWS it has 0.5 m over it, so it is only a problem at springs and near LW. Anchor in 2 m due W of Raz Island, and about a cable off the W shore. Exposed in winds between E and S. This is the only really useful anchorage, but La Tchue, another ½ mile to the SW, is a pleasant place to drop the hook for lunch in settled offshore weather: there are fascinating coloured rocks on the northern part of the bay. Finally, Hannaine Bay on the W side of the island just south of Clonque Fort, is a useful refuge from strong NE winds. From Braye, proceed down the Swinge until the peak of the high Noire Pute is visible just clear of the mainland, turn onto that transit until Clonque Fort bears NE, then steer just S of the fort into the bay, anchoring in 3–5 m in good shelter from all winds with an E component.

Burhou

Chart No. 60

The anchorage at Burhou should only be used during the SW-going tide, but it can be useful for a boat approaching Alderney from the SW by the Swinge and finding herself too late on the tide. The gap between Burhou and Little Burhou must be identified and approached on a course of about 10° (True), say 15° (mag): anchor in the middle of the bay between the two islands in about 4 m. (Note that the gap is spanned by drying rocks, but it is easy enough to distinguish these from 'permanent' land.) This position is right out of the tide, and protected from swell except in strong winds between SE and SW.

Coming from the east, give Noir Houmet, the southernmost islet S of Burhou, a berth of 2 cables until on the approach line, and then turn into the anchorage. It will be found that the overfalls of the Swinge can be avoided on the SW stream by keeping well over to the Burhou side: on that side of the channel they do not begin until a cable or so W of the approach line.

Burhou is uninhabited, but there is a cottage that can be hired, and a huge variety of birds nest there.

94 Burhou: just entering the anchorage. Use only on the SW stream.

Passage Notes: To and from Guernsey

Charts Nos. 807, 808 and 3654

It has already been mentioned that if approaching from the NE against a SW wind, tide-race conditions may be met almost anywhere between Cap de la Hague and Guernsey, and in such conditions it is important to avoid crossing the Banc de la Schole or Alderney South Banks. Coming from this direction, Sark is often sighted some miles before Guernsey is seen, while Herm is indistinguishable from Guernsey until well on in the approach.

The Great Russel channel (between Herm and Sark) is very much clearer and easier than the Little Russel E of Guernsey, and in poor visibility it is often worth using, either cutting across to Guernsey south of the Lower Heads buoy or, if things are very bad, using one of the anchorages on Herm or Sark until the weather improves. In good visibility, however, the Little Russel presents no problems. The Grande Amfroque with its two beacons (BW horizontal striped and white) is always easy to identify NE of Herm: from not less than 2 miles N of this one may steer W, counteracting any southerly set until the BW vertical striped Tautenay beacon is bearing 210° (True), say 215° (mag), then steer to pass ½ mile W of it, and then close W of the Roustel beacon if bound for St Peter Port. From the NW, the Grandes Brayes, a mile N of the NE point of Guernsey, may be approached to within ½ mile, from where steer to pass ½ mile E of Platte Fougére beacon (tall and lighthouse shaped, BW horizontal striped), and so S for the Roustel. S of Roustel, pass ½ mile W of the unmistakable squat Brehon tower and so to St Peter Port entrance. S of St Peter Port there are no problems for the careful navigator. Charts 807 and 808 carry sketches of the main beacons and towers in the areas they cover.

Passages to Alderney are dealt with under the passage notes for that island. The secret of successful passages to Jersey is to get out of St Peter Port or Beaucette while the tide allows, and pick up a mooring buoy in St Peter Port harbour or anchor in Havelet Bay or Saints Bay until it is time to leave. The ideal departure time from Saints Bay is 5 hours before HW St Helier, which allows a generous 5 hours of fair tide to cover the 25 minutes earlier. By the time it is possible to get out of either marina the tide is beginning to run north in the Little Russel and it is far too late for an ordinary yacht to set out for Jersey.

Chart No. 808

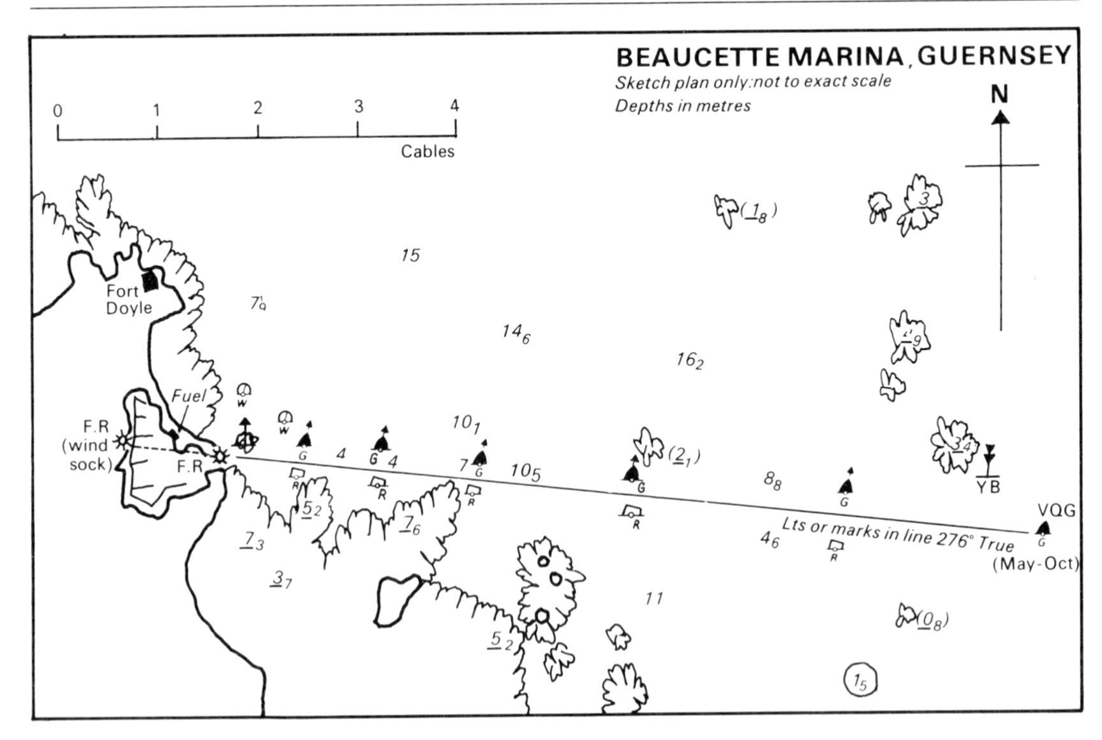

Plan 36 Beaucette Marina, Guernsey.

Lying near the NE point of Guernsey, the marina is approached from just S of the Petite Canupe beacon, which lies $1\frac{1}{2}$ miles W of Tautenay, and about $\frac{3}{4}$ mile S of Platte Fougère. Be warned that this unlit S cardinal beacon is tallish but very skinny and has very small topmarks, so it is quite difficult to spot.

From just S of this buoy the leading line (276° True) can be seen to the west: it consists of a red stripe on the rocks at the N side of the entrance in line with the windsock staff, which also has orange crossbars on it. Keep to this transit: there are red and green channel buoys, but these can float some way off the proper line, especially near LW. The sill in the entrance dries 2.4 m (tide gauge in entrance) and there are two mooring buoys NE of the entrance on which one may wait for water. The entrance is only 8 m wide at half-tide, and should not be attempted in strong winds between N and E. Otherwise the marina can be entered with average draft 2 hours before or after LW neaps, when there will be 1.9 m over the sill: at springs one must be at least $2\frac{1}{2}$ hours from LW, at which time there will be 1.6 m. For tidal details see St Peter Port.

There are 50 visitors' berths, and the harbourmaster always seems to be able to find another space somehow. In high season, though, it is worth ringing in advance, tel: 45000. There are good showers and toilets in the harbour building. The harbour also has a food shop, telephone, the only floating launderette I have ever seen, and one of the most celebrated restaurants on

95 Beaucette Marina entrance. The rear mark is the windsock staff, above the right of the white HM office: the front one is the red mark framed in white just behind the depth gauge.

the island. Water and electricity on the pontoons, fuel pontoon: arrange at harbour office, 7-day service. They listen on VHF Channels 37 and 80. Repairs can be arranged. It is an interesting and unusual place, an old quarry blasted through to the sea. Do not bother dropping your anchor if the engine fails: the water is almost bottomlessly deep!

St Peter Port, Guernsey

Charts Nos. 3140, 808, 3654, and 2669

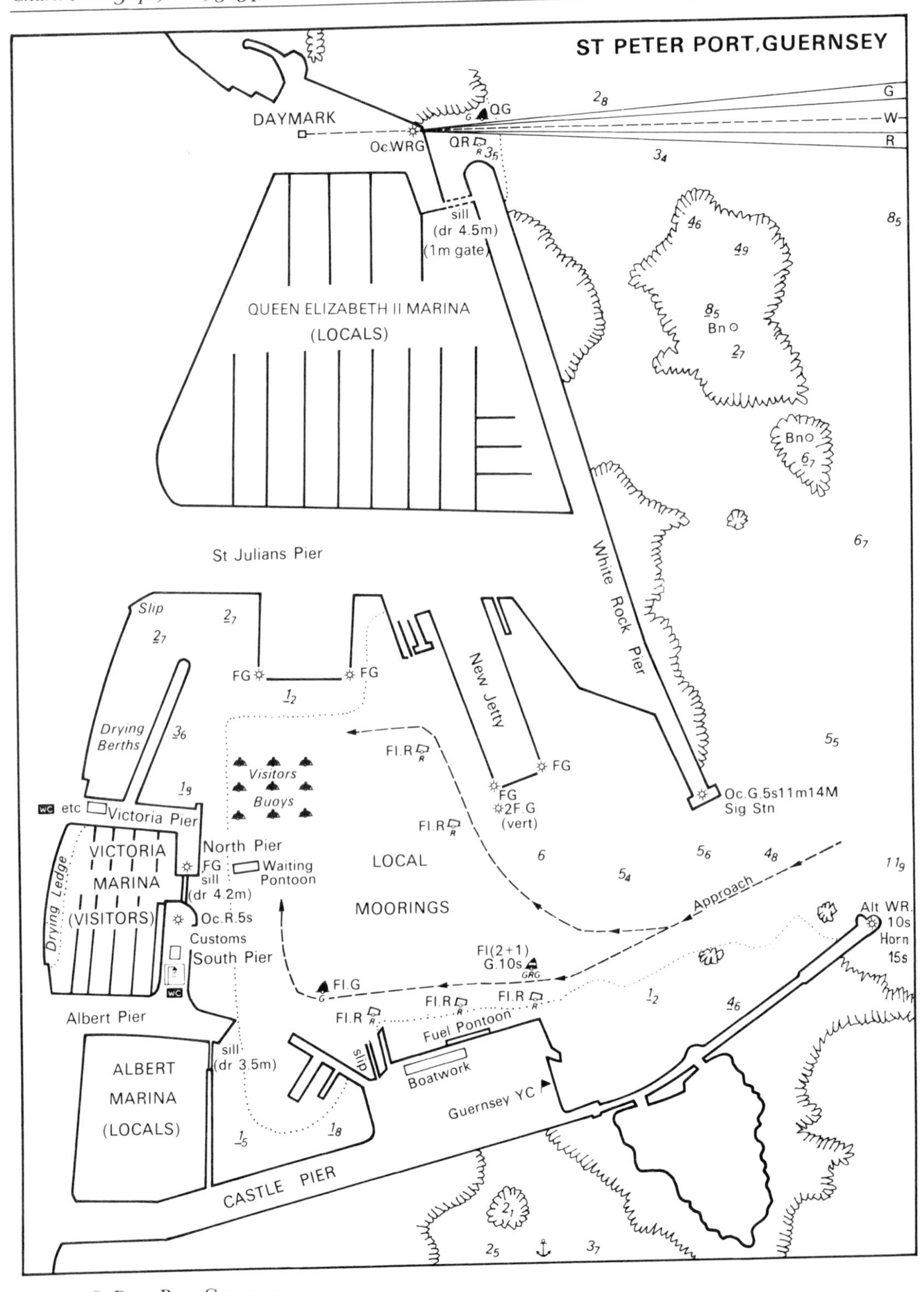

Plan 37 St Peter Port, Guernsey.

96 St Peter Port from the NE. The white tower near the left of picture is at the south side of the entrance: the north pierhead, to the right of it, is less conspicuous.

The main town and harbour on Guernsey, St Peter Port has a character entirely of its own, and recent improvements have made it one of the best and most convenient Channel Islands yacht harbours.

Tidal notes

Heights: 9.0 m MHWS, 1.0 m MLWS, 6.7 m MHWN, 3.5 m MLWN.
HW is HW St Helier (springs), HW St Helier +0.12 (neaps). LW is LW St Helier − 0.8 (springs), +0.02 (neaps). Outside the harbour the N-going stream begins at HW St Helier $-2\frac{1}{2}$, and the S-going at HW St Helier $+3\frac{1}{2}$.

Approach and entrance

The approach has been covered in passage notes: I would just add that a good lookout must be kept in the approaches, as traffic, particularly the hydrofoil, can appear with little warning. Waypoints: from the north, 49°32′.0N, 2°27′.5W, then steer south into the Little Russel Channel. From the south, 49°24′.0N, 2°30′.5W and steer north into the Little Russel. A red light from the N pierhead prohibits entry or departure: strictly speaking yachts under 15 m LOA and motoring are exempt from this signal, but if deciding to ignore it they should certainly have their eyes skinned. Best entry is slightly S of midway between the pierheads, then steer for the buoyed channel just N of the fuel pontoon (see plan) leaving a GRG and then a G buoy, both FlG, to starboard before turning N for the outer moorings and marina entrance. Port control operates on VHF Channel 12.

97 St Peter Port. The marina in Victoria Basin, showing the sill.

Berthing
Harbour control launches normally meet arrivals and direct as to berthing. In crowded periods it may be necessary to wait a day or more on a mooring buoy in the outer harbour before getting a berth in the marina: between June and early September there are pontoons between the visitors' buoys marked on the plan. The marina sill dries 4.18 m, which means it has about a metre over it at half-tide, so most yachts can get in and out about $2\frac{1}{2}$ hours either side of HW, less for deep-draft or at neaps. There is a clear tide-gauge in the entrance. In the marina, boats berth alongside, usually two or more abreast on the S pontoons. Visitors wishing to stay for more than 4–5 days can apply for a vacant berth in the Queen Elizabeth II Marina: they pay in advance and the berth becomes their own for the period. It is quiet, but the facilities are a long walk. Visits to the Victoria Marina are limited to 14 days.

Facilities
Water on all pontoons. Electricity only on the South Pier pontoon. Large toilet and shower block at the SE corner of the basin: showers open 0700–2100, toilets to 2245, and also on the Victoria Pier. Drying grids on the W side of the basin. Fuel pontoon in the outer harbour on Castle Pier: this dries at LWS but is usable by most boats most of the time. It can be very rough there in strong northerly winds. The main chandler, Boatworks +, have their buildings there and operate the fuel berth. Fuel also in Queen Elizabeth Marina, immediately to starboard on entry (open to all). Boatworks + are also a Class A chart agent, can do hull,

motor and spar repairs, electronic sales and servicing, and can organise sail repairs, tel: (0481) 26071. They can slip boats up to 20 tons, and crane to 32 tons. Closer to the marina is Marquand Bros, who have been chandlers in their premises overlooking the Victoria basin for 150 years, and Navigation and Marine Supplies, 100 yards further N, who sell charts, nautical books and navigational equipment. The Royal Channel Islands Yacht Club has premises above the Crown pub opposite the NW corner of the marina: it opens 1030–1430 and 1800–2200 (Sundays 1200–1400 and 1900–2200), sandwiches and cooked lunches at the bar Mondays to Saturdays and suppers Mondays to Thursdays, good value. The club always offers a warm and friendly welcome to visiting yachtsmen. Tel: 723154.

General

The town offers excellent and convenient shopping, with very low duties on wines and spirits (but note that off-licences are not allowed to open on Sundays). There is a huge covered market with meat, fish, vegetable and fruit stalls, and also a few selling delicatessen, bread and all fresh produce. There are restaurants of all standards and price ranges, and the Yacht Inn opposite the roof of Castle Pier, Tel: 720969, can be recommended for accommodation if changing crews.

Guernsey was peacefully annexed to Normandy in 933, so it was part of the power that conquered England in 1066. When King John lost Normandy 150 years later it remained loyal to him rather than return to its French allegiance, and this formed the basis of some of the privileges, such as exemption from UK taxation, which it still enjoys.

Other parts and anchorages on Guernsey

(Note: visitors arriving from outside the Bailiwick should first have cleared Customs at St Peter Port or Beaucette.) Half-way between Beaucette and St Peter Port is Guernsey's second harbour, St Sampson. The outer basins dry 3.6 m, the inner ones over 5 m. Local yachts use it quite a lot, but there seems little point in a visitor going there, as it is very commercial and rather dirty. Grande Havre, on the N coast of the island, provides an attractive anchorage sheltered from all but N winds: the approach with the E side of Rousse Point in line with Victoria Tower is not easy for a stranger to identify, but near LW the approach can easily be identified by the offlying Rousse de Mer reef (dries 6.8 m): pass close E of this and then SSE into the bay. A crew member in the bows is advisable.

Havelet Bay, just S of St Peter Port entrance, is a popular anchorage: pass no more than 100 m S of Oyster Rock (marked by beacon with an orange 'O') and then steer 095° (mag) into the bay. Anchor in 2.5 m clear of moorings. But I never use it myself, finding it crowded and disturbed by passing traffic: much better is the bay to the W of Jerbourg Point, whose NE corner is called Petit Port. The Mouillière rock in the middle only covers at MHWS or higher, and if it is visible the entrance is simple. Saints Bay on the W side of the main bay is best in winds from SW to N; Petit Port in those from N to ESE. In S winds neither these nor Havelet Bay are tenable. Icart Bay, W of Saints Bay, also offers an attractive anchorage in offshore winds. The W side of the island is fringed by a mass of offshore rocks, and yachtsmen are advised to keep well clear of it.

Herm and Jethou

Chart No. 808

Herm

Numerous transits marking clear passages are shown on chart 808. Approaching from the west (say St Peter Port) the easiest is the Alligande Passage: once the Alligande beacon, $\frac{1}{2}$ mile SE of Brehon, is identified (it has an 'A' topmark) the first transit (Vermerette beacon in line with the end of Herm Pier) is easily seen; when clear of the Epec beacon turn onto 308° (True), leaving the Percée rocks to port. The main Herm anchorage is off the W coast of the island, a cable NW of Rosiére steps in about 1 m (i.e. 2 m at LWS), but yachts capable of drying may also find room in the little harbour 2 cables further N. It has about 1.5 m at MHWN, 3.8 m at MHWS. The fairway to Rosiére steps must not be obstructed. When the Vermerette beacon's base is awash, there is 1 m at the pierhead.

The other anchorage is on the E side of the island in Belvoir Bay. The approach is relatively straightforward from the south or east, as Noir Pute never covers and can therefore always be used as a landmark. Anchor as close in as the tide allows: the anchorage is exposed to any wind with east in it, and is really only suitable for a picnic stop. Nowadays it is often used for speedboat racing, when Gull Bay, NW of Selle Roque, will be found quieter.

There are a few shops, a hotel, restaurant and pub on the island.

98 Herm: the small harbour on the west side of the island.

Jethou

Short-term anchorage can be found off the E coast of Jethou, cable N of the beacon on Grande Fauconniére, but the holding is uncertain and the boat should not be left unattended. The jetty at the north of the island is in constant use by commercial launches. The island is privately owned and landing is not allowed.

99 The anchorage in Belvoir Bay, Herm.

Sark

Chart No. 808

Navigation around Sark is easier than it may look at first glance at the chart, as a relatively high proportion of the reefs have islets that never cover, and can therefore always be seen. As anywhere in the Channel Islands, it is important to keep the current height of the tide constantly in mind, to know which rocks are visible, which safely deep, and which lurking dangerously just below the surface; but granted this, the island's waters present problems merely of straightforward pilotage, although a constant lookout must be kept for unexpected cross-sets.

Harbours and anchorages

The only enclosed harbour on Sark is Creux, on the E shore. This is very small and used by fishermen and ferries: it is theoretically permissible for yachts to use it (stern to E wall, bow to anchor, keep clear of the steps) but certainly in the high season for visitors it is wiser not to. Just to the S of the entrance, off Les Laches, is a fishermen's mooring: yachts may not use this nor anchor nearby. Just to the north is La Maseline harbour. The bay is now full of moorings: two of these are for visitors, but they have been known to drag so I would only trust them in good weather. La Maseline is sheltered except from E winds, but there always seems to be a good deal of swell and wash, and I have never found it very comfortable. Another $\frac{1}{2}$ mile to the north, La Grève de la Ville is open from north to east, and also suffers

100 Sark. Maseline harbour from the lighthouse. Sadly, the bay is now full of moorings.

from swell. There is a road from Creux and Maseline to the town, which is in the middle of the island, some 100 m above sea level: the track from La Grève is more suitable for mountain goats.

On the W side of the island, Port la Jument offers a charming anchorage for a picnic, but being totally open to the winds from between west and north, I would hesitate to sleep there except in really settled easterly weather. Proceeding S, there is a most exciting passage between Brecqhou and Sark called the Gouliot Passage. This is only 70 m wide, but deep and clean, and the tide runs through it without undue turbulence when one considers that the rate can exceed 10 knots! The southerly stream begins at about 4 hours after HW St Helier, and the northerly about 3 hours before, and one should aim to make the passage during the first or last half hour of the fair tide at springs, or the first or last hour at neaps.

South of the Gouliot one can turn immediately east into Havre Gosselin, where there are a few private moorings, but still room for one or two yachts to anchor. The little bay is well sheltered, but I should think the reflected swell must be pretty severe in SW gales. Stairs and a lane lead to the central town.

Port des Saies, to the south, offers a pretty picnic anchorage as does Port Gorey on the SW shore of Little Sark, but both are exposed to winds from W and SW, and I would not leave a boat unattended in either, much less spend a night.

Finally, round Little Sark to the SE coast are perhaps the best, and certainly the most commodious, pair of anchorages, Dixcart and Derrible Bays. Both of these offer excellent holding, unlike the other anchorages of the island, and perfect shelter except from between

101 Havre Gosselin, Sark. The top left yacht has just passed through the Gouliot Passage, behind the islet at the top centre.

102 The Derrible Bay anchorage, Sark: Dixcart Bay is just the other side of the first headland.

ESE and SSW. Derrible Bay is calmer than Dixcart in westerlies, but the climb up to the upper level of the island is really fierce, whereas that from Dixcart is relatively gentle. Both anchorages are very beautiful, but I must admit a preference for Derrible, rock staircase and all.

All stores are available in the little town, but most people will prefer to pop over to St Peter Port or somewhere else where the walk back to the boat is rather shorter. No facilities of any kind at sea level. Beautiful bathing beaches in the last two bays.

Tidal rises are almost exactly as for St Peter Port (page 154).

Passage Notes: Jersey Approaches and Coastal Passages

Charts Nos. 3655, 1136, 1137 and 1138

The majority of British yachts who visit Jersey, the largest of the Channel Islands, do so from Guernsey or Sark, which is convenient, as this involves making landfall on the W coast of the island, which is clear of offlying dangers more than a mile from shore. Notes on the timing of departure from those islands on passage to Jersey will be found in 'Passage Notes: To and from Guernsey'. From Guernsey a course can be shaped direct for La Corbière; coming from Sark it is wise to aim for a point a couple of miles W of there, as there is an unfavourable eddy up the W coast of Jersey if one keeps too close in. Once W of Corbière, the inshore passage is easily followed. Steer to pass ½ mile south of Pt de la Moye (a mile E of Corbière light) and from there to pass close S of the light off Noirmont Point, taking care to pass N of the N cardinal buoy (Q) marking the Grande Four rock. Passing close N of another green buoy a mile to the east, one may then continue E until on the St Helier leading line.

This passage can be very rough in wind-over-tide conditions, especially near springs, when the SE coast should be given a berth of at least 2 miles until St Helier can be approached on a bearing of 023° (True).

The N coast of the island is perfectly clear apart from inshore rocks and the two major offshore reefs, the Pierres de Lecq and the Dirouilles, both of which are visible at all times, as they have rocks that never cover. So boats wishing to visit Gorey or St Catherine Bay will often come in on Grosnez Point and then run along the N coast (beware drying rocks extending two cables off Belle Hougue Point) and round to the E coast.

The really tricky passage in Jersey is that between St Helier and Gorey, round the SE corner of the island. The great reef of the Violet Bank dries for more than 2 miles offshore from La Rocque Point, and other groups of drying rocks are scattered in groups running ESE almost to the French coast. The shortest way round the points is by the Violet Channel, and this presents no navigational difficulties in good visibility, but conditions can be rough enough even in moderate weather to cause difficulties for an average cruising boat in wind-over-tide conditions. Indeed in strong easterlies it may be wiser to time things so as to go the long way round the W and N of the island: a boat leaving St Helier about 5 hours after HW there will enjoy a mainly fair tide going clockwise round to Gorey. However, neither Gorey nor the St Catherine anchorage are to be recommended in easterlies in any case.

To take the Violet Channel, leave St Helier on the leading line until the Gros du Chateau rocks, conspicuous twin rocks just W of Elizabeth Castle, are in line with the BW mark on the foreshore between St Helier and St Aubin. Once E of the Hinguette buoy (R can, Fl(4) R 15s), steer to pass ½ mile S of the big YB Demie de Pas beacon (Fl WR 12s), and from there steer 110° (True) for some 4 miles to the Canger Rock W Cardinal buoy (Q(9) 15s). This is where the true Violet Channel begins, and the worst seas are likely to be met over the next 2–3 miles.

Pass about ¼–½ mile N of the Canger buoy, and alter course to 080° (True) for the next buoy, RW vertical stripes (L Fl 10s). This is usually visible once past the Canger: be sure to keep on the line between them and counteract any cross-sets. From the RW buoy (named 'Violet' although this is omitted from some charts) a course of True N will lead into clear water, but be careful not to be set onto the Seal Rocks (dry 1.5 m) 3 cables NW of the Petite Anquette, marked by a beacon. Bound for the French coast, perhaps Portbail or Carteret, pass between the Petite and Grande Anquette beacons and so into clear water.

It is possible to save another $1\frac{1}{2}$ miles by a variant, passing 2 cables S of La Conchiere beacon, then steering 045° (mag) to pass a cable W of the beacon on the NW part of Brett Rocks, continuing the course into deep water. This route passes over rocks awash at LAT, but as the best streams are achieved by leaving St Helier $2\frac{1}{2}$ hours before HW, they will be 7 or 8 m under when using the channel.

Proceeding north for Gorey, the outermost rocks off the east coast of Jersey are well marked by beacons and R can buoys, all to be left to port going N.

Saint Helier, Jersey

Charts Nos. 3278, 1137 and 3655

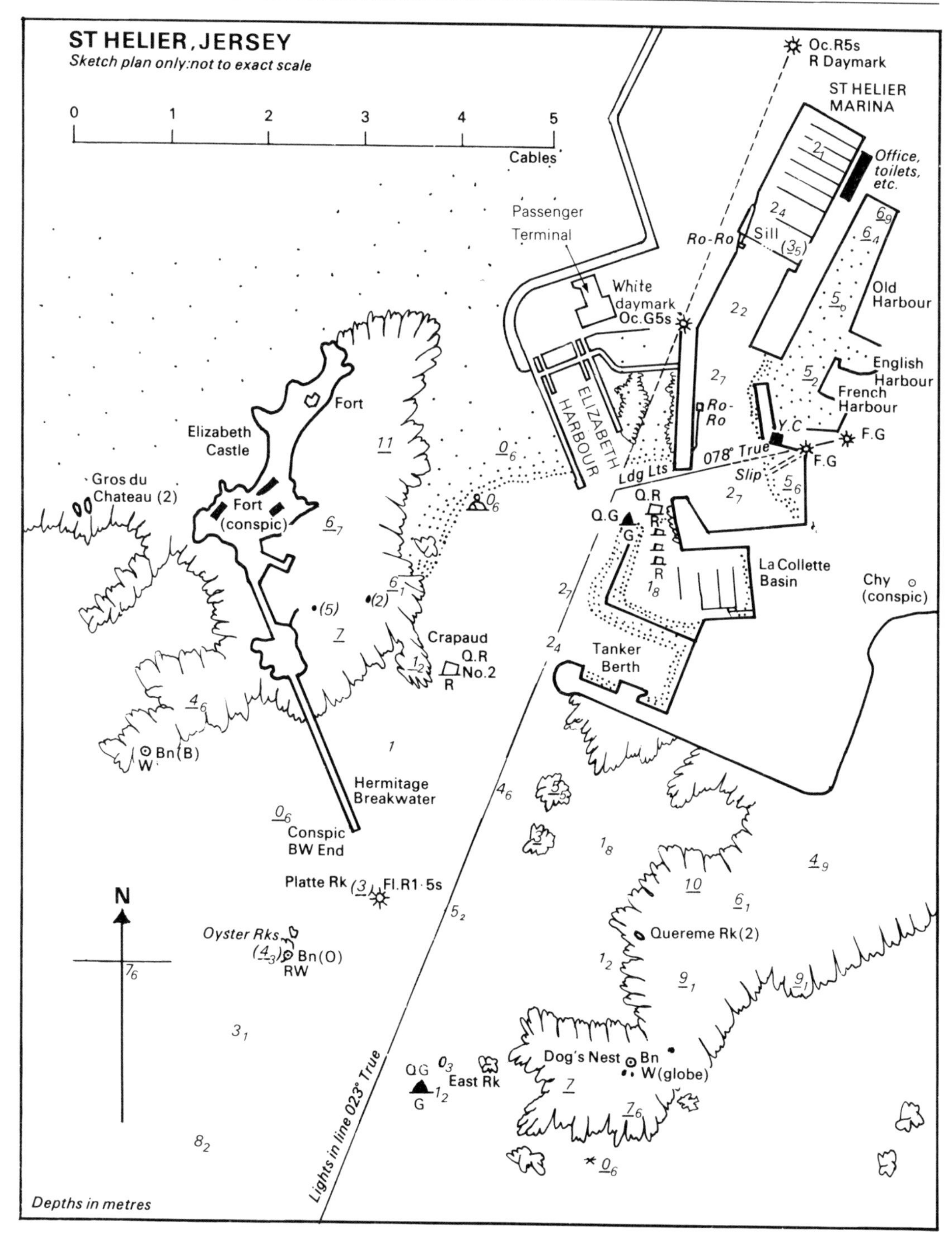

Plan 38 St Helier, Jersey.

103 St Helier approach. The Hermitage breakwater is on the left.

St Helier, Jersey

The main town and port of Jersey, St Helier offers comfortable but often overcrowded accommodation in a tidal marina.

Tidal notes

Heights: 11.1 m MHWS, 1.3 m MLWS, 8.1 m MHWN, 4.1 m MLWN.
In the offing, the stream is E-going on the flood, W-going on the ebb.

Approach and entrance

The outer approaches have already been dealt with in the Jersey passage notes above. From the west, one may steer for the brightly painted end of the Hermitage Breakwater which runs S from Elizabeth Castle until the Oyster Rocks and Platte beacons are identified (the former is a thin RW pole, and not easy to spot). Pass 100 m S of both of these, then steer NNE for the harbour entrance. From the east, pass a cable S of the Demie de Pas beacon (Fl WR 12s), a cable N of the red Hinguette buoy, and then steer 341° (True) with Gros du Chateau rock in line with the BW patch on the sea wall between St Helier and St Aubin until on the leading line for the harbour, when it is safe to turn onto 023° (True) and enter. Waypoints: from Guernsey, 49°10′.0N, 2°16′.0W gives a good approach to the inshore passage (see page 163). From the south, 49°08′.0N, 2°06′.5W puts the boat close to the leading line with the shore mark in line with Gros du Chateau. The leading line is marked by conspicuous white (front) and red (rear) daymarks on Albert Pier, which will easily be seen from this position: at night

104 St Helier: the entrance to La Collette yacht harbour. The red buoy must be left to port, which looks most alarming from this angle.

they are lit, Oc G 5s (front) and Oc R 5s (rear). The harbour operates on Channel 14, and boats with VHF should contact Port Control before entering or leaving. There are traffic signals on the Victoria Pierhead: a green light means that vessels may enter but not leave; red allows departure but not entry; red and green no movement. These signals apply to the main harbour, not La Collette, which is a separate basin to the south, and yachts under power may ignore them if flashing amber lights are also displayed, but must stay well over to their starboard side and keep clear of commercial traffic.

Berthing: La Collette basin

The La Collette basin is available at all times, being dredged to 1.8 m, which is over 3 m at MLWS. The entrance is buoyed: the fairway is only about 25 m wide and looks narrower. It involves a very sharp turn to starboard between the green and red buoys at the entrance, after which the remaining red buoys should be left close to port. The entrance has light signals: G permits entry, R departure, G over R no entry, R over G no departure. There is an 18 ton travel lift. On the whole, La Collette is used by boats waiting for water to proceed into St Helier Marina, as it is a long way from town, though convenient for the yacht club, which is on the elbow of South Pier, where diesel tanks can also be filled and Calor cylinders replaced. Berthing at La Collette is also indicated if a departure is to be made during the lower half of the tide. Water on the pontoons, except the holding pontoon. Toilets near the head of the access ramp.

Berthing: St Helier Marina

The main marina has a sill drying 3.6 m above chart datum, with a gate which closes as the tide falls, rising 1.4 m at the moment when there is 2.2 m over the sill, leaving only 0.8 m. A green light shows when the gate is open, a steady red means it is closed. A flashing red (only shown on a falling tide) means that it is about to close: boats must not attempt to cross against a flashing red unless they are already committed to the final approach. This basin is available 3 hours either side of HW. The marina is large and modern and visitors' berths are clearly marked, but at busy times there are usually staff allocating berths in any case. The marina holds the Yacht Harbours Association's Gold Anchor award.

Facilities

Showers and toilets at the top of the access ramp. Water and electricity on the pontoons. 35 ton fixed and 15 ton mobile crane. Fuel in outer harbour below yacht club (see plan). South Pier Shipyard, near the club, are class 'B' chart agents, have a wide range of chandlery, and can do repairs (including electronics in-house) and rigging, tel: 31907. The buildings behind the Folly pub (between English and French harbours) house a sailmaker and several marine engineers. Channel Islands Yacht Services at 8 Commercial Buildings (tel: 71511) also stock chandlery and some charts and will do engine repairs. Don't miss the friendly St Helier YC (see plan), open from 0900 Monday to Saturday, 1000 Sunday, until midnight. The bar closes 1400–1600 Monday to Friday. Otherwise, beware the dreaded Jersey weekend: most shops and businesses close Saturdays as well as Sundays.

General

There is a good shop at the marina selling provisions, wines and spirits (though as in Guernsey the latter may not be sold on Sundays): open seven days. Otherwise the shops are 200 m or so to the north, rather hard to find among the streets full of banks, which is the island's main industry from all appearances. There are numerous restaurants of all standards up to the award-winning Victoria's at the Grand Hotel, Peirson Road: in the better ones it is well worth booking ahead. While on the island, do not miss Gerald Durrell's famous zoo at Trinity, and the Occupation Museum at St Peter is also worth a visit. This is housed in a seven-chambered bunker. There is a smaller Occupation Museum in St Helier at 9 Esplanade.

Gorey

Charts Nos. 3655 and 1138

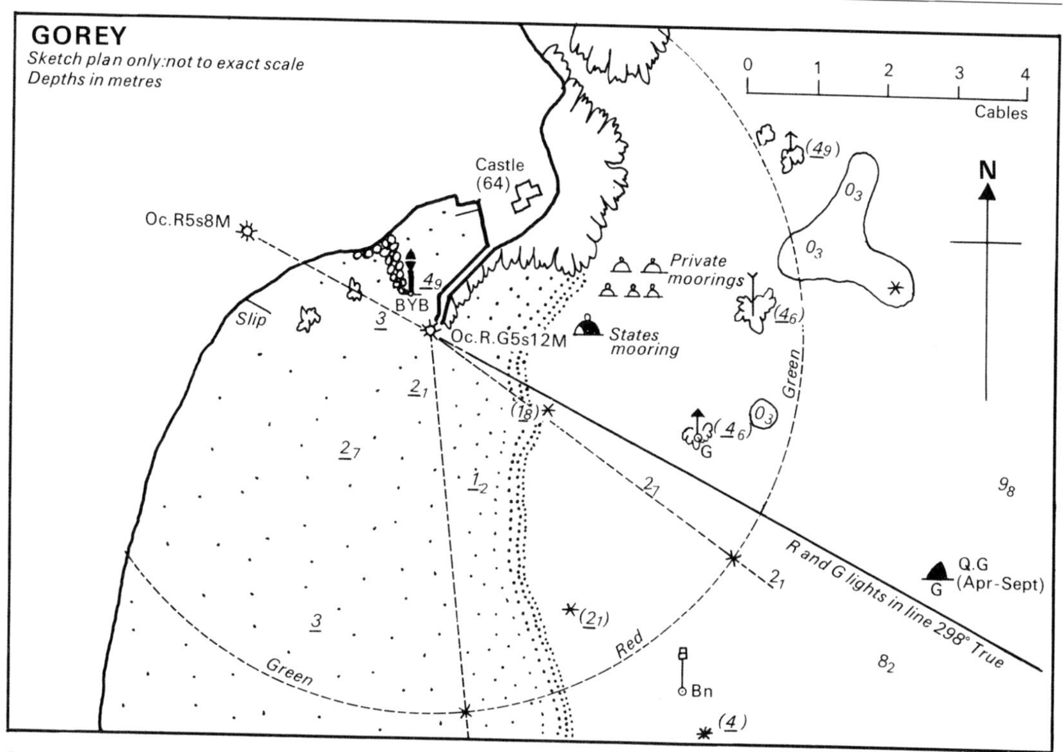

Plan 39 Gorey, Jersey.

Dominated by the magnificent Mont Orgeuil Castle, this drying harbour does not have a great deal of room for visiting boats, and those that do go inside must be prepared to take the ground.

Tidal notes

Heights: 11.1 m MHWS, 1.4 m MLWS, 8.0 m MHWN, 4.1 m MLWN.
HW is HW St Helier (springs), HW +0.10 (neaps). LW is LW St Helier +0.10. 3 miles offshore, the NW-going stream begins at HW St Helier $-\frac{3}{4}$ and reaches a maximum of 2.2 knots at HW St Helier $+1\frac{1}{2}$. The SE-going stream begins at HW St Helier $+5\frac{1}{2}$ and reaches a maximum of 2.4 knots (springs) at HW St Helier $-3\frac{1}{2}$.

Approach and entrance

The inner harbour dries $3-4\frac{1}{2}$ m, and so should not be approached below half-tide, when there is $3-1\frac{1}{2}$ m inside. At this level, few of the offshore hazards present any great difficulty, and those that might are marked by beacons, so the pilotage is quite easy. Make the final approach from the green conical buoy $\frac{3}{4}$ mile SE of the harbour. At night the leading lights (rear Oc R 5s, front Oc G 5s on the line, with a red sector beginning just S of the line) give

105 The approaches to Gorey, Jersey, the entrance left centre.

a convenient approach line from the buoy, which is lit QG. Enter round the head of the breakwater and steer N into the harbour.

Berthing

Yachts dry on 12 buoys just W of the pierhead, or at the N end near the slip. There is room for a maximum of six boats along the wall, which is the only place where a keel boat can safely dry. There are also 2 mooring buoys for visitors E of the harbour entrance, but these dry and are exposed to winds from the SE, and so are only suitable for bilge-keeled or flat-bottomed boats in settled weather.

The harbour operates on Channel 74 VHF. There are showers etc in the harbour, and diesel can be taken alongside from Gorey Yacht Services by appointment, tel: 53958. They also do repairs: enquire at their office by the Dolphin pub at the top of the harbour. The charming little town has shops and restaurants, chandlery etc. It is also a Customs clearing port. The harbour can be uncomfortable or even dangerous in strong winds between east and south.

Other anchorages in Jersey

Note: none of these anchorages should be used before Customs have been cleared in St Helier or Gorey. Continuing anti-clockwise from Gorey, a popular anchorage is tucked in just S of the great breakwater that extends from Verclut Pt, a mile N of Gorey. Coming from the south, the rocks in the middle of St Catherine Bay must be avoided: there is a beacon on the

106 Gorey. There is room for just a few yachts to dry out along the wall, otherwise they must have legs or bilge keels and dry on a mooring.

most easterly part of the reef, but the rocks extend well to the N of the beacon, so care must be taken to keep well E of the beacon until the breakwater is nearly end-on, before turning to enter the N part of the bay. Anchor about a cable S of the breakwater: good shelter except in winds from between E and S.

A mile to the NW, Rozel Bay offers an anchorage sheltered except in winds from between north and east. There is a tiny fishing harbour where it is occasionally possible to dry (the entrance dries nearly 2 m), or a good anchorage outside in W or S winds. Shops, restaurants, bus service to St Helier.

Anchorage can be found on the N coast in Bouley or Bonne Nuit Bays: each has a shop, and the latter has another very small drying harbour. The W coast is exposed to any wind with a westerly component, and would only be used by a yacht as temporary anchorage to shelter from an easterly gale.

On the south coast, St Aubin offers craft that can take the ground an alternative to St Helier. Approaching at half-tide or above, make good a course NNW from Diamond Rock buoy for about a mile, when the channel buoys will be seen marking the best water into the harbour. Visitors dry alongside the N quay. The Royal Channel Islands YC has its headquarters here: showers etc. and meals available and a friendly welcome guaranteed. Shops and restaurants in the town, and frequent buses to St Helier some 3 miles to the east on the other side of the bay.

As mentioned earlier, no visitor to Jersey should leave there without visiting Gerald Durrell's famous zoo at Les Augres Manor, which does such magnificent work in maintaining breeding colonies of endangered species. It can easily be reached by bus from any of the main coastal towns, and a visit makes a memorable outing.

Les Ecrehou

Chart No. 3655

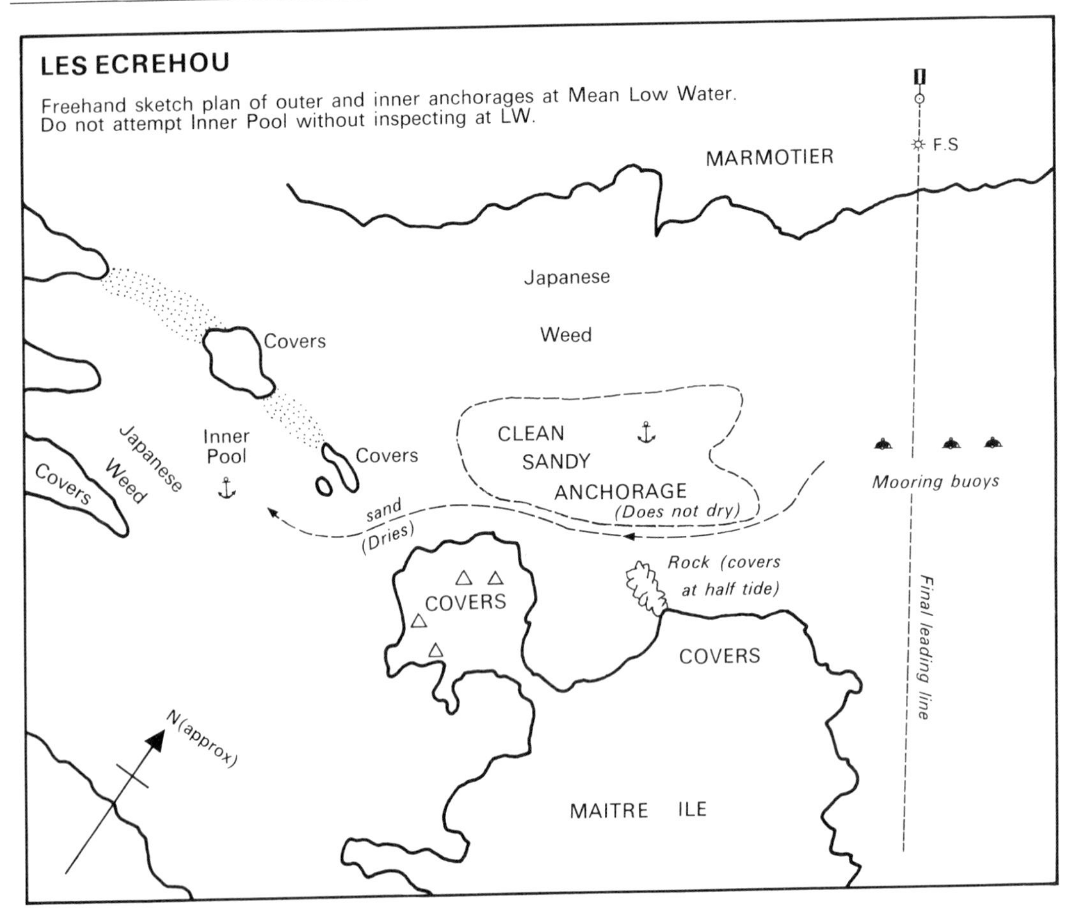

Plan 40 Les Ecrehou Anchorage.

I have always hesitated to include the anchorages in the uninhabited rock groups in the Channel Islands area in this book as they tend to be difficult of access and unsuitable for overnight stays. In any case, the risk of a sudden reduction in visibility is always present, and in the approaches to the Minquiers or the Casquets anchorages this can cause serious problems even to the most experienced navigator. However, a visit during 1987 to the Ecrehou reminded me that the approach to this anchorage presents few problems in identification owing to the distinctive shape of the Bigorne rock, while the final approach is along a well-marked leading line. However, the pilotage is certainly not for the inexperienced, and a visit should not be attempted in conditions when there is a likelihood of fog or bad weather.

This group of rocks and islets provides a fascinating anchorage for a picnic, or an overnight stay in settled good weather. If possible avoid weekends, when the anchorage is often crowded.

Tidal notes

Heights: 10.9 m MHWS, 1.3 m MLWS, 8.4 m MHWN, 3.8 m MLWN.

HW is HW St Helier +0.04 (springs), +0.12 (neaps). LW is LW St Helier +0.10 (springs), +0.20 (neaps). The N-going stream begins at HW St Helier $-\frac{1}{2}$, the S-going at HW St Helier $+5\frac{1}{2}$. The early flood stream can be fierce among the reefs until the lower rocks cover.

Approach and entrance

A stranger should aim to arrive on the final approach at HW St Helier +3, as before this the streams make it difficult to keep on the transits. From Gorey this is simple. From St Helier, leave at HW −1, take the Violet Channel, and waste a little time if necessary. Approaching the islands, identify Bigorne rock, 5 m high with a distinctive pointed top, and approach it on 022° (True), say 028° (mag). On this course it will appear to be exactly between two other flattish islets (see photo). Keep on this line with Bigorne in the middle of the gap (it may be necessary to steer well to starboard of course to stay on the transit) until Marmotier, the island with the houses on it, passes behind the nearer Maitre Ile and comes out to appear to its right. From this range it is just possible to see the marks for the final transit: a vertical black board with a division down the middle, and a white flagstaff. Bring these into line and enter

107 Les Ecrehou. Bigorne, the pointed rock in the middle of the group, kept showing (as here) in the centre of the gap between Grande Galère on the left and Sablonière on the right, is the first leading line.

the anchorage. If the marks are not spotted immediately, steer to pass a cable E of Maitre Ile and proceed until they are identified.

Berthing

There are three mooring buoys, which are private but may be borrowed if free, although be ready to move if the owner returns. Immediately W of the buoys, slightly over towards the Maitre Ile side, there is a wide area of clean sandy bottom with ample water for anchorage. The Marmotier side has heavy Japanese weed. There is a non-drying inner lagoon that is even better protected: the approach round a sand-pit projecting from the Marmotier shore is simple once studied at LW, and it would be a preferable place to spend a night. There are patches of Japanese weed here too: it is wise to check your weed-trap after a visit here.

General

There is no longer a permanent inhabitant of the island, but several of the fishermen's huts are kept repaired and are occupied in summer. The visitors bring what they need, and no supplies or water are available. The anchorage is often crowded at weekends in July and August, but at other times there are few visitors, and it is an enchanting place to visit. One way of timing a visit which I find works very well is to leave Jersey on a morning tide, spend 6 or 7 hours in the Ecrehous, and then continue to Portbail or Carteret on the next tide. If doing this, it is worth noting that the transit of the flagstaff and board leads out safely to the

108 Les Ecrehou anchorage. *Gully-Gully* is lying to one of the private mooring buoys. The markers for the final approach line (black vertical boards in line with white flagstaff) are clearly visible.

SSE, so it is unnecessary to turn onto the Bigorne transit. Indeed approaching the islands from E of south, perhaps from the Iles Chausey or Granville, it is safe to steer on Marmotier on a bearing of 335° (mag) until the marks are identified, and then bring them in line and complete the approach.

Charts Nos. 3656, 3659

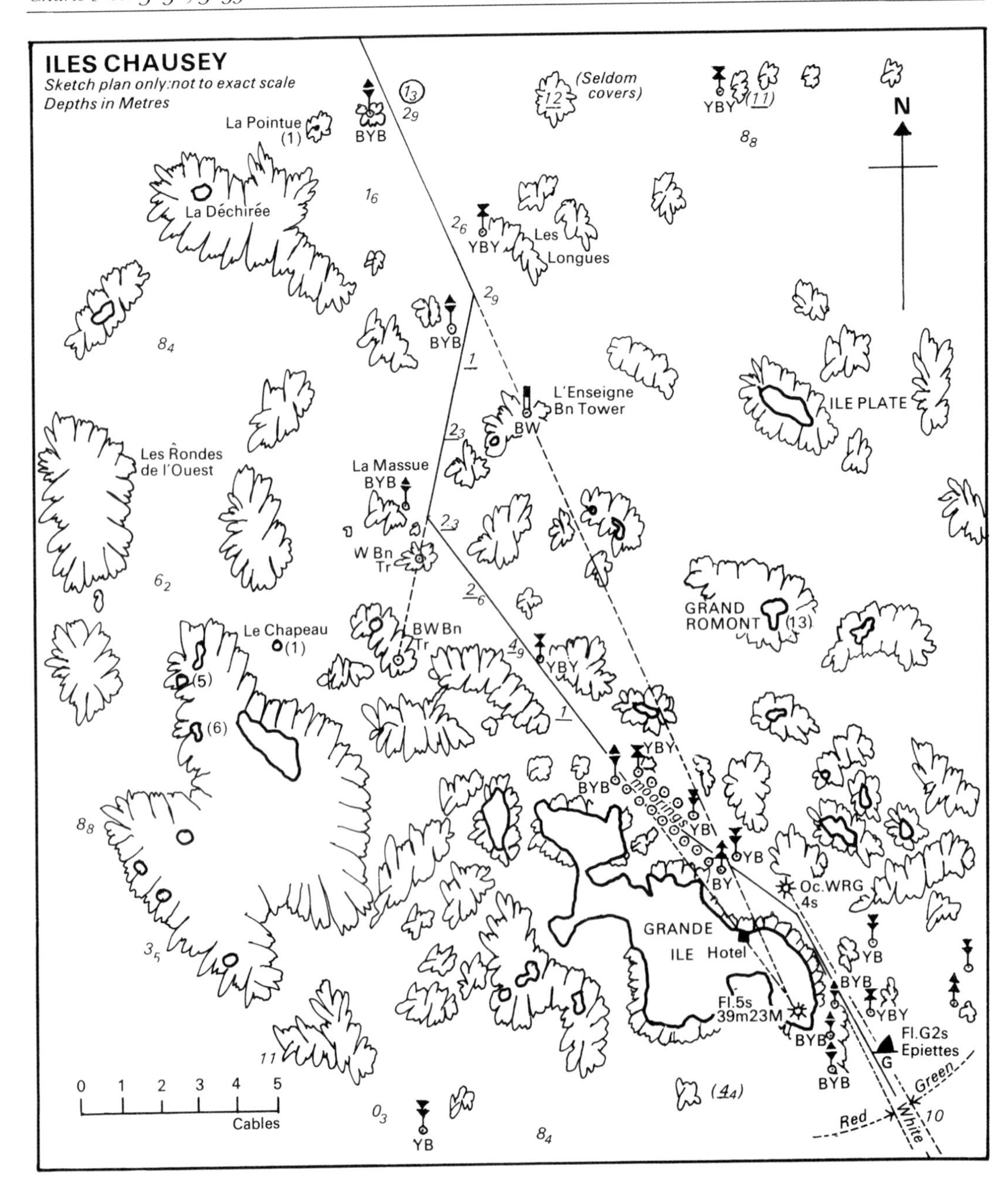

Plan 41 Iles Chausey.

The one group in the Channel Islands that belongs to France, these islands offer an interesting haven which can be used in most conditions, and deserve in my opinion to be better known by the British yachtsman. Ten miles WNW from Granville, they can provide a useful staging point as well as being worth a visit in their own right.

Tidal notes

Heights: 13.0 m MHWS, 2.0 m MLWS, 9.9 m MHWN, 4.9 m MLWN.
HW is HW St Malo +0.09. LW is LW St Malo +0.12.

Approach and entrance

The main approach is from the south, and strangers are well advised to make their first entry from that direction even if they are coming from Jersey. In that case the boat should pass close E of the NE Minquiers buoy, and then make good a course of True south until W of Grande Ile, the main island in the group, when course can be altered to pass S of it to the entrance of the haven, which lies on the E side of the island. The rocks extending W of the island are well marked by beacons. The final approach is made from the Epiettes buoy (green conical, Fl G 2s), leaving three E cardinal beacons to port, and a W and then a N cardinal to starboard. Then the light beacon is left to starboard (it is a conical structure of iron girders) and course is altered a little to port so as to leave a S cardinal beacon to starboard and a N cardinal to port and enter the anchorage. At night, the W sector of the inner sectored light provides a safe line into the anchorage.

109 Iles Chausey: The main lighthouse and the entrance to the harbour.

110 Iles Chausey: looking south from the moorings.

The channel which passes right through the rocks and islands from north to south provides an approach from the north at half-tide or above, when there is 2 m or so in the shallowest part: I would advise a stranger to explore it for the first time by *leaving* the islands by the northern route. Ideally the large-scale French chart (No. 829) should be carried, although it is possible to navigate with British Admiralty 3656 or 3659, the former best if entering the sound from the north, the latter if leaving from the south. The lighthouse on the southern point of Grande Ile is 39 m high, and can be seen from well N of the northernmost rocks: approach this on 155° (True), say 160° (mag), until the BW Enseigne beacon tower is identified, when this in line with the lighthouse can be used as an approach transit. Coming in on this transit, an E cardinal beacon will be seen close to starboard, then Les Longues W cardinal beacon to port. Some 400 m further on another E cardinal beacon is left to starboard, and then course is altered to 193° (True), say 198° (mag), for La Massue beacon. Two white beacon towers provide a transit line for this part of the channel. When La Massue is abeam, a course straight for the lighthouse leads down the remainder of the channel, leaving W cardinal beacons to port and E cardinal to starboard. With the large-scale chart the pilotage is easy, although a watch must always be kept for cross-sets. Leaving the anchorage and going north through the channel is far easier, as every beacon and transit is approached and identified before it is needed: the lower the tide the better, subject to the depths given above, as more of the rocks are visible.

Berthing and facilities

There are two lines of mooring buoys laid down by the Port de Plaisance de Granville, and visitors should moor between two buoys on one of the trots. They are attached to a heavy ship's chain, so it is safe to double-up if necessary. Note that some of them dry at LWS, so keel boats should do their sums before making their choice! It is also permissible to anchor in the channel anywhere N of the jetty used by the ferries. The stream runs N through the sound for the whole of the flood and during the first half of the ebb: it reaches nearly 3 knots on the flood at springs. The southern entrance has strong cross-tide, and can be rough in strong southerlies, and the moorings can be very uncomfortable in strong winds blowing up or down the sound, especially near HW. There are two hotels on Grande Ile and one (rather expensive) shop. Visitors should not land on the other islands, most of which are bird sanctuaries with restricted access. This is a most unusual and interesting place with a unique character of its own, and in good weather I think most people will find it well worth a visit.

My thanks are due to Messrs Kelvin Hughes, class 'A' chart agents of 145 The Minories, London EC3N 1NH, tel: 071-709 9076, Fax: 071-481 1298, for their patience in allowing me the run of their vast chart library to correct the current edition, and also to do the research for this appendix. All the charts and books mentioned below are available from them, or of course from most major yachting chart and booksellers, with the exceptions noted.

Charts

The plans in this book do, of course, reduce the number of large-scale charts which need to be carried, and in conjunction with them it is possible to get away with medium-scale coverage. Using British Admiralty charts, starting from Calais and ignoring passage charts from home ports, I would suggest a minimum would be: 1892, 2451, 2146, 2613, 2669, and 3659. However this gives sparse coverage of the tricky waters of North Cotentin and the Channel Islands, and to do more than visit the major ports one would want to expand the list to include 1106, 3654, 3655 and 60. 2700 also makes the channels between St Malo and Granville easier. This is all that is needed unless you propose to engage in really intricate rock-hopping!

Alternatively, the area is covered by charts published by Imray, Laurie, Norie & Wilson. The numbers are C31 (Boulogne–Le Havre), C32 (Le Havre–Cherbourg), and C33a and 33b, covering the north and south Channel Islands with the adjacent French coasts. They have the advantage of including tidal stream diagrams.

A further option is Stanfords No 1, 'English Channel East' (Calais to Cherbourg) and No 16, 'Channel Islands', covering Cherbourg to St Malo, but the scale here is too small to allow of much detail, and I would prefer to consider them only as passage charts. They are, however, printed on a very good quality waterproof paper – an excellent idea.

Finally, not available from Kelvin Hughes, there are the French *Cartes-Guide de Navigation Cotiére*, whose brightly coloured format confuses me but is admired by some. They are readily available in all French yachting ports: the numbers required (from Calais to St Malo) are 1010, 1011, 1012, 526, 527, 528, 1014, 534, 535. The date of issue used to be very inconspicuous on the lower right-hand corner of the back cover, though some new editions carry the date on an outer envelope. Even newish editions can be very out of date: I would avoid them except in emergency. However, readers intending to go up the Seine may want to have the *Carte-Guide*, 'La Seine du Havre à Paris'. Kelvin Hughes do stock that one.

It is quite easy and not expensive to keep one's charts up to date. *Notices to Mariners* are available free at chart agents, or the condensed yachtsman's version can be bought for a small subscription. Keeping them up to date is much cheaper than buying new ones, and much safer than sailing with uncorrected old ones.

Tidal streams

As much information as practicable has been included in this book, and most almanacs give tidal stream charts, although they are often rather small and inadequate for estimation of position say on a Channel crossing. The area is covered by the Admiralty in two atlases: NP 264, 'Channel Islands and Adjacent Coasts of France', and NP 250, 'English and Bristol Channels'. An alternative is Michael Reeves-Fowkes' *Yachtsman's Tidal Atlas*, Vol 1 (covering down as far as Cherbourg), Vol 2 (Cap d'Antifer to Brittany) and Vol 3, called 'Ports and Approaches'. This is particularly useful, giving large-scale coverage of Guernsey, Jersey (west), the Alderney Race, St Malo, Le Havre and the entrance to the Seine. My advice would be to buy that, and use the two Admiralty atlases for the general coverage.

When using tidal stream charts based on HW Dover, do remember that if the Dover table used is in GMT, 2 hours must be added to bring the time to French summer time. If the Dover table has already been adjusted to BST, then it is only necessary to add one hour.

General

I would never willingly sail without the *Admiralty Pilot* for my area: the painstaking descriptions of every yard of the coast can be invaluable, and they provide a lot of useful and interesting background information. This area is covered by two volumes: the *Dover Strait Pilot*, whose continental coverage starts at Scheveningen, reaches our area at Calais and continues as far as Cap d'Antifer, and the *Channel Pilot*, which covers the rest of the area including the Channel Islands. The *Cruising Association Handbook* (of whose 1981 edition I was the editor) also contains much useful information, as does the *Channel West and Solent Almanac* for the area from Antifer westwards. That is an Adlard Coles Nautical publication, as are their new *Pilot Packs*. These are books of spiral bound harbour charts, with port and pilotage information printed opposite. Pack 1 covers Great Yarmouth to Littlehampton and Ijmuiden to Carentan, and Pack 2 Chichester to Portland, the Channel Islands and St Vaast to Erquy.

I hope that this book will help its readers to enjoy safe and successful cruising in this varied and beautiful area. I am always most grateful to readers who write to point out mistakes (even when these turn out to be changes or developments since the closing date for the edition quoted) or offer differing opinions or new ideas. Any such letters may be sent to me care of the publishers, and will be gratefully received. Meanwhile, happy cruising!

Index

Southampton
R. Hamble
Portsmouth
Chichester Har.
Bright
Lymington
Poole
Christchurch
Cowes
Yarmouth
ISLE OF
WIGHT
Bembridge
Weymouth
St. Catherine's Point
30′
Portland Bill
E N G L I S H C
50°
Cap
De La
Hague
Anse St Martin
Omonville-
la-Rogue
Cap Barfleur
BURHOU
ALDERNEY
Goury
Barfleur
Cherbourg
St Vaast
Dielette
I. ST.
MARCOUF
30′
St Peter
Port
HERM
SARK
GUERNSEY
Cotentin Peninsula
Quinéville
Grandcamp
Carteret
Portbail
LES ECREHOU
Carentan
Isigny
Port-
En-Bessin
Courseulles
Cab
Ouistreham
Bayeux
JERSEY
Gorey
St Helier
Cae
49°
MINQUIERS
ILES
CHAUSEY
Granville
Rothéneuf
St Malo
2°30′W
2°W
30′
1°W
30′